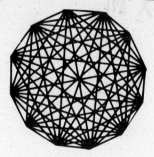

HUMAN BEHAVIOR
IN THE SOCIAL ENVIRONMENT

A Social Systems Approach

THIRD EDITION

HUMAN BEHAVIOR
IN THE SOCIAL ENVIRONMENT

A Social Systems Approach

THIRD EDITION

RALPH E. ANDERSON
IRL CARTER

ALDINE

Publishing Company

New York

ABOUT THE AUTHORS

Ralph E. Anderson is a Professor in the School of Social Work at the University of Iowa. He received his B.A. at the University of Minnesota in 1950 and his M.S.W. at the University of Nebraska in 1953.

Irl Carter is Associate Professor in the School of Social Work at the University of Minnesota. He received his B.A. at Parsons College in 1955, M. Div. from Drake University in 1960, M.A. (in Social Work) at The University of Iowa in 1965, and a Ph.D. in Social Foundations from the University of Iowa in 1975.

Third Edition published 1984
Aldine Publishing Company
200 Saw Mill River Road
Hawthorne, N.Y. 10532

Library of Congress Cataloging in Publication Data

Anderson, Ralph E.
　Human behavior in the social environment.

　(Modern applications of social work)
　Bibliography: p.
　Includes index.
　1. Social systems.　2. Social institutions.　3. Human
behavior.　I. Carter, Irl　II. Title.　III. Series.
HM51.A54　1984　　　306　　　　83-25783
ISBN 0-202-36035-0
ISBN 0-202-36036-9 (pbk.)

TABLE OF CONTENTS

1 THE SOCIAL SYSTEMS APPROACH

2 APPLICATIONS OF A SOCIAL SYSTEMS APPROACH

3 CULTURE AND SOCIETY

4 COMMUNITIES

5   ORGANIZATIONS

6   GROUPS

7   FAMILIES

8   THE PERSON

9   EPILOGUE

Table of Contents

ACKNOWLEDGMENTS

The persons most responsible for this book, other than ourselves, are those of our students who stimulated us to think more clearly and to attempt to teach more effectively. These students, now our professional colleagues, will recognize ideas and examples that emerged from these interactions.

Of those colleagues who have contributed thoughtful suggestions and raised important questions we are again deeply indebted to Gary R. Lowe for his perceptive, critical, and thorough review of the manuscript and prospective changes. We are also especially grateful to Eleanor Anstey and Dennis Falk for their valuable comments. We are appreciative of the invaluable assistance of Beverly Sweet for preparing the manuscript, and Jane Pederson for graphics.

We continue to be especially indebted to the late Gordon Hearn for breaking the ground and sowing the seed.

We would also like to acknowledge Portland State University for allowing us to use a photograph of the sculpture "Holon."

INTRODUCTION TO THE THIRD EDITION

In the ten years since this book first appeared, social systems approaches have been incorporated across a wide range of disciplines and professions. Such acceptance indicates an increasing rate of cross-fertilization among the social sciences and related applied fields. This portends well for acceleration and consolidation of knowledge development in the human services.

This revision reflects this broader acceptance as we attempt to present more clearly the fundamental concepts of this approach, while adding recent contributions to this expanding body of knowledge. Throughout this past decade we have received feedback from many readers: faculty, students, and practitioners. These criticisms and suggestions have strongly influenced our revisions.

While continuing to strive for breadth and brevity we have added new diagrams and figures intended to better illustrate certain concepts. In response to suggestions from readers we have also introduced a short story to be used to demonstrate applications of systems ideas. Literary sources in chapter bibliographies have been augmented to include film versions of plays.

We have added an epilogue since the time is overdue to begin an examination of the philosophical underpinnings and the implied values of such a social systems approach to understanding human behavior. The epilogue is intended to stimulate thought and to suggest some possible directions for exploration of these fundamental issues.

Our experience, and the experience of others, have confirmed our statement in the first edition that the sequence of use of the chapters is best determined by the user(s). All possible sequences have been recommended by instructors who use this book. This book continues to be "open" and incomplete. We still expect instructors to supplement this volume with relevant readings, according to their purposes. We welcome your suggestions and criticisms.

INTRODUCTION

But *you* gotta know the territory!
Meredith Willson, *The Music Man*

This book is an attempt to map the territory of human behavior. It is intended to introduce students in the human services to ideas and theories that are fundamental to understanding human behavior. Students in social work, education, nursing, home economics, child development, and other professions providing human services require an acquaintance with a vast body of knowledge about the behavior of humans. Today it is not possible to present enough information in one book to accomplish this. In our teaching and in our students' learning, we have found that we came nearest to accomplishing this task by writing this book and using it as a global map of human behavior. It designates the major levels of knowledge of human behavior and enables students to recognize the human systems that most concern them. It is designed as a textbook to organize human behavior content into an understandable whole.

Along with most of our students, we have found this book useful as a large-scale map in a "survey" of human behavior. We know from our experience that its utility in a particular sector of human behavior may be limited. Since this is true, "small-scale maps" are provided in the suggested readings described at the end of each chapter. These sources provide more detailed explorations of particular human systems. This book, however, serves to place knowledge of human behavior within a broad context to remind us that one's theory and one's practice are "a piece of the continent, and a part of the main," as John Donne so aptly put it (see Chapter 1).

The manner in which this book and the more specialized resources fit together varies with the terrain. For example, a great many books and articles deal with organizations as systems, and it is fairly clear how the large-scale systems map and the small-scale maps of organizational behavior can be integrated. However, the integration of the two scales is less clear as they converge in the behavior of persons — where the relationship of the part and the whole is always at issue. One recurrent question, for example, is whether a person should be regarded as the basic unit (the focal system), a system capable of being subdivided, or should be regarded only as a subunit of society. There is disagreement about which scale to use, which perspective to take. Our intent is to demonstrate that these are all legitimate perspectives, to be used selectively in accord with criteria explicated in this book.

Our objectives in this book are to explain how our map is designed and to prove its utility. We have sought an "umbrella" theory under which various theoretical perspectives would fit; or, to shift the metaphor, a "skeleton" framework upon which various theories can be affixed and fleshed out toward a comprehensive theory of human behavior. In our experience, no single theoretical construction can encompass all aspects of human behavior. Courses in human behavior have had various organizing themes including:

1. *Normal vs. abnormal behavior.* This perspective provides knowledge of individual and family dynamics, which is invaluable in understanding and dealing with individual behavior but is of doubtful validity when applied to groups, institutions, communities, and societies.

2. *Developmental patterns of the individual.* This perspective includes groups, communities, and society but only from the standpoint of their effects on the development of the person. Inherent in this approach is a view of the person as an "adjuster" or an "adapter." Human behavior is seen as adjustment to social stresses. Intervention possibilities are dichotomized, *either* working toward helping the person to adjust to the social situation *or* attempting to change the social situation so that it would be less stressful to the person.

3. *Social processes.* This perspective emphasizes knowledge of the social and cultural patterns that provide the social context of development and behavior. Such understanding is essential to social planning but omits the uniqueness of the individual and patterns of living.

Each of these perspectives and others have served as a structuring theme for ordering knowledge of human behavior. Each enables scrutiny of various theories and hypotheses. Each, however, has limited applicability to the broadening base of human services. There has been an exponential increase of social science knowledge, which varies widely in its quality and reliability. This increase requires a more comprehensive integrative framework than that provided by any of the previously employed organizing schemes. What is now required is an approach that will foster an integration of psychoanalytic, psychological, and developmental perspectives with the burgeoning discoveries from the many disciplines that study human behavior. We have found that social systems is that approach.

The social systems approach is probably best described as a "way of thinking," a "theory about theories," or a "hypothesis about theories," since there is not yet sufficient research to establish it as a theory of human behavior. It is a particular variation of general systems theories, which crosses physical, natural, and social sciences. Emerging findings in many disciplines buttress the validity of general systems theories.

A social systems approach has several advantages.

1. *It is comprehensive.* It offers greater possibilities for description and integration of seemingly disparate theories into a single framework than any other approach we know.

2. Even though it does not map adequately all sectors of human behavior, it does *provide suggestive leads.*

3. It has the potential for *providing a common language* to various disciplines, both within and across disciplines. Students interested in psychotherapy, education, community development, and administration may find social systems a useful common framework. To use a social work practice example, the psychotherapist may not be vitally interested in community development, believing that significant changes occur within individuals; the community developer may believe that significant changes occur only when groups act; while the administrator may believe that change is real only when it is structured and solidified in an institution or program. We believe that each is partially right and partially wrong. Like the proverbial blind men examining the elephant, each has part of the truth. Yet these three social work specialists can see the relationships between and among their localities if they share a knowledge of social systems. Each might still prefer his or her own domain, but would be aware that it was a "part of the main." They would recognize that interactions of persons, groups, and organizations are integrally related in a common system. It is our conviction that human services have lacked such an integrative approach far too long, even though we recognize the historical reasons for the delay.

4. A final advantage is *parsimony.* Social systems theory allows the student to reduce the "blooming, buzzing confusion" of theories of human behavior and methods of practice to a framework that can be mastered. Herein lies the danger, of course. Through reductionism the student may be content with the global map, flying from continent to continent, coast to coast, without encountering the precipices, mudholes, and arid wastes upon which many a theory has foundered. Systems theory cannot replace detailed knowledge of at least some particular sectors of human behavior. After all, people live through the processes of human interaction, not on maps.

This book attempts to describe a systems skeleton and then locate important human behavior concepts upon it. The instructors and students who use this book must flesh out the skeleton so that the approach will be directly applicable to the practice of each respective profession.

HOW TO USE THIS BOOK

This book is, then, a large-scale map, intended to be supplemented in each particular sector of human behavior by more detailed maps. We have used it in this way with both graduate and undergraduate students. We have guided students through the courses in modular fashion, selecting theories that made sense to us and to the students and indicating where each more detailed theory meshed with the large-scale map.

The first chapter acquaints the student with our social systems approach. The essential systems characteristics are introduced and explained. These concepts, which serve to draw the map, reappear in the subsequent chapters. They are the key ideas that together form the social systems approach of this book.

The subsequent chapters are modules — they can be taught as discrete units, requiring only the first chapter as precedent. The arrangement of the chapters is one feasible way of ordering human systems, in descending order of magnitude. If instructors using this book prefer other sequences, the order can be changed or even reversed. By so doing, this course might better integrate with others being taught during the same term, or might better convey a particular theme being emphasized. For instance, instructors in colleges of education may decide to deal with the chapter on the person prior to chapters on group or family.

We have found it advantageous to use other texts with this book to provide additional threads of continuity throughout the general map, to assure degrees both of latitude and longitude, and to provide a single small-map source for each human system examined. For continuity crossing all human systems we have used *The Autobiography of Malcolm X*, Tillie Olsen's *Tell Me a Riddle* and *One Flew Over the Cuckoo's Nest* by Ken Kesey. For specific systems we have assigned, for example, Erikson's *Identity: Youth and Crisis* for the chapter on the person; Billingsley's *Black Families in White America* for the chapter on family; and E. T. Hall's *Beyond Culture* for the culture module. Again, many choices are open to the instructor.

Suggested readings, with brief commentaries on their particular utility, follow each chapter. The readings actually used will depend on the instructor and students involved and on the clock and calendar time available. If the students are unfamiliar with the content germane to particular human systems (such as family, groups), the supplemental materials should be selected with this in mind. For students acquainted with particular content, supplemental readings can give deeper insights into theoretical writings and related research.

The glossary is designed for easy reference to the key concepts used throughout this book. Although most readers will be familiar with most of the terminology, our usage may be unfamiliar. The reader should consult the glossary because these are the definitions used throughout.

This book is intended to be an open system. We assume that each instructor will add and substitute books, articles, films, or other learning aids. This flexibility allows the book to be used in graduate schools, four-year colleges, community and junior colleges, and perhaps in-service training programs.

In other words, this work comes to you incomplete. It not only suggests that students and instructors add their own input to this study of human behavior; the book *requires* it. We hope that this social systems approach to the study of human behavior will be a step toward an integrated body of social science knowledge that will reflect both the complexity of social forces and the uniqueness of the person.

HUMAN BEHAVIOR
IN THE SOCIAL ENVIRONMENT
A Social Systems Approach
THIRD EDITION

THE SOCIAL SYSTEMS APPROACH

No man is an island, entire of itself; every man is a
piece of the continent, a part of the main; if a clod be
washed away by the sea, Europe is the less, as well
as if a promontory were, as well as if a manor of thy
friends or of thine own were; any man's death
diminishes me, because I am involved in mankind;
and therefore never send to know for whom the bell
tolls; it tolls for thee.

John Donne, Devotions XVII

This well-known passage expresses the sense of this book's systems theme,
a theme that will be referred to as the *systems approach*, or *systems model*.
Since our approach is in fact a loose cluster of theories, hypotheses, and
speculations emerging from various disciplines, the phrase *systems theory* is
inaccurate and should be avoided. Some of this eclectic body of knowledge
has been validated by observation and experiment; some is merely logical
and suggests hypotheses for investigation. Howard Polsky classed systems
theory as metatheory, that is, theorizing about theories; and as a model
applicable to any dynamic, patterned activity (Hearn, 1969:12). Joe Bailey
stated, "' Systems theory' is really a misnomer. It is really a complicated and
elaborate metaphor for describing what seems to be an inevitable way of
thinking" (Bailey, 1980:73).

Much of the utility and explanatory power of a social systems approach
derives from the manner in which the metaphor fits with the thinking about
the reciprocal relatedness of persons and their social environment. Gordon
Hearn established that a systems approach is particularly well suited to the
profession of social work, as exemplified by the following:

1

> The general systems approach . . . is based upon the assumption that matter, in all its forms, living and nonliving, can be regarded as systems and that systems, as systems, have certain discrete properties that are capable of being studied. Individuals, small groups—including families and organizations—and other complex human organizations such as neighborhoods and communities—in short, the entities with which social work is usually involved—can all be regarded as systems, with certain common properties. If nothing else, this should provide social work education with a means of organizing the human behavior and social environment aspects of the curriculum. But beyond this, if the general systems approach could be used to order knowledge about the entities with which we work, perhaps it could also be used as the means of developing a fundamental conception of the social work process itself (Hearn, 1969:2).

We suggest this conception is useful to other professions as well, for example, psychology, nursing, education, communication, and medicine.

The general systems approach seems to apply to all phenomena, from subatomic particles to the entire universe. We will confine ourselves to one part of the systems approach—social systems—which comprises knowledge about persons, groups of persons, and the human and nonhuman environs that influence social behavior and are influenced by persons.

Auger asserts that a systems approach enables the nurse

> . . . to evaluate the status of the person who is ill and the significance of changes that may or may not have occurred in patterns of behavior. This content will help the student to develop a broader concept of the relationship between health and illness, the wide variations of "normal" behavior, and changes that may occur as a consequence of illness and/or hospitalization (Auger, 1976:x).

Peter R. Monge has argued that a systems perspective provides the best theoretical basis for the study of human communication. His reasons for doing so "are based upon my belief that a discipline as young as ours would make a serious mistake to preclude alternative perspectives. That perspective which incorporates the others is, at least until more information is available, the one best suited to guide us in our quest for knowledge about human communication" (Monge, 1977:29).

In his essay recommending a new model for biomedicine, George L. Engel stated, "When a general-systems approach becomes a part of the basic scientific and philosophic education of future physicians and medical scientists, a greater readiness to encompass a biopsychosocial perspective may be anticipated" (Engel, 1977:135).

The social systems model explained in the next pages provides the organizing principles for this book. The model enables the reader to recognize similar or identical ideas (isomorphs) emerging from different ancestry and provides a scheme for classifying such related ideas.

I. THE SYSTEMS MODEL

A widely used sociology text states:

> By far the most widely used analytical model in contemporary sociology is that of a social system. System models of various kinds are used in many fields besides sociology, so a social system can be thought of as a special case of a more general system model. A social system is not, however, a particular kind of social organization. It is an analytical model that can be applied to any instance of the process of social organization from families to nations. . . . Nor is the social system model a substantive theory—though it is sometimes spoken of as a theory in sociological literature. This model is a highly general, content-free conceptual framework within which any number of different substantive theories of social organization can be constructed (M. Olsen, 1968:228).

The model itself is probably most easily and efficiently introduced by the basic metaphor common to the sciences: the atomic or molecular model, which is composed of interacting units, each with its own parts, each unit being part of some larger whole.*

Buckley defines a system as "a complex of elements or components directly or indirectly related in a causal network, such that each component is related to at least some others in a more or less stable way within a particular period of time" (Buckley, 1967:41). The model is not descriptive of the real world. It is only a way of looking at and thinking about selected aspects of reality. It is analogous to a map or transparency that can be superimposed on social phenomena to construct a perspective in order to show the relatedness of those elements that constitute the phenomena. It is a means to make "sense" of seeming chaos or puzzlement, a way of thinking, and an approximation. A systems model draws attention to dynamic patterns of relatedness of part to whole, foreground to background, and object to environment.

A social system is a special order of system. It is distinct from atomic, molecular, or galactic systems in that it is composed of persons or groups of persons who interact and mutually influence each other's behavior. Within this order can be included families, organizations, communities, societies, and cultures. The social systems model must be validly applicable to all forms of human association.

> Very briefly, a social system is a model of a social organization that possesses a distinctive total unity beyond its component parts, that is distinguished from its environment by a clearly defined boundary, and whose subunits are at least partially interrelated within relatively stable patterns of social order. Put even

* We call your attention to the logo, which symbolizes the model, on the cover of this book.

more simply, *a social system is a bounded set of interrelated activities that together constitute a single entity* (M. Olsen, 1968:228–229).

Having said that systems exist at all "levels," from individual persons to cultures and societies, we should specify what we see as the "basic unit" of a social system. Within sociology, there has been polar divergence on designation of the unit of primary attention. The macrofunctionalists such as Talcott Parsons tended to view the totalistic system, the society, as the prime focus and to view the behavior of the system and its components as being determined by the total system's needs and goals. At the opposite pole, the social behaviorists and social interactionists, such as Max Weber, G. H. Mead, Don Martindale, and Herbert Blumer began with the smallest unit of the system, the behavior of the individual person. In this view, the acts of the individual persons tend to cluster into patterns, or role consensus, and the social system is constructed out of these patterns. They concluded, as did Parsons at an earlier point in his theoretical evolution, that the social system is merely an agglomeration of these acts by persons. Gintis expresses this in free verse:

The social system
Consists of the structured interaction
Of individuals.
This structuring
Takes the form
Of a concrete number of alternatives
Ordering the way the individual may relate
     to his social environment
These alternatives are called "roles". . .
                         (Gintis, n.d.:23)

Churchman sums up this view by stating that "for the behavioral scientist . . . the 'whole system' is made up of the behaviors of the individual persons. Once individual and social behavior have been examined in detail, then one can discover in the operation of behavior the nature of the whole human system" (Churchman, 1968:200). Thus, of the two polar positions among social systems theorists, one is holistic, viewing persons as units within the social system and behaviorally determined by it; the other is atomistic, viewing systems as the accumulated acts of individuals.

These polarized positions are encountered in professional education and in professional practice as "social change" versus "individual change." The social change emphasis is grounded in the macrofunctionalist view that behavior is primarily determined by the larger social systems. A clinical or individual change emphasis derives its theoretical legitimacy from the belief that society is constructed from the behavior of its smallest units.

We hold that both polar positions must be taken in examining human affairs. There must be simultaneous attention to both the whole and the part. Our point of view is that each social entity, whether large or small, complex or simple, is a *holon*.* The term is borrowed from Arthur Koestler, who coined it to express the idea that each entity is simultaneously a part and a whole. The unit is made up of parts to which it is the whole, the suprasystem, and, at the same time, is part of some larger whole of which it is a component, or subsystem. Koestler said that, like the god Janus, a holon faces two directions at once — inward toward its own parts, and outward to the system of which it is a part (Koestler, 1967:112ff; 1979:23–51). What is central is that any system is by definition both part and whole. We have found the concept of holon particularly useful. It epitomizes a consistent theme in this book. No single system is determinant, or is system behavior determined only at any one level, part, or whole.

One visual image of this was sculpted by Don Wilson as a tribute to Gordon Hearn and is permanently on display on the Portland State University Campus in Portland, Oregon (see Figure 1). Hearn was, as noted earlier, pivotal in introducing social systems ideas.

The idea of holon as used in this book extends Koestler's proposition of whole–part relationships to include certain corollaries. First, the system approach requires the designation of a *focal system*. The focal system sets the perspective; it is the system chosen to receive primary attention. Holon then requires the examiner to attend to the component parts (the subsystems) of that focal system and simultaneously to the significant environment (the suprasystems) of which the focal system is a part, or to which it is related. For example, a family may be identified as the focal system. If viewed as a holon, attention must simultaneously be given to both its members and its significant environment, such as schools, community, work organizations, other families, and neighborhood. To deal only with the interactions among family members (the family as whole) ignores the functions of family interactions with large systems (the family as part). A simple series of diagrams illustrates this (see Figure 2).

The causal network referred to in the preceding quotation from Buckley does not imply one-way causation. Causation is multiple and multidirectional. A change in any part of the causal network affects other parts but does not determine the total network. In other words, behavior is not determined by one holon (seen as whole or part) but rather by the interaction and mutual causation of all the systems and subsystems, the holons of differing magnitudes.

* *A note to the reader:* We know you will encounter difficulty incorporating "holon" into your speaking vocabulary. Be undaunted; the important thing is that you incorporate its meaning into your thinking so that you always view a social system as both a whole with parts and as part of other wholes; that it always has partness and wholeness.

FIG. 1. This sculpture, entitled "Holon," effectively conveys the wholeness of the part and partness of the whole. One may think about the further permutations of what is pictured here and what other systems and systems relationships this work suggests.

The Social Systems Approach

Consequently, we take the position that it is not useful to think of human behavior as understandable through searching for linear cause-effect relationships. It then serves little purpose to ask the question "Why?" persons do what they do. A "why" question demands a causal explanation, that is because. . . . A more useful form of inquiry is "How?" An excellent example of a systems model that is nonlinear is Forrester's "world dynamics" model, adapted in the controversial study *Limits to Growth* (Meadows *et al*, 1972). Forrester's model recognizes that factors interact in complex *loops* (see glossary), avoiding the use of an over-simplistic causal chain. Alan Watts takes a stronger position: "Problems that remain insoluble should always be suspected as questions asked in the wrong way, like the problem of cause and effect. Make a spurious division of one process into two, forget that you have done it, and then puzzle for centuries as to how to get the two together" (Watts, 1966:53). Happenings or phenomena frequently are labeled "problems" when it is recognized they do not fit theory, belief, or expectation. The "problem" may be a function or consequence of the way of thinking; alter the perception and the "problem" becomes something else.

Our stance, then, rather than being either holistic or atomistic, may be described as contextual, interactional, transactional, pluralistic, or perspectivistic (Bertalanffy, 1967:93). The latter term connotes that causation, or the significance of an event, is relative to the focus one has at the moment of assessment; that the interpretation one places upon events depends upon where and who one is and the perspective one has upon the focal system. "What we perceive, or overlook, in the field of our potential experience depends on the framework of concepts we have in our minds" (Ichheiser, 1949:2). Einstein expressed the idea more simply: "It is the theory which decides what we can observe" (Watzlawick, 1976:63).

If one is a social behaviorist, one sees what happens to individual persons as most important. If one is a macrofunctionalist, the essential consideration is what happens to the total system (supra-system, usually the society). Our viewpoint, a functionalist one, is that one's perspective at a particular time is what determines one's view of the nature and importance of an event. As events are viewed from other times, or by other observers, meanings are likely to change. Robert Merton, a sociologist, states that

> . . . the theoretic framework of functional analysis must expressly require that there be SPECIFICATION of the UNITS for which a given social or cultural item is functional. It must expressly allow for a given item having diverse consequences, functional and dysfunctional, for individuals, for subgroups, and for the more inclusive social structure and culture (Loomis and Loomis, 1961:265).

Thus the view we take here requires the specification of the focal system, the specification of the units or components that constitute that holon, and

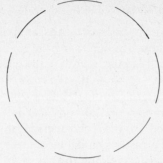

(a) Family

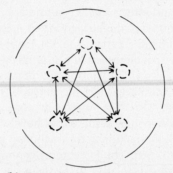

(b) Family looking inward (whole)

Environment

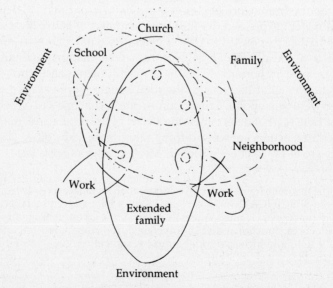

(c) Family looking outward (part)

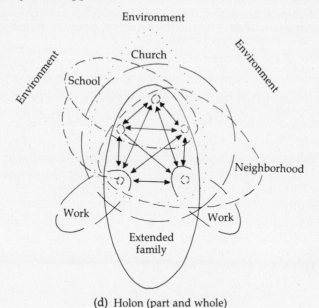

(d) Holon (part and whole)

FIG. 2. Diagrams of a Family System.

specification of the significant environmental systems. The components and environment will have meaning in their effects on the focal system and, of course, the focal system will have meaning in its effect on its component parts and its environment. Further, to achieve an objective description of the focal system, one must state one's own position or relation to the focal system. Such a view is philosophically consistent, we think, with the basic metaphor described by Einstein, that perceptions of events are relative to the position of the observer.

(all things are relevant?)

II. ENERGY

Consistent with the atomic metaphor, we suggest the basic "stuff" of a system is energy. Just as atoms and molecules are composed of energy, so also are social systems.

The smallest molecular particle gets its dynamic movement from the fact that it consists of a negative and positive charge, with tension—and therefore movement—between them. Using this analogy of the molecular particles of matter and energy, Alfred North Whitehead and Paul Tillich both believe that reality has the ontological character of negative–positive polarity. Whitehead and the many contemporary thinkers for whom his work has become important see reality not as consisting of substances in fixed states but as a process of dynamic movement between polarities (May, 1969:112).

The dynamic movement between polarities accounts for the genesis of energy. What occurs in social systems are "transfers of energy" between persons or groups of persons. The energy in this dynamic process is not directly observable. Its presence is inferred from the effects upon the system and its parts. There is some disagreement among systems theorists as to whether energy is a valid concept for social systems. For example, Gregory Bateson did not like analogies of energy since such analogies were derived from nineteenth-century physics, he termed it "misplaced concreteness' (Lipset, 1980:171).

Our use of energy, then, is analog and construct. In this sense, energy may be defined as "capacity for action," "action," or "power to effect change." As previously stated, the presence of energy is inferred from its effect on the system and its parts.

The question becomes: "Is energy an inclusive enough concept to denote the life of a social system?" We suggest it is, providing the meaning goes beyond the precise idea of active force. To borrow again from physics, the broader meaning includes both information and resources as "potential energy." The nature of both information and resources includes the capacities to activate or mobilize the system and to serve as energy sources. "The interplay of people on the job, of husband and wife, of nations at war are all social systems that involve the sending and receiving of energy/information. System action will be examined as this movement of energy/information (1) WITHIN a system and (2) BETWEEN a system and its environment" (Monane, 1967:1–2). To disqualify information as energy is to deny its reality; information is nothing if it provides no potential for action. Hence we proceed on the assumption that social systems do have energy, and that energy transfer is a prime function of all social systems.

Bertalanffy's discussion may assist in resolving the question of the legitimacy of energy as applicable to social systems (Koestler and Smythies, 1971:71–74). He said that living systems must be thermodynamically open, that is, exchange energy across their boundaries and be information carriers. We interpret this to mean that energy and information are not identical, but that they are complementary and inseparable in living systems. Both are necessary although neither is sufficient. Energy must be structured in order to be useful; information, just as its root meaning implies, gives form to the energy. Bertalanffy, however, notes that the issue is not yet completely clarified.

One of the first social scientists to apply systems ideas to his discipline was James G. Miller, a psychologist, who wrote that "systems are bounded regions in space–time involving ENERGY INTERCHANGE among their parts'' (J. Miller, 1955:514). In his last published work, Sigmund Freud said of the concept of energy:

> We assume, as the other natural sciences have taught us to expect, that in mental life some kind of ENERGY is at work; but we have no data which enable us to come nearer to a knowledge of it by AN ANALOGY WITH OTHER FORMS OF ENERGY. We seem to recognize that nervous or physical energy exists in two forms, one freely mobile and the other, by contrast, bound; we speak of cathexes and hypercathexes of the material of the mind and even venture to suppose that a hypercathexis brings about a sort of synthesis of different processes — a synthesis in the course of which free energy is transformed into bound energy. Further than this we have been unable to go (Freud, 1949:44 – 45) (Emphasis ours).

The exact nature of human energy is undetermined and depends in part upon the particular system being examined. Within a person, we refer to psychic energy; we could analogously refer to the social energy of a family, group, organization, or community. What is meant is the system's capacity to act, its power to maintain itself and to effect change. The energy derives from a complex of sources including the physical capacities of its members; social resources such as loyalties, shared sentiments, and common values; and resources from its environment. Environmental resources may provide information, ideas, and manpower.

For example, a military organization's energy would include the persons available for service, the military hardware it possesses (weaponry, transportation facilities, communications equipment), money appropriated for its use, and public sentiment favoring support of the military (such as "support our boys" campaigns). Other energy sources may be ideological support for military activity ("we must make the world safe for democracy") and legal or diplomatic sanction to conduct war (as provided by a declaration of war, a United Nations declaration as in Korea, or the Gulf of Tonkin resolution which expanded the United States involvement in Vietnam). All of these constitute energy sources available to the military system to perform its assigned tasks.

Energy sources for a personality system, to give a further example, could include: food; the physical state of the body; intellectual and emotional capabilities; emotional support from friends, family, or colleagues; cultural sanction for one's beliefs and activities; recognition of one's status by society and one's superiors in an organization; and perhaps most important, one's own sense of worth and integrity.

At this point, essential concepts that bear on the topic of energy in a social system should be introduced. *Entropy* has to do with the tendency of an unattended system to move toward an unorganized state characterized by decreased interactions among its components, followed by decrease in usable energy. Entropy is a measure of the quantity of energy not available for use. *Synergy* refers to increasingly available energy within a system derived from heightened interaction among its components. Whether or not the law of entropy is applicable to organic and social systems has been a lively issue among general systems thinkers. Erwin Schrodinger, a physicist, postulated the mind-boggling concept of *negentropy* to counter the tyranny of the Law of Entropy. He stated, "What an organism feeds on is negative entropy" and argued that living organisms "build up" instead of run down as they create complex structures from simple elements (Anderson, 1981:90). Biologist Szent Gyorgyi coined the less complicated term *syntropy* to connote an innate drive in living matter to protect itself, to seek synthesis and wholeness.

Entropy is a concept from physics that does not apply precisely to social systems.

> Physical processes follow the second law of thermodynamics, which prescribes that they proceed toward increasing entropy, that is, more probable states which are states of equilibrium, of uniform distribution and disappearance of existing differentiations and order. But living systems apparently do exactly the opposite. In spite of irreversible processes continually going on, they tend to maintain an organized state of fantastic improbability; they are maintained in states of NON-equilibrium; they even develop toward increasingly differentiation and order, as is manifest both in the individual development of an organism and in evolution from the famous amoeba to man (Bertalanffy, 1967:62).

An example of the usefulness of the notion of entropy can be seen in the concluding phases of the Vietnam War. As opposition to the war gained momentum, energy available for making war became disorganized and depleted. In unknowing recognition of this process, the phrase "winding down the war" was employed. That phrase is a fair description of entropy, worded as if it had been planned and controlled.

Synergy is appropriate to open, living systems (and thus to social systems). One advertisement proclaimed, "We're synergistic. We do a lot of things at Sperry Rand. And we do each one better because we do all the rest." An open system does not deplete its energy, but it actually compounds energy from the interaction of its parts. Abraham Maslow credited Ruth Benedict with the first application of the idea of synergy to social interaction. She used it to denote the amplification of goal-directed activity where there was a fit between the individual goals of persons sharing a culture and the goals of the culture (Maslow, 1964:153–164). The concepts of *entropy* and *synergy* should not be employed literally in regard to social systems but rather used as analogies in describing the characteristic of certain systems.

For example, it may be apparent that a certain organization is becoming increasingly static and predictable and could be described as characterized by entropy. Another organization may be increasingly unpredictable and fluid, with internal shifts of concentration of energy and power that result in "dynamic growth"; this could be described as characterized by synergy. The same analogy could be applied to a person as well. Rigidity and maintenance of psychological defenses could be evidence of entropy, while absorption of new stimuli and constant adaptation to the environment, with resultant stimulation of new attachments and ideas, could be evidence of synergy or syntropy. These somewhat esoteric terms (*entropy, synergy, negentropy,* and *syntropy*) are useful in describing and understanding the vitality, resources, and organizational state of any particular human systems. Both energy and entropy are imported and exported across systems boundaries. One system's (person's, town's, organization's, nation's) energy may be another system's entropy. A prime example is the chronic controversy attendant to waste disposal, whether it is household or nuclear. High concentrations of energy collection and use is inevitably bound to high concentrations of entropy. Exporting entropy is a modern-day dilemma. There is no solution since it is not a problem, so it is truly a dilemma (Anderson, 1981:91).

Systems require energy in order to exist and carry out system purposes. This can be diagrammed simplistically as occurring through four energy functions (Fig. 3). This diagram is intended to illustrate the interrelatedness of energy functions and is applicable to all human systems.

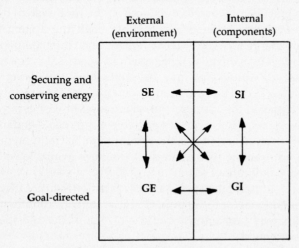

FIG. 3. Four energy functions (S: securing; G: goal; E: external; I: internal). (See glossary for definitions of terms.)

A. Functions SE and SI

The first pair of functions (cells *SE* and *SI*) pertain to the securing of energy. SE represents the function of securing energy from outside the system, that is, importing energy from the environment. This importing function roughly corresponds to Parson's idea of "adaptation" (Parsons, Bales, and Shils, 1953:182). The SE function involves GE as well, since the importation of energy occurs through a transactional process between the human system and the environment. SI denotes securing energy from inside the system and requires access to energy sources from one or more component parts of the focal system. A variety of possible outcomes are probable with SE and SI functions. The SE function is well-illustrated by the fossil fuel situation facing industrialized nations in the recent past and the forseeable future. If less fuel is available externally (imported oil), more must be conserved and secured internally (SI function) through domestic oil, wood, coal, or solar energy to achieve national goals.

Following the shortages and price increases in the world oil markets, the United States established policies to foster conservation and to further resource development. One means of accomplishing the latter was to extract oil from shale. Government and industry merged resources to mobilize this potential energy source. Recently, oil supplies have exceeded demand and prices have stabilized, consequently Exxon quickly shut down its ambitious oil shale works near Parachute, Colorado.

If internal system energies are in short supply and energy from the subsystems is critically needed, energy-consuming frictions and conflicts among subsystems must be prevented or reduced. If the focal system has a surplus of energy available from its components, then the system can tolerate diversion of energy into subsystem conflicts. Such intercomponent conflicts may be, to focal system goals, the lesser of two evils. Diversion of energy to suppress one subsystem may be preferable to allowing the subsystem to go unchecked. The operation of defense mechanisms of the personality is an example of this. Suppression of impulses or wishes may be preferable to allowing them free expression, which in turn could endanger the "survival" of the personality, that is, the focal system. Racial supremacy in a nation is another example. Although the amount of available energy required to maintain conditions of segregation and second-class citizenship for a racial minority (United States) or a racial majority (South Africa) is great and thus dysfunctional for the attainment of some goals, continuation of the system as it is may take priority because of fear of the anticipated consequences of changing it.

Parsons refers to this function of securing energy internally as "integration" (Parsons *et al.*, 1953:182), which means reduction of internal conflict to maximize available energies to direct toward the goals of the focal system. This phenomenon can be seen in those circumstances where a system is in danger of being destroyed or radically changed. Pulling together, tightening the ranks, and forgetting past differences are found in the family, city, and the nation when circumstances or events threaten continued existence. Such was the rationale given for both former President Ford's pardon of former President Nixon and President Carter's granting of amnesty to Vietnam-era draft evaders. Reduction of conflict within a personality in order to achieve better ego orientation to reality, thus heightening the likelihood of achieving goals, is yet another example.

B. Functions GE and GI

The second pair of basic functions (cells GE and GI of Figure 2) pertain to the use of energy, that is, the uses to which energy is put. One of the characteristics of living systems is the purposefulness of activities. They operate in a goal-directed manner. This pair of functions may be called goal achievement or "goal attainment" (Parsons *et al.*, 1953:182). As in the first pair of functions, these too are performed both internally and externally; GE refers to goal-directed activity outside the system and is interrelated with SE, SI, and GI. The holon attempts to carry on transactions with the environment to achieve its own goals as whole and as part. It seeks to achieve as much reliability and control over the system–environment linkages as possible. The American Medical Association, for example, collects money and efforts from its constituent parts (its membership) in order to engage in lobbying activities to influence and control its environment to achieve system goals. The child mobilizes internal resources to please his/her parents and to achieve the goal of gaining love, status, and a position of some influence within the family system, which is the child's primary environment.

GI refers to goal-directed activity inside the system. Here energy is employed to subordinate the subsystems to the goals of the focal system, by whatever means possible, in order to be consistent with the nature of the system and the surrounding environment. This is similar to Parson's labeled function of "pattern maintenance" (Parsons *et al.*, 1953:182).

The declaration of a state of martial law in a nation is an example of goal-directed activity within the system. With system survival at stake, energies are directed inward to reduce or eliminate disequilibrium, which is perceived as threatening the continued existence of system patterns. Military takeovers of Chile, Argentina, Poland, Lebanon, and Afghanistan are examples. A professional organization requires its members to align their goals and patterns of behavior with the goals and patterns of the system. If members fail to do so, they are subject to expulsion or disciplinary measures. Social workers are regulated by a code of ethics and subject to sanctions by the National Association of Social Workers; psychologists are regulated by the American Psychological Association. A family system that holds a goal of educational achievement will direct energies to control a member who rejects education as a goal.

C. Interrelatedness of Energy Functions

Emphasis should be placed on the fact that these four functions are not discrete; that is, a system performs two or more of these functions at the same time. In any exchanges between whole and parts, all partners receive some energy and have some goals met. The reciprocal nature of the transactions and exchanges should be kept in mind. If one function is dominant, the other functions are neglected to the detriment of the total system. For example, the family system that concentrates energy only on the SE function through securing and importing energy from the external environment may experience internal disintegration. This may take the form of both parents devoting excessive time and energy to jobs at the expense of internal family functions. An excellent example of the condition of a person–system concentrating all energies on internal functions is Paul Simon's lyrics, "I Am A Rock":

> I've built walls;
> A fortress deep and mighty
> That none may penetrate.
> I have no need for friendship—friendship causes pain.
> Its laughter and its loving I disdain.
> I am a rock . . . I am an island.
>
> Don't talk of love.
> I've heard the word before.
> It's sleeping in my memory.
> I won't disturb the slumber of feelings that have died;
> If I'd never loved I never would have cried.
> I am a rock . . . I am an island.
>
> I have my books.
> And my poetry to protect me.
> I am shielded in my armor.
> Hiding in my room, safe within my womb
> I touch no one and no one touches me.
> I am a rock.
>
> I am an island.
> And a rock feels no pain.
> And an island never cries . . . (Simon, 1965).*

The energy functions portrayed in this song can be diagrammed in the style introduced in Chapter One, II "Energy" or "by Figure 4."

* Reprinted with permission of the publisher. Copyright 1965, Paul Simon.

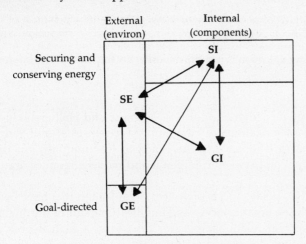

Fig. 4. "I Am A Rock" Energy Functions (S: securing;
G: goal; E: external; I: internal).

III. Organization

Just as energy is the basic "stuff" and the necessary element of a system, organization is the sufficient element. A total absence of organization would mean a total absence of system. Randomly distributed energy cannot be mobilized to further the purposes of the system. A more or less closed system, a rock for instance, can only be immobile because its energy is unorganized. In order to move the rock, energy must be exerted from outside the system. A social system, to be so classified, must have a degree of organization. The word *organization* refers to the grouping and arranging of parts to form a whole, to put a system into working order. System organization secures, expends, and conserves energy to maintain the system and further its purposes.

Monane, in discussing the cybernetic concept of organization, asserts that it pertains to intrarelatedness, that is, the degree of impact of a component's actions upon the actions of the other components within the system. He distinguishes between high and low organization. In a highly organized system—a family—the components are strongly interdependent; what one does is crucial for others. In systems of relatively low organization—a metropolis—components are independent and autonomous (Monane, 1967:21). Monane's notion of high organization and low organization are similar to E. T. Hall's conception of "high" and "low" context.

A high-context (HC) communication or message is one in which most of the information is either in the physical context or internalized in the person, while very little is in the coded, explicit, transmitted part of the message. A low context (LC) communication is just the opposite; i.e. the mass of the information is vested in the explicit code (Hall, 1977:91).

The comparative sets of "high and low" of Monane and Hall are akin to Tönnies (1957) characterizations of community (*gemeinschaft* and *gesellschaft*) as explained in Chapter 4,I, "As Kinds of Communities" of this book; and the distinction between traditional and modern families drawn in Chapter 7.

Thus, there are two polar aspects of system organization that have been applied to communities, organizations, and families. One side of the duality is less formal, based on relationships over time with a high degree of interdependence among components, and where meaning is largely derived from the particular context. The other side of the duality has system organization based in formalized structures, with explicitly stated expectations of required behaviors, and relatively autonomous components. In reality, all systems will organize with some mixture of these two polar aspects.

The founding of a social system, that is, the delineation of a new entity from its environment, can generally be expressed in the familiar phrases, "Let's get organized," "Let's get it together." The first action of the components of a burgeoning system must be to order randomly distributed energies. The Constitution of the United States organizes the component systems into a suprasystem. The Preamble sets forth the general purpose for forming a new system and then specifies system goals:

We the People of the United States, in Order to form a more perfect Union, establish Justice, insure domestic Tranquility, provide for the common defence, promote the general Welfare, and secure the Blessings of Liberty to ourselves and our Posterity, do ordain and establish this Constitution for the United States of America.

The various articles and amendments of the Constitution specify the conditions of intrarelatedness of the components (states and individuals) to the system. The goals of the national system as specified in the Preamble are, and must be, congruent with the goals of its components. It was precisely this organization and interrelatedness that were at issue in the Civil War (or War Between the States), Nixon's "new Federalism," and the effort of the Reagan administration to defederalize many of the "general welfare" programs. Revenue sharing was designed to decentralize federal control, and that has been followed by a weakening of the federal regulatory agencies; both are attempts to redefine relationships and linkages between the federal government and the various component states. The Equal Rights Amendment was an attempt to redefine organizing principles prescribing the relationships between system and its components and among system components. Ultimately, the Watergate issues dealt with the balance among the three branches of the Federal government.

Organization is a concept that does not implicitly carry the message of ever increasing complexity, although complex systems with a higher order of differentiation usually require complex organization. "A complex society is not necessarily more advanced than a simple one; it has just adapted to conditions in a more complex way" (Farb, 1968:13). A personality with complex defenses is not necessarily better or worse than an "uncomplicated" personality, but certainly the two function differently. There is a rapidly expanding literature advocating reduction of scale and specialization in society (Illich, 1973; McRobie, 1981; Schumacher, 1973; Slater, 1974). Such authors propose reorganizing society in various ways in order to promote less complex lifestyles.

The measure of the effectiveness of organization is its capacity to enable the fulfillment of the system's goals as well as the goals of the component elements of the system. (See discussions of "effectiveness" and "efficiency" in Chapter 5,II, "A. Goal Direction.") Effective organization enables the energies of the system not only to be generated and purposefully used but also to secure energy from the environment (i.e., SE and GE functions).

Disorganization of a system—whether person, family, or neighborhood—does not mean totally unorganized. It means not sufficiently organized. The system's energies are not in working order; the components of the system do not stand in sufficient relatedness to one another; energies are randomly distributed and expended; the system is tending toward a state of entropy. Vernacular terms for this in a person are *spaced out,* or *losing it.*

In the Freudian personality system, id, ego, and superego are the triad of organizers that need to work in harmony with the ego dominant. If the id were dominant, energies would be directed toward goals not in keeping with the goals of the total system. If the superego were dominant, energies could not be sufficiently mobilized to fulfill total system goals.

Erikson's (1963) formulation of identity can be viewed as the expression of an organizing principle that enables the components of the personality to "get together" to fulfill the goals of the person. The "identity crisis" is defined on the bipolar dimension of "identity versus diffusion" (see Chapter 8, I, A, "1. Erikson" regarding polarities). In systems terms this could be expressed as organization versus disorganization. The word *identity* is defined as personality components drawn together to form a working whole; *identity diffusion* refers to disharmony among personality components, that is, randomization. The person diagnosed as schizophrenic is seen as a disorganized system—he or she is not together.

The family with problems is generally a disorganized family. The members (internal energy sources [SI, GI] are operating in a system-defeating manner. Among the possible reasons for family disorganization are the following:

1. The goals of one or more members are in opposition to system goals.
2. The elements of organization (communication, feedback, role expectations) are disrupted or unclear.
3. Available energies from within the system are not sufficient for the demands on the system.
4. The family is not adequately organized to obtain additional energy from outside its own system.
5. Pressures from the environment (the suprasystem) exercise a disorganizing influence on the family system (e.g., oppression).
6. Energy is denied or not available from the suprasystem.

In conclusion, the dimension of organization — the fact of organization — is characteristic of all social phenomena that can be designated as social systems. If there is no organization present, there is no system. If organization is insufficient or dysfunctional for the goals of the system, the term *disorganization* is used. Organization refers to the ordering of the energies of the component parts in some fashion that results in a whole.

Energy and the organization of energy are then the prime characteristics of social systems. We now discuss in more detail aspects of social systems that follow from these prime characteristics. All systems are composed of energy interchange. Monane points out (1967: Chapter 2) that structural and functional aspects of social systems are merely descriptions of this basic interchange. Those processes of energy interchange that are slower and of longer duration and thus appear to the observer to be relatively static can be called *structural*; those processes that are of relatively fast tempo and short duration can be called *behavioral*. This is a distinction employed by John Dewey, whose discussion is worth reading (Dewey, 1966). We call these processes behavioral rather than functional to avoid confusion with the energy functions discussed earlier. Those processes that change slowly over time, but are not apparently static (that is, they move faster than structural but slower than behavioral changes), we label *evolutionary* aspects. For example, a structural change in the family may be from extended family to nuclear family over centuries; evolutionary change may be from traditional nuclear family to single-parent families over decades in the twentieth century; and behavioral change includes any particular family's functioning during its life cycle.

Characteristics of social systems are discussed under the structural, evolutionary, and behavioral headings.

IV. EVOLUTION OF SOCIAL SYSTEMS

As with other dimensions of social systems, change and maintenance are not diametrically opposed in reality. Systems never exist in a condition of complete change or complete maintenance of the status quo. Systems are always both changing and maintaining themselves at any given time. The balance between change and maintenance may shift drastically toward one pole or the other, but if either extreme were reached, the system would cease to exist. As Alfred North Whitehead said, "The art of progress is to preserve order amid change and to preserve change amid order." This is similar to Erikson's (1963) "bipolarities" of personality growth and Piaget's (1932) "assimilation" and "accommodation" discussed in Chapter 8, I, B, 1, "c. Schemas."

A. Steady State

Steady state, a systems concept borrowed from physics, is the most adequate term available to describe what Laszlo refers to as "the particular configuration of parts and relationships which is maintained in a self-maintaining and repairing system. . . . It is a state in which energies are continually used to maintain the relationship of the parts and keep them from collapsing in decay" (Laszlo, 1972:37).

Steady state occurs when the whole system is in balance. In such a state, the system is maintaining a viable relationship with its environment and its components, and its functions are being performed in such fashion as to ensure its continued existence. The word *steady* is somewhat confusing because it implies some kind of fixed, static balance. The balance is, however, dynamic and always changing to some degree (as just noted concerning change – maintenance). The use of the word *state* in its singular form also is mildly confusing. Actually, the concept involves a series of states in which the system, as a complex of components, adapts by changing its structure. It is not exactly the same, but somewhat the same, from one time to another. The steady state is modified along with the system's goals and the system's purposive, self-directive efforts to maintain integrity. Steady state is characterized by a sufficient degree of organization, complexity, and openness to the environment.

The concept of steady state applies to all social systems. One example of it is Erikson's (1963) concept of *identity*, which is a steady state of the personality system. Menninger's view is consistent with this. He devotes an entire chapter to demonstrating how systems concepts are compatible with psychiatry and the succeeding chapter to a discussion of ego's function in maintaining steady state (Menninger, 1963: Chaps. 5 and 6).

The terms *equilibrium* and *homeostasis* have meanings similar to steady state but with important differences. They denote a fixed balance in which some particular adjustment is maintained, and the structure of the system is not altered significantly. Steady state does not include a fixed balance; the system can find a new balance and new structure radically different from the previous one.

The three terms may be illustrated by analogy to transportation, using the human body and the means of transportation to form a system. Equilibrium is like a teeterboard. Balance can be achieved, but the limits of being in balance are narrow. No movement is possible on a balanced teeterboard. To maintain balance, it is necessary to protect it from environmental factors such as wind or swaying. A possible exception may be acrobats on a tightwire, but even in this case, it is hazardous to attempt to move a fixed balance. This was illustrated by the tragedy of the Wallenda family when their pyramid of balancing acrobats fell from the high wire and several of them were killed.

Homeostasis denotes a more variable balance; that is, the system's balance may change within some limits. Balance is maintained by movement and by encounter with the environment. Homeostasis may be illustrated by a motorcycle. The rider has some latitude and remains upright by leaning against centrifugal force (leaning into a curve) or by altering the machine's center of gravity on a banked curve by tilting the machine. Within some limits, which are determined by weight of the machine, wind velocity, speed, and road angles, the bike is maintained in balance. *Zen and the Art of Motorcycle Maintenance* (Pirsig, 1975) contains a description of the delicate art of balance, both of a motorcycle and a personality.

Steady state is movement and balance like that of *Around the World in 80 Days*—a narrative in which various forms of transportation are used to traverse the planet. The balance changed, and even its structure changed. Phileas Fogg depends on transportation throughout his trip, but the mode changes from balloon to train, to ship, to raft, to foot. In each successive form, a moving balance is maintained, but to maintain movement the form varies with the environment.

The concept of *ecological balance* also is appropriate here. Forms or structures may change in and of themselves and in relation to one another in order to survive, but there are strong tendencies for the system to continue in some form.

Buckley (1967: passim) calls the two tendencies involved in maintaining balance "morphostasis" (or structure-maintaining) and "morphogenesis" (structure-changing). Again, no system reaches either extreme, although it may tend toward one pole or the other. All systems must maintain a shifting balance between status quo (morphostasis) and change (morphogenesis) and likewise a balance between order and disorder. Ardrey demonstrates this principle in his discussion of the relationship between civil rights and civil liberties:

> If the social contract represents a delicate balance between a degree of order that the individual must have to survive and a degree of disorder which society must have to ensure fulfillment of its diverse members, then a significant ascendancy of violence from any quarter tends radically to revise the contract. No triumph of disorder can be other than temporary. When order has been destroyed by one force, so will it be restored by another (Ardrey, 1970:254).

When order destroys or prohibits disorder, other forms of disorder will emerge.

Another important distinction in steady state, equilibrium, and homeostasis is that equilibrium demands a minimum of stress and disturbance and seeks minimal interchange with the environment. The verses previously quoted from "I Am A Rock" are the expression of a person seeking a state of equilibrium. Homeostasis also requires minimal stress and disturbance but does require interchange with the environment. Steady state does not require minimal stress; social systems may prosper from stress and disturbance. In fact, human systems tend to seek situations that are stressful as a means toward "building up" (negentropy) or to "seek synthesis and wholeness" (syntropy). You well may be experiencing stress as you are studying these systems concepts. More than likely you have encountered this book as a consequence of your actively seeking to acquire information/energy as you seek steady state. Interchange is essential to the existence of steady state. Equilibrium implies closed and static systems, homeostasis implies open and static systems, and steady state denotes open and changing systems (see Table I). What we mean by steady state is the continuing

TABLE I. Comparison of equilibrium, homeostasis, and steady state

	Equilibrium	Homeostasis	Steady state
Stress	Least possible	Minimal	Optimal and necessary
Structure	No change	No change	Wide possibility of change
Interchange with environment	Least possible	Minimal	Optimal and necessary
Openness	Closed	Minimal	Open

"identity" of the system, its continuity with the previous states through which it has passed, and through which it will pass in the future.*

V. STRUCTURAL CHARACTERISTICS

This discussion of structural characteristics is related to the preceding sections, "I. The Systems Model," especially the discussion of holon, and "III. Organization."

A. Boundary, Linkage, and "Open" and "Closed" Systems

In order to be identified as distinct from its environment, a system must have some limits, that is, locatable boundaries. Consistent with our view that energy or activity is essential to social systems, we define a *boundary* as being located where the intensity of energy interchange is greater on one side of a certain point than it is on the other, or greater among certain units than among others. The intensity of energy transfer between units within the boundary is greater than the intensity of exchange across the boundary. For example, members of a family are distinguished not only by blood relationships, but also by frequency and intensity of personal contact. A neighbor would usually be considered outside the boundary, but may become "a member of the family" by participating in family activities and sharing emotional ties of the family. An adopted child is another example of a person not related by blood who crosses the boundary and is incorporated within it.

Boundaries can be defined only by observation of the interaction of the parts of the system and the environment. Some boundaries are visible because of their impenetrability, for example, the rigid personality that permits little interchange with the environment. Some religious orders have boundaries defined clearly by behaviors such as dress, marital status, and allegiance to group beliefs. The Old Order Amish are set apart by dress, modes of transportation, and style of beard. The fact that boundaries may change is evidenced in the Roman Catholic Church by changes in dress (the abandonment of some traditional nuns' habits) and by some changes in group beliefs (attitudes toward birth control, ecumenical relationships to other denominations, and the roles of women).

It is important to distinguish between the location of a boundary and its nature. Boundary does not necessarily mean barrier. A social system may have a readily discernible boundary and yet be very open to transfers of

---

* There is a familiar saying, "The more things change, the more they remain the same." If one explains that from a social systems perspective, the idea of steady state will be clearer.

energy across its boundary (e.g., the boundary of male–female). Another example is the boundary between generations that has become an important tenet in systems approaches to family therapy (Bowen, 1978; Minuchin, 1974).

Other boundaries are difficult to identify because interchange is frequent and intense across the boundary. For example, "Who is a Jew?" is a question both unsettled and important to the nation of Israel.

The boundaries of being "American" were at issue during the Vietnam War. For some persons, support of, or opposition to, the Vietnam War constituted a boundary. Usually no single interaction defines a boundary. Obviously, more than one criterion is involved in being "American:" such behaviors as paying taxes, voting, and acknowledging "American" values and responsibilities are some criteria to be considered. The issue of amnesty for draft evaders raised the question of such boundaries in a tangible and dramatic form. President Carter attempted to resolve the issue by granting amnesty under a broad construction of the boundaries of "American."

When two systems exchange energy across their boundaries they are *linked* or have *linkage* with each other. Their linkage may be for a very limited and peripheral purpose or may constitute a vital linkage (e.g., a family's association with the economic system). A family's memberships in social clubs and civic groups may be important links to community activity and resources. Their religious affiliation may be a vital social, emotional, and ideological link as well.

Energy transfers by way of linkages are rarely, if ever, one way. Reciprocity of energy, or true exchange, is present in virtually all linkages. The church, club, or industry draws energy from its linkage to the family, hence, industry's willingness to contribute to families' welfare through Social Security, United Fund drives, mental health campaigns, or ecological improvements. Increasingly, industry is providing services directly in support of family welfare (e.g., day care, social services, and retirement preparation). (See discussion of organizations' relationships to other systems in Chapter 5, this volume.) Similarly, the church maintains its role as prime defender of family and marital stability; the linkages are vital and central.

Open and *closed* are largely self-explanatory terms. A system or its significant environmental systems can be receptive or nonreceptive to the movement of energy across boundaries. In actuality, of course, no system is completely open since it would then be indistinguishable from its environment. Nor is a system ever completely closed — it would cease to exist. We use open and closed with these reservations in mind; what is really meant is "relatively more open" or "relatively more closed" than some other system or than some standard by which we are judging the system. A person is an open system, but from a teacher's or counselor's point of view, may be less open (or more so) than is desirable for his or her own growth. For example, a child may be less open to interaction with peers than he or she "should" be and more open to interaction solely with parents than is expected at his or her age. Community organizers might wish for a social agency to be more open to ghetto residents and less open to interchange solely with white, middle-class clientele. This latter example illustrates that it is often not sufficient to generalize that a system is open or closed. It is frequently crucial to specify "open to what?" and "closed to what?"

B. Hierarchy and Autonomy*

Parts of systems are related to each other in various ways. One of these kinds of relationships is vertical or hierarchical, meaning that parts are arranged in the order in which energy is distributed. For example, parents in a family have greater access to the family's income than do the children. Because they receive larger shares of public good will and public resources, state universities have an advantage over welfare and penal institutions in receiving public funds. This was modified somewhat in recent years by public reaction to campus protests and because college teachers and students became identified with controversial social issues such as the nuclear "freeze," abortion, and women's rights. Universities are perhaps lower in the social hierarchy now, whereas community colleges have risen somewhat in access to public funds (energy).

Another hierarchy is that of power and control. Some parts control others by regulating access to resources or by regulating communication. For example, the executive officer of an organization has rank not only by title but by virtue of controlling the allocation of responsibilities and resources. Power wielded by the members of the White House staff who control presidential appointment schedules and screen incoming information is yet another example. H. R. Haldeman was an extreme example during the Nixon administration. The "gatekeeper" function is of central importance to a system; it is the locus of control of the flow of information and the crossing of the system boundary from both inside or outside. In contrast to Presidents Nixon and Johnson, it appeared that Jimmy Carter sought to establish a greater degree of openness of information flow through personal contact. President Reagan has established clear gatekeeping channels for both access and information.

A third form of hierarchy is that of authority. Some parts serve as sources of sanction and approval through acting as "defenders of the faith" (a phrase applied to the monarchs of England, whose status far exceeds their actual power). Religious institutions and schools serve this function. Within a family, part of the mother's role has traditionally been that of imparting and representing certain values of the society, hence Mother's Day has been

---

* Hierarchy and autonomy are emotionally laden words; please refer to the definitions in the glossary.

observed with a certain prescribed reverence and respect. Fathers, traditionally, also have imparted certain societal values; there has been some
change from "macho" values to father's role as counselor, friend, and "pal"
or confidante.

A fourth form of hierarchy is a required sequence in which development
must occur. Some events or functions must occur before others can be seen
to. One example of this is Maslow's hierarchy of needs within the person:

> . . . needs or values are related to each other in a hierarchical and develop-
> mental way, in order of strength and of priority. Safety is a more prepotent, or
> stronger, more pressing, more vital need than love, for instance, and the need
> for food is usually stronger than either. . . . [a person] does not know in
> advance that he will strive on after this gratification has come, and that
> gratification of one basic need opens consciousness to domination by another,
> "higher" need (Maslow, 1968:153).

The physiological development of the human organism follows a hierarchical pattern of emergence and integration. Similar forms of hierarchy are
found in Erikson's developmental tasks (1963) and Piaget's cognitive stages
(1932), both of which are discussed in Chapter 8, this volume.

There are, then, several varieties of hierarchies. Most frequently we will
discuss hierarchy in one of the forms just described. We will discuss
instances in which the hierarchy is one of control and power and in which
the parts are dependent upon other parts for some vital resources. The
relationship in these instances will be that of subordination – superordina-
tion, or submission – dominance. That is, the hierarchies most often examined will be those in which control is exerted in a "chain of command" (e.g.,
bureaucracies, communities with elected leadership); or personality in
which ego functioning provides control and direction.

Not all parts, however, exist in such chains of command. Some parts are
relatively autonomous from a centralized control agent. Children are relatively autonomous after reaching legal status as adults, yet they remain part
of their parents' family. In classic cases of "split personality" or dissociative
reaction, some significant portions of the personality function autono-
mously without control by the ego. The military organizations of some
Latin American and South American countries function largely indepen-
dently of the elected political hierarchy and are autonomous. Such autonomy in a social system may mean great power, as in the case of a military
organization that is increasingly less responsible to the rest of the society, or
it may mean irrelevance and powerlessness. This is seen, according to some
observers, in the case of a caste or racial minority such as black or Native
Americans.

It should be noted that, as Miller says, "It is the nature of organizations
that each subsystem and component has some autonomy and some subor-

dination or constraint, from lower level systems, other systems at the same level, and higher level systems" (J. Miller, 1965:222). In one way, this repeats what was said earlier about holons and the fact that causation is mutual; each system is both a superordinate whole and a subordinate part.

C. Differentiation and Specialization

The terms *differentiation* and *specialization* are similar but not the same. Differentiation means "dividing the functions" (Loomis and Loomis, 1961), that is, assigning functions to certain parts and not to others. Specialization adds the further stipulation that a part performs only or predominantly that function.

Differentiation is not the same as, but is always related to, allocation or distribution of energy. For example, assigning particular societal goals (GI function) to the Department of Health and Human Services is not the same as providing the necessary appropriations. Income maintenance of the elderly, as provided for in the Social Security Act, cannot be realized without the allocation of necessary revenues; the current debate over Social Security illustrates this very well.

Differentiation may apply to any of a large number of aspects of system functioning. There may be differentiation by age in regard to earning income for the family. Typically, adults are expected to earn, teenagers are expected to provide their own spending money, and the elderly and children are not expected to be self-supporting.

As a society becomes more complex, it becomes necessary to differentiate functions. Modern professions, such as nursing, home economics, social work, and law enforcement have come into being as part of the evolution of particular societies. In these societies, problems of social welfare and problems in social relationships are the concern of the newly minted professions developed to handle them.

There are several other important facts about differentiation that merit discussion. As a social system becomes differentiated, at some point the need arises to reintegrate and to establish communication between the differentiated parts. The more differentiation occurs, probably the more internal exchange of energy/information is necessary. This is one of the seemingly unsolvable problems in governmental provision of human services. There has been a high degree of differentiation of function without accompanying specialization that has resulted in the necessity of increasing amounts of energy being devoted to communication. A whole "industry" has been spawned to coordinate functions. Despite that, not because of it, services remain largely uncoordinated, duplicative, and random as experienced by the consumer/citizen.

Differentiation may be reversible; a system may reorder its structures to perform functions more satisfactorily (e.g., the belated efforts of the United

States automobile industry to modify the assembly line). The highly specialized assembly line had provided the means to mass produce automobiles and greatly increase the volume of sales. Now, in order to redress the resultant problems of quality control and alienation, the industry is merging and combining previously differentiated and specialized functions (e.g., through autonomous work groups and dismantling specialization). In a sense, the field of medicine is acting similarly in broadening specialties (e.g., family practice or the nurse practitioner).

There are levels of differentiation according to the stages of development of the social system; the more complex, the more fully the functions are differentiated among the parts, and this leads to discussion of specialization. As noted earlier, specialization means exclusivity of function — as a popular song puts it, "I can handle this job all by myself." Professions stake out their boundaries (who shall administer medication, who shall give legal advice, who shall approve adoptions, who is an expert witness in court). In that sense, professions are specialties, but they are not completely specialized in that all of them are performing integrative SI and GI functions in the society.

An example of societal specialization from ancient history is found in a manual for farmers written in the second century B.C.: "tunics, togas, blankets, smocks, and shoes should be bought at Rome . . . tiles at Venafrum, oil mills at Pompeii and at Rufrius's yard at Nola" (Lenski, 1970:255). This might have been the first paid commercial or the first consumer protection announcement in history. Occupational specialization is most pronounced in modern industrial society, but in Paris in 1313, there were already 157 different trades listed on the tax rolls (Lenski, 1970:256).

The extent of occupational specialization in modern society has become problematic. As Darwin and later scientists proved, the utility of specialization is always dependent on particular environmental conditions. When these conditions shift, the highly specialized adaptation is no longer functional. Similarly, if technology replaces or supercedes a specialized occupation, the previous workers are no longer valued or needed (e.g., local telephone operators and service station attendants).

As with differentiation, specialization is necessary to perform functions, but certain dangers also arise: "The more highly specialized a group's activities the more its need for the products of other groups and more important systemic linkage becomes. The ultimate of the kind of systemic linkage occasioned by cooperative specialization is reached in centralization" (Loomis and Loomis, 1961:228). These authors give specific examples:

> There is a certain amount of risk involved in a unit's devoting itself solely to a specialized commodity or other output. The family producing and partially socializing children risks the chance that the school will not perform its function. The schools risk the chance that collective families will not provide

essential facilities. The husband–father may prefer poverty on a subsistence farm to the risks of uncertain or disadvantageous systemic linkage with an outside wage-paying production unit. That the production of imperative outputs and their orderly interchange will not be a random affair, the social systems at any one hierarchical level are systematically linked to social systems of a higher level (Loomis and Loomis, 1961:417).

Thus we have come full circle to hierarchy as an aspect of structure.

VI. BEHAVIORAL ASPECTS OF SOCIAL SYSTEMS

Behavioral aspects are those energy interchanges that are of shorter duration and faster tempo. Three of these seem to us most significant: They are related to the basic energy functions, but not identical, and they are the subfunctions that seem to be most important for this book.

A. Social Control and Socialization

Social control and *socialization* occur in all systems and can have the purpose either of securing energy for the system from its components or of achieving goals; in other words, either the SI, GE, or GI functions. This process of securing energy or expending it to achieve goals can be done in either a coercive or cooperative fashion. The system can secure energy or achieve goals coercively either by threatening the component's survival and functioning or its goal achievement, or cooperatively by supporting the component's goal and encouraging its harmony with the system's goal. An example of this would be the "gentle persuasion" that a church can apply to its members to summon their efforts in supporting the church's goals, such as a building fund, yearly budget, or attendance at a revival. Or the church may employ coercive means — excommunication or expulsion from membership — if the member interferes with the church's goals by refusing to recruit new members, refusing to rear children in the faith, or failing to contribute financially.

This coercive control is usually labeled "power" (see the discussion of power in Chapter 5,II, "C. Power and Control"). Traditionally, the helping professions have espoused cooperative approaches, holding up the value of "self-determination," but in practice, decisions sometimes are made for clients. When these decisions are forced upon the client and fulfillment of the client's own goals or the client's access to needed resources is threatened, the professional person is using power and is an agent of coercive social control.

One form of social control is socialization. This is the induction of persons into the social system's way of life, whether the system is a family, community, or society. A bargain is struck: The system "promises" support of or noninterference with the person's goals as long as they are consistent with the system's goals. Some deviance may be permitted so long as it does not seriously interfere with the system's goals. The purpose of socialization is to get the work of the system done; the more successful the socialization, the less control is necessary because the person's goals will be harmonious with or identical to the system's goals. A certain degree of aggressiveness is tolerated and sometimes valued in our society, and it is expressed in approved ways. If we interfere with society's functioning by threatening people's lives, disrupting transportation, or preventing policemen from performing their tasks, we are liable to be controlled in some manner consistent with our "offense."

B. Communication

Communication is discussed in Chapter 3,II, "C. Language," in regard to symbols and language and in the appropriate chapters for functions of communication in communities, organizations, and families. Here we only wish to point out the necessity of communication. As Monane (1967: 42–44) says, transfer of energy/information is essential in a system. Organization of a system depends upon the effectiveness of communication. Monane (1967:59) also says that we usually think that communication will spread emotional warmth and bring the components of the system closer together. It certainly may, but it is just as likely to alienate and separate people by its content. The point is that *communication* is the transfer of energy to accomplish system goals. The effect of communication depends upon the context in which communication occurs. For example, the communication "You're under arrest!" hardly seems likely to encourage affection—it expresses control. The professionals who say they "communicated" with their clients usually means that positive affect was conveyed. But the professional and client also communicate when the energy exchange exerts control as in "Stop it, Jimmy, I won't let you run away!"

Systems develop means to send and receive information. *Feedback* is the primary means by which systems accomplish self-direction and seek goals. Feedback is a term which has been bankrupted in popular usage. "Give me your feedback" or "I really want your feedback" are corruptions that at best deal with only one aspect of feedback (see Glossary, p. 229 for further definition). Feedback is not, as the popular definition suggests, merely the echo received in response to one's actions, as is a radar blip. In cybernetics and systems thought, feedback includes not only the echo but the adjustment made to the echo.

In social systems thinking, feedback is the set of ideas to account for how any system accomplishes adaptation and self-direction. Feedback has been referred to as the secret of natural activity. It refers to the process of interaction wherein information is received and processed; behavior is validated (morphostasis) or changed (morphogenesis). Feedback enables a system to constantly monitor and adapt its own functioning, which is the means to steady state.

The use of the quality terms *positive* and *negative* in describing the nature of feedback varies among systems authors. Some view positive feedback as that which impels behavior in desirable directions and negative feedback as discouragement. Watzlawick, Beavin, and Jackson describe negative feedback as characteristic "of homeostasis (steady state) and therefore plays an important role in achieving and maintaining the stability of relationships. Positive feedback, on the other hand, leads to change, i.e. the loss of stability or equilibrium" (Watzlawick, Beavin, and Jackson, 1967:31). Others, including the authors of this book, label feedback as positive if it confirms or encourages existent behavioral patterns. Negative feedback, then, discourages or invalidates current behavior; it, therefore, encourages change, and the adaptive response is one of change.

One kind of example of use of feedback processes is the planned "news leak" or material attributed to "a White House source." Information is released in order to assess what the reaction would be to official statements, actions, or shifts in policies. If there is minimal public reaction or favorable reaction, the adaptation is to proceed in the suggested direction. If reactions are negative, that is, unfavorable, the adaptation is to modify or cancel the proposed course of action or to postpone to a more auspicious time. Effective use of such "trial balloons" and the inherent aspects of feedback cycles enable a system to steer a course toward its goals with minimal need to rescind actions in the face of opposition. This whole process is feedback.

Feedback operations and mechanisms are familiar to people in the human services. Some commonly encountered concepts are: reaction formation and overcompensation; looking-glass self and generalized other; positive reinforcement; cycle of poverty; dynamic modeling; deviation amplifying, deviation counteracting, and deviation reduction mechanisms.

An example of deviation-amplifying feedback is the following: A boy from a poor family wears clothing that makes a negative impression; and his teachers conclude that he probably is not very intelligent. They treat him as though he is not; and he responds to this, confirming their view, in order to "get along." His behavior confirms their opinion, they provide him with less attention and simpler, intellectually less demanding material. He performs at this level, and when he is tested, the tests confirm that he does not perform as well as the other children. The teacher continues to regard him as less capable than other children, and he continues to fall behind. Eventually, he withdraws or is expelled from school.

This example can also serve to illustrate the differing uses of "positive" and "negative" labeling of feedback. As this boy is confirmed in and accepts the position of "poor student," the status becomes a central element of his conception of himself. Each time he receives further recognition of his being an inadequate or unwanted student, that is "positive" feedback. It is "positive" since it validates his self-conception. In this instance, "negative" feedback would be information that impels him to reappraise himself and change sufficiently in order to impel others to revise their expectations of him. Since such change is more difficult than remaining the same, the first adaptation to this sort of negative feedback is to accentuate the familiar patterns of adaptation. Thus with the boy in the example, a teacher or counselor may ambitiously attempt to use strategies to manipulate the feedback cycle through informing the youth that he really is capable of better performance and then become discouraged when the boy's response "proves" he is a poor student. Again, the point being emphasized is that feedback processes are not simple causal chains; they are complex cycles of mutual interactions.

Feedback is as integral a part of all teacher–student relationships or all counselor–client relationships as it is of all human relationships. Therapy consists, in part, of interpreting signals from the client and "feeding back" carefully selected responses that are neutral, positive, or negative to stimulate the occurrence of behavior that is consistent with the goals of the two-person therapeutic system. The therapist assumes the client will be similarly interpreting and feeding back.

C. Adaptation

Feedback could be considered identical to adaptation, but adaptation is discussed separately to emphasize two points. First, *adaptation* is viewed by some theorists (including Parsons) as being of paramount importance because systems must adjust to their environment. While it is true that there must be adjustment between systems and environment, we reject the view that the adjustment must be made only by the system and not by the environment. (Our position was stated earlier in the discussion of holon.) Therefore, we do recognize the importance of feedback as a mechanism of adjustment but do not make adaptation the primary function.

Second, adaptation takes two forms: *assimilation* and *accommodation*. These are discussed in Chapter 8 in the section on Piaget. These two terms indicate whether the system accepts or rejects the incoming information without any change on the part of the system, or whether it modifies its structure in response to the incoming information. In reality, systems do both of these at the same time in some mixture; as with other polarities, no system does one or the other entirely.

CONCLUSION

This chapter has introduced those concepts we judge to be essential to a social systems approach to understanding human behavior. These are fundamental ideas that will be developed further in subsequent chapters. A few other key concepts will be introduced in later discussions of particular systems.

It is important to note in conclusion that *evolutionary, structural,* and *behavioral* aspects are three ways to slice the same apple; they are not separate but complementary dimensions of a system. A board that is long, wide, and thick is not three separate boards; nor can one dimension exist without the others.

SUGGESTED READINGS

Auger, Jeanine Roose.
   1976   *Behavioral Systems and Nursing.* Englewod Cliffs, N.J.: Prentice-Hall.
      Application of general systems concepts to nursing practice. Discussion of physical and psychological subsystems. Useful diagram of subsystems and functions as well as results of system imbalance.
Bertalanffy, Ludwig Von.
   1967   *Robots, Men and Minds.* New York: Braziller.
      The author is generally acknowledged, by himself and others, to be the "father of general systems." This book deals with the central conceptualizations.
Buckley, Walter, ed.
   1968   *Modern Systems Research for the Behavioral Scientist.* Chicago: Aldine.
      A comprehensive collection of the major writings of general systems theorists. The reader needs an understanding of the basic terminology before tackling this work.
Capra, Fritjof.
   1977   *The Tao of Physics.* New York: Bantam Books, Inc.
      A creative attempt to reconcile Eastern philosophy and Western science. A search for unity which extracts the commonalities of world view in these seemingly disparate cosmologies.
Engel, George L.
   1977   "The Need for a New Medical Model: A Challenge for Biomedicine" *Science* v. 196n 4286, April 1977, pp. 129–36.
      A nicely constructed argument for a systems approach for medical training and practice.
Hearn, Gordon, ed.
   1969   *The General Systems Approach: Contributions Toward an Holistic Conception of Social Work.* New York: Council on Social Work Education.
      A seminal monograph that established the relevance of the general systems approach to social work. The articles by Hearn, Gordon, and Lathrope provide essential background to a social systems approach to the nature and knowledge of social work.
Koestler, Arthur
   1979   *Janus: A Summing Up.* New York: Random House.
      In this book Koestler further develops his conception of holon and expands the applications.

Koestler, Arthur, and J. R. Smythies.
  1971 *Beyond Reductionism: New Perspectives in the Life Sciences.* Boston: Beacon.
  This is for the student who wants to delve into the complex issues inherent in
  general systems. It is a report of an international symposium held in Alpbach
  in the Austrian Tyrol in 1968. The invitations were confined to "personalities
  in academic life with undisputed authority in their respective fields." They included Jerome Bruner, Bertalanffy, and Piaget.

Laszlo, Ervin.
  1974 *A Strategy for the Future: The Systems Approach to World Order.* New York:
  George Braziller, Inc.
  An exploration of the potentials of a systems approach to world order. Especially relevant are pp. 3–30, and pp. 203–225.

Rogers, Martha E.
  1970 *An Introduction to the Theoretical Basis of Nursing.* Philadelphia: F. A.
  Davis Company.
  An excellent introduction to a theory for nursing cast within a systems framework. Unit II, pp. 39–78, is particularly recommended.

Saxton, Dolores F., *et al.*, eds.
  1977 *Mosby's Comprehensive Review of Nursing* (ninth edition). St. Louis: The
  C. V. Mosby Company.
  Review of concepts and sources fundamental to the practice of nursing.
  Chapter 5, "The Behavior Sciences" includes systems ideas and is an excellent
  listing of concepts applicable to all levels of social systems.

Zukav, Gary.
  1979 *The Dancing Wu Li Masters.* New York: William Morrow and Company,
  Inc.
  Another stimulating attempt to reconcile differing ways of knowing. A book
  written for lay persons, explaining the evolution of the quantum relativistic
  physics of today. Stresses that experience is never limited to two options; there
  is always an alternative between every "this" and every "that."

LITERARY SOURCES

Forster, E. M.
  1954 *Howards End.* New York: Random House.
  This symbol-laden novel with its oft-quoted theme, "Only connect," beauti-
  fully describes systemic properties. It is one of many literary sources that are
  available for testing out the ideas presented in this chapter. An example, "Only
  connect the prose and the passion, and both will be exalted, and human love
  will be seen at its height. Live in fragments no longer. Only connect, and the
  beast and the monk, robbed of the isolation that is life to either, will die."

Mailer, Norman.
  1979 *The Executioner's Song.* New York: Warner Books, Inc.
  Mailer's biography of Gary Gilmore written in novel form is an excellent
  portrayal of the complexity of a person's part/whole aspects interacting across
  the range of systems: family, group, organizations, communities and society.

Romains, Jules.
  1961 *Death of a Nobody.* New York: New American Library.
  One of many literary works that portray the interlacing of human systems as
  they converge through a particular system, in this instance, a person whose life
  seemed of little consequence.

APPLICATIONS OF
A SOCIAL SYSTEMS
APPROACH

Systems ideas are best learned through applications to human situations. It is our contention that most people in the human services tend to think systemically as they view humans in their social context. The first chapter introduced the fundamental terminology and contained illustrations of application. This chapter provides a human situation drawn from literature, followed by a few suggested ways of applying systems thought to the story.

As you read *A Tree. A Rock. A Cloud* by Carson McCullers,* think about the applicability of concepts introduced in Chapter 1.

> It was raining that morning, and still very dark. When the boy reached the streetcar café he had almost finished his route and he went in for a cup of coffee. The place was an all-night café owned by a bitter and stingy man called Leo. After the raw, empty street the café seemed friendly and bright: along the counter there were a couple of soldiers, three spinners from the cotton mill, and in a corner a man who sat hunched over with his nose and half his face down in a beer mug. The boy wore a helmet such as aviators wear. When he went into the café he unbuckled the chin strap and raised the right flap up over his pink little ear; often as he drank his coffee someone would speak to him in a friendly way. But this morning Leo did not look into his face and none of the men were talking. He paid and was leaving the café when a voice called out to him:
> 'Son! Hey Son!'
> He turned back and the man in the corner was crooking his finger and nodding to him. He had brought his face out of the beer mug and he seemed

* Paul Engle, distinguished American poet and critic and editor of the annual O. Henry Awards anthology, *Prize Stories*, considered *A Tree. A Rock. A Cloud* to be "the most perfect short story in modern American literature" (Jaffe and Scott, 1960).

suddenly very happy. The man was long and pale, with a big nose and faded orange hair.

'Hey Son!'

The boy went toward him. He was an undersized boy of about twelve, with one shoulder drawn higher than the other because of the weight of the paper sack. His face was shallow, freckled, and his eyes were round child eyes.

'Yeah Mister?'

The man laid one hand on the paper boy's shoulders, then grasped the boy's chin and turned his face slowly from one side to the other. The boy shrank back uneasily.

'Say! What's the big idea?'

The boy's voice was shrill; inside the café it was suddenly very quiet.

The man said slowly: 'I love you.'

All along the counter the men laughed. The boy, who had scowled and sidled away, did not know what to do. He looked over the counter at Leo, and Leo watched him with a weary, brittle jeer. The boy tried to laugh also. But the man was serious and sad.

'I did not mean to tease you, Son,' he said. 'Sit down and have a beer with me. There is something I have to explain.'

Cautiously, out of the corner of his eye, the paper boy questioned the men along the counter to see what he should do. But they had gone back to their beer or their breakfast and did not notice him. Leo put a cup of coffee on the counter and a little jug of cream.

'He is a minor,' Leo said.

The paper boy slid himself up onto the stool. His ear beneath the upturned flap of the helmet was very small and red. The man was nodding at him soberly. "It is important," he said. Then he reached in his hip pocket and brought out something which he held up in the palm of his hand for the boy to see.

'Look very carefully,' he said.

The boy stared, but there was nothing to look at very carefully. The man held in his big, grimy palm a photograph. It was the face of a woman, but blurred, so that only the hat and the dress she was wearing stood out clearly.

'See?' the man asked.

The boy nodded and the man placed another picture in his palm. The woman was standing on a beach in a bathing suit. The suit made her stomach very big, and that was the main thing you noticed.

'Got a good look?' He leaned over closer and finally asked: 'You ever seen her before?'

The boy sat motionless, staring slantwise at the man. 'Not so I know of.'

'Very well.' The man blew on the photographs and put them back into his pocket. 'That was my wife.'

'Dead?' the boy asked.

Slowly the man shook his head. He pursed his lips as though about to whistle and answered in a long-drawn way: 'Nuuu—' he said. 'I will explain.'

The beer on the counter before the man was in a large brown mug. He did not pick it up to drink. Instead he bent down and, putting his face over the rim, he rested there for a moment. Then with both hands he tilted the mug and sipped.

'Some night you'll go to sleep with your big nose in a mug and drown,' said Leo. 'Prominent transient drowns in beer. That would be a cute death.'

The paper boy tried to signal to Leo. While the man was not looking he screwed up his face and worked his mouth to question soundlessly: 'Drunk?'

But Leo only raised his eyebrows and turned away to put some pink strips of bacon on the grill. The man pushed the mug away from him, straightened himself, and folded his loose crooked hands on the counter. His face was sad as he looked at the paper boy. He did not blink, but from time to time the lids closed down with delicate gravity over his pale green eyes. It was nearing dawn and the boy shifted the weight of the paper sack.

'I am talking about love,' the man said. 'With me it is a science.'

The boy half slid down from the stool. But the man raised his forefinger, and there was something about him that held the boy and would not let him go away.

'Twelve years ago I married the woman in the photograph. She was my wife for one year, nine months, three days, and two nights. I loved her. Yes . . .' He tightened his blurred, rambling voice and said again: 'I loved her. I thought also that she loved me. I was a railroad engineer. She had all home comforts and luxuries. It never crept into my brain that she was not satisfied. But do you know what happened?'

'Mgneeow!' said Leo.

The man did not take his eyes from the boy's face. 'She left me. I came in one night and the house was empty and she was gone. She left me.'

'With a fellow?' the boy asked.

Gently the man placed his palm down on the counter. 'Why naturally, Son. A woman does not run off like that alone.'

The café was quiet, the soft rain black and endless in the street outside. Leo pressed down the frying bacon with the prongs of his long fork. 'So you have been chasing the floozie for eleven years. You frazzled old rascal!'

For the first time the man glanced at Leo. 'Please don't be vulgar. Besides, I was not speaking to you.' He turned back to the boy and said in a trusting and secretive undertone: 'Let's not pay any attention to him. O.K.?'

The paper boy nodded doubtfully.

'It was like this,' the man continued. 'I am a person who feels many things. All my life one thing after another has impressed me. Moonlight. The leg of a pretty girl. One thing after another. But the point is that when I had enjoyed anything there was a peculiar sensation as though it was laying around loose in me. Nothing seemed to finish itself up or fit in with the other things. Women? I had my portion of them. The same. Afterwards laying around loose in me. I was a man who had never loved.'

Very slowly he closed his eyelids, and the gesture was like a curtain drawn at the end of a scene in a play. When he spoke again his voice was excited and the words came fast—the lobes of his large, loose ears seemed to tremble.

'Then I met this woman. I was fifty-one years old and she always said she was thirty. I met her at a filling station and we were married within three days. And do you know what it was like? I just can't tell you. All I had ever felt was gathered together around this woman. Nothing lay around loose in me any more but was finished up by her.'

The man stopped suddenly and stroked his long nose. His voice sank down to a steady and reproachful undertone: 'I'm not explaining this right. What happened was this. There were these beautiful feelings and loose little pleasures inside me. And this woman was something like an assembly line for my soul. I run these little pieces of myself through her and I come out complete. Now do you follow me?'

'What was her name?' the boy asked.

'Oh,' he said. 'I called her Dodo. But that is immaterial.'

'Did you try to make her come back?'

The man did not seem to hear. 'Under the circumstances you can imagine how I felt when she left me.'

Leo took the bacon from the grill and folded two strips of it between a bun. He had a gray face, with slitted eyes, and a pinched nose saddled by faint blue shadows. One of the mill workers signaled for more coffee and Leo poured it. He did not give refills on coffee free. The spinner ate breakfast there every morning, but the better Leo knew his customers the stingier he treated them. He nibbled his own bun as though he grudged it to himself.

'And you never got hold of her again?'

The boy did not know what to think of the man, and his child's face was uncertain with mingled curiosity and doubt. He was new on the paper route; it was still strange to him to be out in the town in the black, queer early morning.

'Yes,' the man said. 'I took a number of steps to get her back. I went around trying to locate her. I went to Tulsa where she had folks. And to Mobile. I went to every town she had ever mentioned to me, and I hunted down every man she had formerly been connected with. Tulsa, Atlanta, Chicago, Cheehaw, Memphis. . . . For the better part of two years I chased around the country trying to lay hold of her.'

'But the pair of them had vanished from the face of the earth!' said Leo.

'Don't listen to him,' the man said confidentially. 'And also just forget those two years. They are not important. What matters is that around the third year a curious thing begun to happen to me.'

'What?' the boy asked.

The man leaned down and tilted his mug to take a sip of beer. But as he hovered over the mug his nostrils fluttered slightly; he sniffed the staleness of the beer and did not drink. 'Love is a curious thing to begin with. At first I thought only of getting her back. It was a kind of mania. But then as time went on I tried to remember her. But do you know what happened?'

'No,' the boy said.

'When I laid myself down on a bed and tried to think about her my mind became a blank. I couldn't see her. I would take out her pictures and look. No good. Nothing doing. A blank. Can you imagine it?'

'Say Mac!' Leo called down the counter. 'Can you imagine this bozo's mind a blank!'

Slowly, as though fanning away flies, the man waved his hand. His green eyes were concentrated and fixed on the shallow little face of the paper boy.

'But a sudden piece of glass on a sidewalk. Or a nickel tune in a music box. A shadow on a wall at night. And I would remember. It might happen in a street and I would cry or bang my head against a lamppost. You follow me?'

'A piece of glass . . .' the boy said.

'Anything. I would walk around and I had no power of how and when to remember her. You think you can put up a kind of shield. But remembering don't come to a man face forward—it corners around sideways. I was at the mercy of everything I saw and heard. Suddenly instead of me combing the countryside to find her she begun to chase me around in my very soul. *She* chasing *me*, mind you! And in my soul.'

The boy asked finally: 'What part of the country were you in then?'

'Ooh,' the man groaned. 'I was a sick mortal. It was like smallpox. I confess, Son, that I boozed. I fornicated. I committed any sin that suddenly appealed to me. I am loath to confess it but I will do so. When I recall that period it is all curdled in my mind, it was so terrible.'

The man leaned his head down and tapped his forehead on the counter. For a few seconds he stayed bowed over in this position, the back of his stringy neck covered with orange furze, his hands with their long warped fingers held palm to palm in an attitude of prayer. Then the man straightened himself; he was smiling and suddenly his face was bright and tremulous and old.

'It was in the fifth year that it happened,' he said. 'And with it I started my science.'

Leo's mouth jerked with a pale, quick grin. 'Well none of we boys are getting any younger,' he said. Then with sudden anger he balled up a dishcloth he was holding and threw it down hard on the floor. 'You draggle-tailed old Romeo!'

'What happened?' the boy asked.

The old man's voice was high and clear: 'Peace,' he answered.

'Huh?'

'It is hard to explain scientifically, Son,' he said. 'I guess the logical explanation is that she and I had fleed around from each other for so long that finally we just got tangled up together and lay down and quit. Peace. A queer and beautiful blankness. It was spring in Portland and the rain came every afternoon. All evening I just stayed there on my bed in the dark. And that is how the science come to me.'

The windows in the streetcar were pale blue with light. The two soldiers paid for their beers and opened the door — one of the soldiers combed his hair and wiped off his muddy puttees before they went outside. The three mill workers bent silently over their breakfasts. Leo's clock was ticking on the wall.

'It is this. And listen carefully. I meditated on love and reasoned it out. I realized what is wrong with us. Men fall in love for the first time. And what do they fall in love with?'

The boy's soft mouth was partly open and he did not answer.

'A woman,' the old man said. 'Without science, with nothing to go by, they undertake the most dangerous and sacred experience in God's earth. They fall in love with a woman. Is that correct, Son?'

'Yeah,' the boy said faintly.

'They start at the wrong end of love. They begin at the climax. Can you wonder it is so miserable? Do you know how men should love?'

The old man reached over and grasped the boy by the collar of his leather jacket. He gave him a gentle little shake and his green eyes gazed down unblinking and grave.

'Son, do you know how love should be begun?'

The boy sat small and listening and still. Slowly he shook his head. The old man leaned closer and whispered:

'A tree. A rock. A cloud.'

It was still raining outside in the street: a mild, gray, endless rain. The mill whistle blew for the six o'clock shift and the three spinners paid and went away. There was no one in the café but Leo, the old man, and the little paper boy.

'The weather was like this in Portland,' he said. 'At the time my science was begun. I meditated and I started very cautious. I would pick up something from the street and take it home with me. I bought a goldfish and I concentrated on the goldfish and I loved it. I graduated from one thing to another. Day by day I was getting this technique. On the road from Portland to San Diego——'

'Aw shut up!' screamed Leo suddenly. 'Shut up! Shut up!'

The old man still held the collar of the boy's jacket; he was trembling and his face was earnest and bright and wild. 'For six years now I have gone around by myself and built up my science. And now I am a master. Son. I can love anything. No longer do I have to think about it even. I see a street full of people and a beautiful light comes in me. I watch a bird in the sky. Or I meet a traveler on the road. Everything, Son. And anybody. All stranger and all loved! Do you realize what a science like mine can mean?'

The boy held himself stiffly, his hands curled tight around the counter edge. Finally he asked: "Did you ever really find that lady?'

'What? What say, Son?'

'I mean,' the boy asked timidly. 'Have you fallen in love with a woman again?'

The old man loosened his grasp on the boy's collar. He turned away and for the first time his green eyes had a vague and scattered look. He lifted the mug from the counter, drank down the yellow beer. His head was shaking slowly from side to side. Then finally he answered: 'No, Son. You see that is the last step in my science. I go cautious. And I am not quite ready yet.'

'Well!' said Leo. 'Well well well!'

The old man stood in the open doorway. 'Remember,' he said. Framed there in the gray damp light of the early morning he looked shrunken and seedy and frail. But his smile was bright. 'Remember I love you,' he said with a last nod. And the door closed quietly behind him.

The boy did not speak for a long time. He pulled down the bangs on his forehead and slid his grimy little forefinger around the rim of his empty cup. Then without looking at Leo he finally asked:

'Was he drunk?'

'No,' said Leo shortly.

The boy raised his clear voice higher. 'Then was he a dope fiend?'

'No.'

The boy looked up at Leo, and his flat little face was desperate, his voice urgent and shrill. 'Was he crazy? Do you think he was a lunatic?' The paper boy's voice dropped suddenly with doubt.'Leo? Or not?'

But Leo would not answer him. Leo had run a night café for fourteen years, and he held himself to be a critic of craziness. There were the town characters and also the transients who roamed in from the night. He knew the manias of all of them. But he did not want to satisfy the questions of the waiting child. He tightened his pale face and was silent.

So the boy pulled down the right flap of his helmet and as he turned to leave he made the only comment that seemed safe to him, the only remark that could not be laughed down and despised:

'He sure has done a lot of traveling.'

A Tree. A Rock. A Cloud can be viewed from a systems perspective as can any human situation. Can you properly consider Leo's restaurant as the focal system with Leo, the boy, the old man, and the other customers as parts, or subsystems? How would the boundaries be described? What are the elements of organization? How would you describe the culture of the restaurant? What larger system(s) is the restaurant part of, or subsystem to: What systems is it linked to? What evidence is there of one or more communities in the restaurant's environment?

Now shift the focus to the old man or the boy. Describe the nature of boundaries and elements of organization. What are the component parts of the "old man system?" What larger system(s) is he now part of? What systems was he part of in the past? What does it mean that he did not use his wife's name?

The answers to these questions will suggest a systems picture of relatively closed individuals, interacting in a social–cultural context that enables people to pursue their own agendas without forming interactional systems that have continuity over time. Thus the restaurant may meet criteria for judging it to be a system, but are the boy and the old man part of it? Some would describe them as "linked" to this system; a few who relish systems jargon may term them to be "throughput." The restaurant is then seen as the setting for their interaction, but they are not integral "parts" of the systemic continuity that all systems must have. The other customers referred to more possibly could be parts of the restaurant system. Certainly Leo is.

The substance of the interaction was obviously of greatest importance to the old man, who insisted on pursuing it in his way. He is actively, and perhaps chronically, organizing and trying to make whole himself and his feelings of intimacy. He does this through explaining himself to himself through explaining himself to others—the status of young boy being particularly vulnerable to hear him out, although Leo is to hear him as well. What does he mean, that his wife was "something like an assembly line for my soul?"

The story effectively conveys not only how the listeners are affected and in turn the old man is affected. The feedback cycle is clear, isn't it?

CULTURE AND SOCIETY

> Men commonly feel according to their inclinations, speak and think according to their learning and imbibed opinions, but generally act according to custom.
>
> Sir Francis Bacon

INTRODUCTION

This chapter explores human behavior at the broadest, most general level —that is, as a species. We will examine ideas from a number of disciplines, ideas that seem particularly pertinent to human services and a systems approach. These disciplines include biology, sociology, linguistics, psychology, ethology, and especially anthropology.

First, we should explain how we use the terms *culture* and *society*. To be consistent with the systems skeleton, we use the term culture in two ways. First and generally, culture refers to those qualities and attributes that seem to be characteristic of all humankind. Culture denotes those things unique to the species *Homo sapiens* as differentiated from all other forms of life. As Jerome Bruner says, "man represents that crucial point in evolution where adaptation is achieved by the vehicle of culture, and only in minor ways by further changes in his morphology" (Bruner, 1968:74). This general usage of culture is employed to underscore the notion that the human evolutionary timetable is unique in that it is through culture that the human is immediately affected by and subject to the evolutionary principle of natural selection. As Konrad Lorenz, the widely known theorist in ethology, puts it, "historians will have to face the fact that natural selection determined the evolution of cultures in the same manner as it did that of the species"

43

(Lorenz, 1963:260). In other words, a culture survives if it can accommodate to changing conditions. If its ways are rigidly matched to a particular set of environmental conditions, the survival of its cultural integrity is dependent on the continuation of those conditions. One reason for the decline and near disappearance of some Plains groups of American Indians is that the buffalo were exterminated by white hunters and there was no adequate substitute.

The human, then, is a social being, uniquely possessing culture. Cultural forms — not the species — are changed, synthesized, radiated, and extinguished. This, of course, does not preclude the possibility of the human species being subject to the laws of species survival as well, but the time scale is quite different for biological evolution. According to this broad definition, then, culture is to be viewed as a macrosystem for purposes of discussion and speculation. Weston La Barre provides arguments for this position (La Barre, 1954: Chap. 1).

A *society* refers to a group of people who have learned to live and work together. Society is viewed as a holon, and within the society, culture refers to the way of life followed by the group (society). This, then, is the second usage of culture — that which binds a particular society together and includes its manners and morals, tools, and techniques.

I. SPECIES AND CULTURE: UNIQUE ASPECTS OF THE HUMAN SPECIES

Human beings have certain attributes in common regardless of time or place. These common attributes can be parsed and explicated in a number of ways. For the present purpose, we will generalize these attributes under four headings: (1) the capacity to think, (2) the family as a biological universal, (3) language, and (4) territoriality.

A. The Capacity To Think

The capacity to think is perceived as the most distinctive attribute as witnessed by our identification of the species as *Homo sapiens* (thinking man). In 1948, Julian Huxley commented that "the first and most obviously unique characteristic of man is his capacity for conceptual thought, if you prefer objective terms, you will say his employment of true speech but that is only another way of saying the same thing" (Huxley, 1964:8). The capacity to think and communicate thoughts sets humans apart from other forms of life. In recent research, it appears that humans are not unique in this ability. Dolphins' language, e.g., is being decoded by means of computer. Gross impairment of these faculties in humans is indeed a grave matter. Much of child-rearing is devoted to the further refinement and development of this capacity (as is apparent in the discussion of cognitive theory in Chapter 8, I, "B. Cognitive Theory"). Perpetuation of tradition and use of tools is dependent upon members of the culture having this capacity.

B. The Family as a Human Universal

The family is biologically based and is the primary social (and socializing) unit. The *fact* of the family is a constant; the *form* of the family is a variable. Anthropological studies have demonstrated convincingly that although the family as a primary socializing unit is a universal phenomenon, there is no "normal" family form. As ethologists have learned about the mating, reproducing, and rearing patterns of a range of species, they have uncovered a number of factors that seem to influence the pairings and groupings of various species. These factors include:

1. The number of offspring per mating — the reproductive rate
2. The length of the gestation period, which influences the number of matings
3. The length of the period of the immaturity of the young, expressed in ratio to total life span

As the first factor reduces (smaller number of offspring per mating) and the other two factors lengthen (gestation and relative length of the time of immaturity), pair bonds and family rearing of the young increase. Among humans, the existence of the family is, of course, a necessary element for the development of culture because culture is transmitted from one generation to the next through teaching, not through the genes (La Barre, 1954: Chaps. 2 and 7).

As La Barre emphasizes, the *cultural form* of family must never be confused with the *biological norm* of the family; the cultural forms vary tremendously (La Barre, 1954:113). The nuclear family, consisting of the biological parents and their offspring, is only one of these forms and not the most prevalent at that. The form of the family is influenced by the culture in which it exists; in turn, the form influences that culture. The human family, then, is a system, a holon, and it has a simultaneous existence as part and whole. Its form organizes the energies of the family members, and it must engage in transactions with its suprasystems.

The following is an example of how cultural aspects influence the family system. Our economic system, with its accent on production and distribution of goods achieved through the standardization of organization of energies toward that goal, requires a mobile work force. Adaptation to this single cultural artifact has been extremely stressful to the form of the family during the past generation and has been amply discussed in both popular and technical literature. The cultural bind experienced by emigrants from

Appalachia is a prime example. To seek and find gainful employment requires a move to an industrial city, but the cultural expectations and norms for expected behaviors remain the same at home. The nature of the mutual obligations between the emigrants and those who remain behind, especially those related to family, require the emigrants' presence at certain times of need. As these occur, the person well may decide to leave the employment situation to "go down home."

The main point here is that the family is a universal characteristic of the human species and is necessary to the maintenance of human culture, but the form of the family varies from culture to culture and among the subcultures within a culture.

C. Language

Etymologists broadly define language as any transfer of meaning, but general usage refers to the spoken and written messages. Appreciation of the universality in the broader sense — that is, any transfer of meaning — is particularly important to those who deal with persons rather than objects. Since persons with troubles often have their troubles because they rely on other means of communication without conscious intent, attunement to unspoken and unwritten language forms is essential. A person may express feelings and ideas with signals rather than with consensual symbols of communication. Consequently, such ideas as "body language" and "listening with the third ear" become important.

There are explicitly arranged language forms other than spoken and written verbal messages. A driver's examination for illiterates uses colors and sign shapes rather than the printed word. On the road, the conventions for indications of one's intent to overtake and pass another vehicle are clearly communicated through codes of blinking lights. The automobile driver can overtake a truck and signal to the truck driver a wish to pass. The truck driver, based on a better view of the road ahead, can signal the driver behind either to remain behind or that it is safe to pass. And the variation from dim to bright lights communicates that the deed has been accomplished. The key to nonverbal language is the consensus of meaning attached to symbols and their manipulations. An important aspect of socialization into a new system is to become acquainted with such symbolization and learn the attached meanings. Excellent examples are the sometimes subtle and complex, silent or audible signals exchanged at auctions.

There are also implicitly understood conventions and symbols that require even more consensual agreement than the explicit symbols. The initiation of a social transaction between two equals can be signaled by the shaking of hands, an embrace, or mutual acknowledgment of deference, such as bowing or removal of hats. The culturally conditioned "embracer" learns very quickly in a "handshaking" culture that the meaning of gesture is culturally defined, not universal.

Communication seems to be present in other life forms as well. The dancing flight of the bee and the singing of the bird to announce territorial prerogatives to other members of their species are well known. Such phenomena seem distinguishable from human language in respect to the thought and meaning signified. The evidence thus far is that the bee and the bird, operating from instinct, evolved for purposes of species survival, whereas the human operates from learning that has evolved for cultural survival.

Etymologists have an interesting time with cross-cultural comparisons of word meanings and in the process provide interesting insights. For example, Mario Pei in his fascinating book, *The Story of Language* (1966), has a section dealing with the symbolism of color and how symbols vary from language to language and from culture to culture. Why are we "blue" when depressed, "yellow" when cowardly, "red" when radically inclined? In Russia, red is beautiful, and both "red" and "beauty" come from the same word root. White is the color of purity and innocence to Americans, but to Russians and Koreans, it is the color of mourning and death. In the Russian civil war, the Reds had a gigantic psychological advantage over the Whites because of the symbolic overtones. This kind of information carries implications for attempts to understand racial conflicts. Those who launched the "Black is beautiful" campaign were attuned to the cultural importance of color symbolism. How much of the unyielding racial prejudice is attributable to the cultural artifact of color symbolism is unknown, but it certainly must be an important factor.

In considering language and thought as species characteristics in man, the thesis propounded by Whorf and Sapir is of note. Their hypothesis is that language structures reality; the form and variability of the language determines how members of the culture will view reality and structure their thoughts (Whorf, 1956). This hypothesis is generally accepted. E. T. Hall, in developing his thesis about territoriality and its importance to people, did an analysis of the words listed in the *Oxford Pocket Dictionary*. He found that 20% of them could be classified as referring to space and spacial relations (Hall, 1969:93).

Bruner says that the Whorf and Sapir formulation serves to set up the pins in the wrong alley. He holds that attention should really be focused on *how* language determines thought, regardless of which language is being considered (Bruner, 1968). There is a close, demonstrable relationship between culture and language. This relationship is not necessarily causal in either direction. As often cited, modern English and American language structures attend closely to the temporal plane. In the study of grammar, tenses are of utmost importance, since time is so essential to aspects of the culture. Some cultures make no provisions for tenses — the precise measurement of time is of little cultural importance to them.

La Barre presents intriguing facts and speculations about language as symbolic communication (La Barre, 1954: Chap. 10). He accepts the

Whorfian hypothesis and states that the structure of reality is, much of the time, merely imputed to reality by the structure of our language. As soon as the human infant learns to speak any language at all, it already has a "hardening of the categories," or "they are different, this we know, for our language tells us so" (La Barre, 1954).

La Barre develops the idea that language is so flexible that a word can put into semantic equation any two disparate objects in the universe. If the society accepts the equation by consensus, semantically it becomes the essence of reality; if the individual does this without societal consensus, the person is schizophrenic and thus not attuned to reality. "A psychotic's truth is one 'I' make it, and cultural truth is what by unwitting vote 'we' make it; but ultimate truth still remains in the outside world of that which is" (La Barre, 1954:266). Robert Merton expressed the same idea in his Thomas Theorem, "If men define situations as real, they are real in their consequences" (Merton, 1957:421). Koestler comments:

> The prejudice and impurities which have been incorporated into the verbal concepts of a given universe of discourse cannot be undone by any amount of discourse within the frame of reference of that universe. The rules of the game, however absurd, cannot be altered by playing that game. Language can become a screen which stands between the thinker and reality. This is the reason why true creativity often starts where language ends (Koestler, 1967a:177).

D. Territoriality

Another dimension of culture that has only recently received much attention is *territoriality*. This concept refers to the tendency of people, in their social systems, to seek and maintain a territory. Some authors deal with territory as primarily spatial (Ardrey, 1966; Hall, 1969), while others stress the interactional aspects (Lyman and Scott, 1967). The definition of spatial and interactional territories is a paramount feature of any culture.

One simple example is the definition of territorial elements as squared or rounded. This choice seems to be simultaneously determined *by* other features of the culture as well as a determinant *of* culture. The "home territories" within a given culture give clues to other aspects of the culture. The sedentary and specialized culture with much differentiation of function tends to organize living and work spaces in squares with specialized uses. The square house has its bedrooms, bathrooms, kitchen, living room, den, and so forth. The nomadic, unspecialized culture lives in round houses (igloo, wigwam, cave, or round hut) without specialized compartments. Arranging territories in squares tends to close boundaries. The increasing use of geodesic domes as homes may signify cultural shifts in our society. Another significant feature may be designs of public schools in "pods," "clusters," or "modules." (For further discussion, see McLuhan, 1965:123–130.)

The spirit of equality, fidelity, and camaraderie embodied in the King Arthur legend is symbolized by the table round. Formal dining tables are usually rectangular, while tables in small, intimate bars are round. Youth's expressions of dissatisfaction with the impersonal, highly structured role relations and specialized functions of the bureaucratic system or organization were expressed in the 1960's in the epithet "square." Dictionaries show that the meanings attached to this epithet by immediately preceding American generations were "justly," "fairly," and "honestly." These meanings reflected the primary purpose of the impersonality of the bureaucratic system—to protect the person from unjust and arbitrary decisions. The Paris negotiations concerning the resolution of the Vietnam War were delayed for many months while it was decided if the talks would be conducted over a rectangular table or around a circular one. In part, this dispute symbolized crucial differences in cultural traditions and beliefs between the contending systems.

Relationships are symbolized by diagrammatic representations intended to concretize interactional territories (Fig. 5a and b). The components in Fig. 5a are arranged in a vertical hierarchy, and each component (person or department) is designated by title or role rather than by name. Specialization and differentiation are designated by these labels. In Fig. 5b, the components would be labeled by name (or number, to protect the innocent). The hierarchy here is represented in the circular plane and conveys positive, negative, and absent patterns of relatedness. Each of these diagrams is illustrative of interactional territorial arrangements and relationships.

It is hypothesized, then, that all holons have a territorial dimension. This territory may be spatial or interactional, not static, objective, or observable.

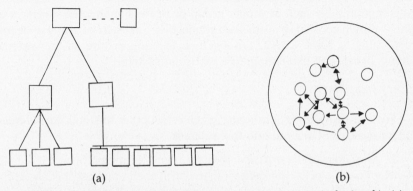

(a)   (b)

Fig. 5. A typical representation of a bureaucratic structure is depicted in (a). A typical sociogram is represented in (b).

It probably is a "sense of territory," and as such is congruent with the particular culture. Territoriality refers to the cultural ways people locate themselves in their universe and establish the boundaries of their various human systems.

II. ANALYTICAL DIMENSIONS OF CULTURE: QUALITIES OF A SOCIETY

Definitions of culture abound and frequently conflict. Kroeber and Kluckhohn (1952) devote an entire book to a listing of definitions of culture. They conclude that the definition given by Edward Tylor in 1871 was as good as any. Tylor's definition is that culture is that complex whole that includes knowledge, belief, art, law, morals, custom, and any other capabilities and habits *acquired by man as a member of society* (Teicher, 1958:450–455). The italicized words represent an important qualification occasionally overlooked by enthusiastic culture determinists. Konrad Lorenz considers this qualification of the utmost importance and states that "human behavior, and particularly human social behavior, far from being determined by reason and cultural tradition alone, is still subject to all the laws prevailing in all phylogenetically adapted instinctive behavior" (Lorenz, 1963:237). Rather than choosing a definition of culture from the myriad that have been offered, or trying to form one, we will discuss five dimensions of culture. These dimensions are expansions on what Jerome Bruner has termed "the five great humanizing forces" (Bruner, 1968:75ff.): toolmaking, social organization, language, management of the prolonged human childhood, and the human urge to explain the world.

These dimensions are important facets of any culture. One can approach the analysis of culture through examining these dimensions regardless of the time and place or kind of culture being studied. With a subculture within a culture, such as a peer group or professional culture, certain of these dimensions may seem less applicable; but each of the five seems applicable to some extent. We are then viewing culture as the ways of doing, being, and explaining, in a particular system.

A. Tools

Tools are amplifiers of human capacities, whether the tools are invented or synthesized. They fall into three classes:

1. Amplifiers of *sensory* capacities; for example, microscopes, telescopes, telephones, clocks, spectacles, radar, conch shells, and psychedelic drugs
2. Amplifiers of *motor* capacities; for example, hammers, wheels, the lever, and rockets
3. Amplifiers of *reasoning* and *thinking* capacities, for example, mathe-

matical systems, logic, the abacus, the computer, and the chalk board (a major educational invention)

Tools, then, are devices, objects, and procedures that are extensions of human natural capacities. The crucial, most important aspect is not the tool itself but rather its function, that is, the use to which the tool is put. A hammer is generally assumed to be of use to pound nails and, if it is a claw hammer, to remove nails as well, but it can also be used as a lethal weapon or to prop open a door or window. Books generally are assumed to be for the purpose of reading, but they can also serve to press flowers, level the short leg of a table, or to impress other people with their owner's literary sophistication. Understanding the tools of a culture includes, therefore, not only understanding their seeming intrinsic or built-in purpose, but, more importantly, how the tools are used (i.e., their purpose to the user). Some years ago one of the authors worked in a small Indian reservation where the occupants had been given a refrigerator for each household and electricity was available. The purpose of food storage by refrigeration was not part of the way of life of this culture. The refrigerators were used for other purposes—for decoration in a few instances—but mostly for storage. They were perceived as attractive boxes with a door, but the "built-in purpose" was not the purpose of the users.

Peter Farb, a cultural anthropologist, has analyzed the evolution of cultures in a remarkably readable book. One of his theses is that a new tool or technique must have a counterpart in social organization or knowledge to become functional. He uses the example of the introduction of the horse into two quite different cultures. The first of these cultures, a hunting tribe, mounted the horses and used them to pursue the buffalo. This amplified human motor capacities, making them much more efficient hunters, and rapidly the culture evolved toward one in which the horse became central. The second culture merely slaughtered the horse and ate it (Farb, 1968:29).

Tools, then, are a key dimension by which a culture may be analyzed. They extend the uses of energies within the cultural system toward fulfillment of the system's goals. It may be equally significant and analytical of a culture that certain tools do *not* exist. For example, the absence of written languages or of the wheel are significant in some North and Central American Indian cultures.

B. Social Organization

All cultures, being social systems, have organization. They may be organized, may be in the process of organizing, or they may be in the process of disorganizing. But in any event, the dimension of organization is present. As previously stated, the structure is not fixed, and any analysis of structure is like a still photo. At the moment of analysis, the social organization of a culture is not what it has been nor what it will become. It is structured in the sense of a system of interacting elements, and any change in one element or single pattern of relationships affects all other elements directly or indirectly.

Evolutionary theory, in its essence, describes the increase of complexity, whether from simple to complex biological organisms or from simple to complex cultures. The social organization of an evolving culture becomes more complex because of an increased volume of interrelationships among the various elements of the culture. A "stagnant culture" is one in which the interrelationships are static and interaction of the cultural elements is unchanging. Some have postulated that bureaucracy will appear as an organizational system when society reaches a given state of complexity, regardless of the form of government. The bureaucracies of ancient China, Rome, the Catholic Church, the Russian monarchy, and most recently American democracy and Russian communism can all be cited as illustrations. Bureaucracy seems to have as a major function the reduction and containment of forces that may lead to change. As such, bureaucracy is probably used as a "buffering" device by all complex societies. The systems term *equifinality* applies to this phenomenon; Beer defines it as "the proven ability of certain OPEN systems to reach the same characteristic result, despite differences in initial conditions, and despite different rules of conduct along the way" (1981:191) (see glossary for further explanation).

Certain important concepts related to social organization are commonly employed. These are the interrelated ideas of *class, status,* and *role.* All societies have schemes of ordering human interaction and ways of defining and communicating expected behaviors. As with definitions of culture, many theorists have proposed hypothetical *social class* structures. In considering the current American scene, Martin Loeb attempts to describe categories of life styles (Loeb, 1961); Hollingshead uses a variety of socioeconomic indices (Hollingshead, 1969); and Kvaraceus orders social classes by values (Kvaraceus, 1959).

T. H. Marshall, an English sociologist, has worked out a scheme based on Max Weber's writings (Marshall, 1964). Marshall believes that there are three aspects operating: economic status, social status, and political power. When the groupings of these three coincide (multibonded), then social class is a visible thing. If the boundaries between the social classes are clear and closed, the result is caste. The idea of social class suggests a group consciousness on the part of members, both of their own groups and other groups, and of their general position in the social scale.

John Rowan follows the classical distinctions of Pitrim Sorokin in characterizing a social class as a multibonded group: "One bond is occupation, including such things as career chances; one bond is income and wealth, particularly important at the extremes; and the third bond is a matter of the collection of rights and duties, of privileges and disfranchisements. These things tend to run together and give a certain social status" (Rowan, 1978:85).

Social status does not necessarily imply the existence of groups at all; it refers to a consensus of social ranking. Status, of course, can be achieved or ascribed, but the organizing mechanisms for acquiring or granting status, as well as the recognition thereof, seem to be present in all cultures. To understand the culture, it is important to know the key determinants of status.

Role relates to and derives from status. Ralph Linton describes role as "the sum total of the cultural patterns associated with a particular status. It thus includes the attitudes, values, and behavior ascribed by the society to any and all persons occupying that status" (Linton, 1945:76–77). The complexity of a status is manifested partly by the complexity and differentiation of role expectations. Bureaucracy is one of the organizational forms devised to reduce this complexity. In the bureaucratic structure, the role often becomes more important than the person occupying the status, but it is only through occupying the status that one can assume the role. Beyond the family, continuity depends less on the person's characteristics and more on the roles he or she occupies and interacts with.

Role expectations, then, are culturally defined by the system and its components and incorporated by the persons filling the role. A culture may allow more or less latitude in deviations from the expected behaviors. Certain cultures rigidly define role behavior, but more often the rigidity or flexibility of role definition is dependent on what else is transpiring within the system. For example, there was a time in United States culture when expected role behavior of a child in relation to the adults in the child's life was expressed by the phrase "children should be seen and not heard." More recently, children are expected to be heard, and if this role behavior is not forthcoming, they are considered withdrawn or at least shy.

In a dynamic, open cultural system, role occupants are constantly seeking flexibility of role definition with or without the encouragement of the culture. As the cultural system is threatened from either external or internal quarters, strings are drawn more tightly on the expected role behaviors.

All persons occupy a complex of roles, the total number of these being influenced by the quantity of networks of interrelationships they are involved in. At any given moment, a person is likely to be more actively fulfilling one or another of the roles but carries them all at one time nevertheless. When a person experiences excessive conflict in fulfilling varying role expectations, or if society judges the person to be failing in this respect, the person and the society both have troubles.

A contemporary example is the strong cultural emphasis on the work-role expectation. Work is quite narrowly defined as contractual employment, profession, or own business, and it is expected that each adult, unless manifestly disabled or past an arbitrary age, will fulfill such a role. The work role is fused with the economic role. There are an insufficient supply of such work roles (i.e., jobs). Even though members of the society accept the prescribed role expectations, a significant number are not able to fulfill the

agreed-upon role. The culturally prescribed remedy is to attempt to gener-
ate more jobs (i.e., work roles). Another culture may seek to broaden the
definition of the work role or separate work from economic participation.

If any significant minority of the members of the society do not do what
the consensus requires for a length of time, the system is in difficulty and
the survival of the culture is in question. In such instances, energies of the
system must be devoted to maintaining the organization and redefining the
expectations of those in the particular status. In the latter years of the
Vietnam War a significant minority refused to fulfill the expectation for
military service. Subsequently, the draft was terminated and expectations
redefined. In certain states in the United States, many people refuse to
accept and abide by the national 55 miles-per-hour speed limit. The speed
limit is not enforced, and the state governments ignore federal edicts.

C. Language

Here again we refer to language in its broader sense, that is, as transfer of
meaning. The structures of language strongly influence the content conveyed—language is composed of symbols and the meanings are learned
and transferred through social interaction. *Symbolic interaction* refers to this
process. The communication of symbols and their attendant meanings
represents the major form of transaction between human systems.

Most of the work of the symbolic interactionists is built on the insights of
George Herbert Mead and Charles Horton Cooley (Mead, 1967; Cooley,
1967). Mead states that we do not simply respond to the acts (including
speech, of course) of others; rather, we act on our *interpretations* of their
intentions and judgments. Gestures are an important kind of symbolic
communication, and we respond to the meanings not necessarily as they
are intended but as we interpret them. When a gesture has a common
meaning (some measure of consensus), Mead terms it a *linguistic element* —
a significant symbol. Common examples include the kiss as an expression of
affection; the drawn-back, clenched fist as threat of aggression; the smile as
an expression of pleasure; and the frown as an expression of displeasure.
Because of the consensus of meaning, we attribute the quality of pleasure to
the smile of the baby even though it may be an expression of gas in the
stomach.

The term *generalized other* is central to Mead's formulation. This refers to
a generalized stance or viewpoint imputed to others that one uses to assess
and judge one's own behavior. "This concept calls attention to the fact that
ongoing conduct is oriented not only to the expected responses of those
physically present, but also to the general expectations as a whole of the
group to which the individual belongs" (Hewitt, 1979:59).

Another key concept is *self.* An individual may act socially toward self as toward others. The self is composed of the *I* and *me*. *I* is the impulsive, spontaneous, and unorganized energizing part of the self. *Me* is the incorporated other. The *I* energizes and provides propulsion, whereas the *me* provides direction, in other words, controls function. These are similar to, but in important ways different from, id and superego. The emphasis is on social rather than intrapsychic functioning.

The "looking glass self" is Cooley's construct and refers to the idea that we interpret what others think of us. It involves the following sequence: (1) the imagination of our appearance to others; (2) the imagination of their judgment; and (3) a self feeling in response to this imagined judgment (e.g., pride or mortification).

The symbolic interactionists, as represented by Mead and Cooley, go far toward explaining the process of transfer of meaning. Their formulations clearly demonstrate that meaning derives from interaction between the sender and the receiver at both verbal and nonverbal levels. These are, in essence, elements of the descriptions of feedback cycle as transacted between human systems. If there is little or no feedback from outside the focal system, then the assessment of appearance and judgment must be projected from the inside. For example, the paranoid person is not able, or is not allowing self, to participate in this feedback cycle with outside systems and must rely on his or her own imagined judgments. As Philip Slater puts it, "Without air we die, without love we turn nasty, without feedback we go crazy" (Slater, 1974:49). It was argued during the 1972 presidential election that a nation–system can find itself in this same situation, with its feedback projected from within, and therefore become isolated and chauvinistic. Subsequent revelations during the Watergate investigations indicated that such isolation and closed feedback cycles were characteristic of the Nixon presidency. This is a frequent criticism of the societal context of Washington, D.C. (i.e., the feedback cycle is overly restricted and tends to be "out of touch").

Language, then, is the vehicle for transfer of meaning between the components of a cultural system and between one culture system and other cultures. That which is considered important enough to symbolize and communicate is as important in understanding a culture as is the understanding of the methods of comunication. In this instance, Marshall McLuhan (1965) seems in error. There is more to the message than merely the medium. Furthermore, language is a means of setting and maintaining cultural boundaries as well as a major means of organizing the energies of the system. Subcultures universally employ their own jargon and argot, and one of the major tasks of socialization into a subculture is to become acquainted with the special language. Certainly the subculture of social work is an example with such jargon as "personal–social needs," "relationship," and "intervention." The special language of a subculture may serve to exclude others from participation in the culture. Because it prevents interaction, this "linguistic collusion" is an effective way to close a boundary. (Incidentally, we hope that this systems approach helps prevent such boundary closures between helping professions, although we recognize the initial difficulty learning the jargon of systems thinking.)

The importance of "screening" and interpreting symbols in working with people is abundantly clear. Much of the literature of the helping professions, for example, is devoted to making the reader sensitive to the possible meanings of the symbols received from the person being helped. Theodore Reik's idea of "the third ear," in which the therapist's own emotional reactions give clues to unspoken messages being sent by the patient, is a time tested example (Reik, 1948). Another example is psychological testing, especially "projective" tests such as the Rorschach, Thematic Apperception, or House–Tree–Person tests. In these tests, the responses of the subject being tested are interpreted in order to provide clues about the subject's personality structure and what treatment methods may be most useful in dealing with this person. In these instances, between the professional person's reception (input) of the symbols and response (output) to them, the interpretation (processing) that occurs is formalized and takes on the character of scientific problem-solving—or at least, this is what professional schools hope their graduates are capable of doing.

In such professional techniques, obviously some standardization of language and symbols is necessary, and thus each theoretical approach, such as psychoanalysis, transactional analysis, or behavior modification, must devote much energy to training professionals in some standard terminology. This is necessary so that the results of professional efforts and the theoretical elaboration of them can be conveyed in some common language. Certainly the history of psychiatry is replete with examples of attempts by Kraepelin, Freud, and others to standardize terminology. Menninger lists such attempts in the history of medicine (Menninger, 1963: Chaps. 1 and 2 and Appendix). A major problem for each of the developing helping professions has been the training of professionals to apply the same labels to similar phenomena so that terms have some consensual meaning —that is, so that one psychiatrist's "schizoid" is not another psychiatrist's "passive–aggressive." Despite such efforts as the American Psychiatric Association's standard nomenclature, however, serious disagreements on interpretations of symbolic behavior do occur within that profession. Consensus of meaning with a high degree of precision is difficult to achieve; if it were not so, probably books such as this would not need a glossary.

D. Child-Rearing: Management of the Prolonged Human Childhood

Anthropologists, sociologists, and psychologists have exhaustively researched forms of child rearing in various cultures. Although most of these studies focus on the family system, many deal with other educative and socializing social systems as well. Writers in ethology compare the human family structures with those of other animals, seeking generalities and unique attributes (Ardrey, 1966; Lorenz, 1963). The human family is always found to be highly organized, in the sense that Monane uses this phrase to connote intense intrasystem relatedness (see Monane, 1967 and our discussion in Chapter 1, "I. Organization"). There is a predominance of sentiment in this interaction rather than only biological need gratification and response, although the two are always related.

The management of the human's prolonged childhood is a major characteristic of any culture and, as such, must fit with other aspects of the culture and interact with these. As a culture becomes more complex and differentiated, so too does child rearing, and other social provisions appear. There are numerous examples in the recent evolution of United States society. As the economic system required greater mobility, the extended family began to dissolve. This was accompanied by the advent of the babysitter. Currently, the demands of the economic system and shifts in role definition of the female are leading to rapid growth of day-care centers and the emergence of the "househusband."

New social institutions, such as day-care facilities, are accompanied by changes in family functions, but this is not necessarily tantamount to family breakdown. These new systems arise to realize more effectively the complex of values of a culture. Usually, certain values are in conflict with certain other values, leading to tension and strain in the various systems. The historical development of the public school is an excellent illustration. The belief that a certain amount of formal education should be the right of every person developed over centuries in a number of places, particularly Western Europe. This was related to values such as "equality" and the "importance of knowledge." An informed citizenry became a national system goal in the first half of the nineteenth century. As the belief became a cherished system value held by a significant portion of the components of the system, provisions were implemented to fulfill the value. This was followed by the adoption of the "common school" in a majority of the states during the decade of the 1850's. Since then, the public school as a child-rearing social subsystem has continued to evolve, becoming more complex and differentiated. The current controversy over the transmission of culture, manners, and morals related to sexual behavior and whether this should be a family or school responsibility, exemplifies the process of culture change and the inherent value conflicts. There is also increasing concern about the role and effect of television and movies upon children as well as a growing controversy over the issue of prayer in the public schools.

E. The Human Urge to Explain the World

This major dimension of a culture is often overlooked or minimized in explication of the concept of culture. Much of the energy of a culture system is expended in this dimension of human existence. Religion, philosophy, science, and superstition are some of these pursuits. The attendant beliefs, rituals, values, and theories are an essential part of a culture. This quest to explain the unexplained can be viewed as an integral aspect of the adaptation of a system to its environment.

In our present-day culture, science continues to be the dominant means of exploring, explaining, and changing our world. (The scientific method, empirical observation, and inductive reasoning are, of course, highly valued only in certain cultures.) It is believed dogmatically that the scientific method or technology can solve all important problems. Major religious organizations in this culture have been responsive to the currently accepted way of explaining the world and have engaged in social problem-solving in the "scientific" way.

In recent years, however, there has been a renewal of interest in other ways of knowing and explaining the cosmos. Popular manifestations include astrology, numerology, and meditation. Adherents of creationism are pressing to juxtapose their explanation with scientism in the curriculum of the public schools.

CONCLUSION

Today, there is recognition by all professions and disciplines concerned with human behavior that culture must be attended to and understood. The concept of culture has become politicized in the past two decades by racial minorities and ethnic groups that have called attention to the vitality and integrity of their own cultures and have reasserted their impact on mainstream culture. At the same time, the "melting pot" description of United States society—an unfortunate metaphor to the extent that it denied subsystems their own distinctiveness and integrity—has been replaced. Some theorists construe our multicultural relationships to be "beyond the melting pot" (Glazer and Moynihan, 1970).

These changes in our thinking about culture have implications for the human services. Without an awareness of the power of culture, it is very difficult to care for, teach, learn from, or assist anyone whose cultural experience has been different significantly from one's own. At the same time, it is difficult to avoid the human proclivity to overgeneralize from the culture to the person (e.g., Latinos are emotional; he is Latino; therefore, expect him to be emotionally unstable). Sharing a common culture does not make people identical. We honor that principle in interacting with other members of our own culture, but with members of a foreign culture, we tend not to expect differences between persons.

The pioneering anthropologists tended to study cultures markedly different from their own, so-called "primitive" cultures. The unfamiliarity allowed them a measure of objectivity in reasoning from symbolic behavior to related meanings. Even so, they were frequently confounded by what they observed or inferred meanings grounded in their own cultural experiences. Margaret Mead, in her intimate autobiography (Mead, 1972), makes the statement that her field studies were conducted so that Americans may better understand themselves. This is consistent with E. T. Hall's contention that to be able to see one's own culture, it is first necessary to experience a foreign one (Hall, 1977). This is true for the simple reason that one's native culture becomes "normal," "sensible," "natural," and "right." Moreover, it feels natural. It feels natural to shake hands, to smile when pleased, to bathe frequently; but, of course, all of these conventions are peculiar to particular cultures.

Almost everyone has experienced the sensation of being "out of culture," as a fish out of water. This may be expressed as: not knowing what to expect from others, vague physical discomforts, longing for the familiar, and disorientation. The traveler in Europe looking for a proper hamburger is a popular example. Coca Cola has gone wherever United States citizens have migrated. In the same vein, in the wake of the earthquake shock in Guatemala City, many people from the United States, without prior plan or communication, congregated in the Dairy Queen parking lot.

How one applies the concept of culture depends on one's vantage point, what one is prepared to see, and perhaps most important, the knowledge used to interpret one's observations. Visualize the three-dimensional atomic model as a system and then consider the study of culture. If you are somewhere within the cultural system you can see some components well, others less well, and others not at all. If you are outside the system your perspective may help you better see the "big picture," but the further out you are, the more danger there is of reductionism and oversimplification. Popular adages express this dilemma (e.g., "they can't see the forest for the trees").

There is no solution to this dilemma. To understand best a culture in any of its forms (e.g., a primitive society, an ethnic group, a peer group, or a profession), observers must strive for objectivity if they are themselves components of the system, or strive for involvement if they are outside the system. It is through this process of reasoning that social work, education, and other human services recently have concerned themselves again with greater involvement in the "client system" and its particular culture, be it family, neighborhood, or community.

SUGGESTED READINGS

Ardrey, Robert.
    Any of his books provide stimulating reading for this chapter. Especially
    recommended are *The Territorial Imperative* (New York: Atheneum, 1966) and
    The Social Contract (New York: Atheneum, 1970).
Blumer, Herbert.
    1967   Society as Symbolic Interaction. In *Symbolic Interaction,* Jerome G. Manis
    and Bernard N. Meltzer, eds. Boston: Allyn and Bacon.
    This article succinctly explains symbolic interaction and reviews the theoretical
    foundation of this school of thought.
Farb, Peter.
    1968   *Man's Rise to His Civilization as Shown by the Indians of North America from
    Primeval Times to the Coming of the Industrial State.* New York: Dutton.
    In this very readable book, with its foreboding title, Farb illustrates how cul-
    tures evolve.
Hall, Edward T.
    1969   *The Hidden Dimension.* Garden City, New York: Doubleday.
    An extremely interesting and stimulating work that deals with the structure of
    experience as it is determined by culture. The particular cultural theme exam-
    ined in the human use of space. (This book has been used as the "small map"
    for this chapter. Students have found the content directly applicable to social
    work situations.)
Hall, Edward T.
    1977   *Beyond Culture.* Garden City, New York: Doubleday Anchor Book.
    Hall's most recent synthesis of his own research and the research of others, and
    his theorizing about culture. His major thesis is that in order to understand
    ourselves and our culture we must experience another culture.
Hewitt, John P.
    1979   *Self and Society.* Boston: Allyn and Bacon, Second Edition.
    A useful source for a symbolic interactionist approach to social psychology.
La Barre, Weston.
    1954   *The Human Animal.* Chicago: University of Chicago. (The 1968 edition has
    minor differences.)
    The author, an anthropologist, examines the culture of man from an evolution-
    ary stance. He combines findings from anthropology, psychiatry, linguistics,
    and human biology into a controversial thesis. His arguments are particularly
    thorough as he deals with family, symbolic communication, and deviant
    behavior. (This book has been used as the "small map" for this chapter and has
    generated much discussion.)
Lewis, Oscar.
    1979   *Self and Society.* Boston: Allyn and Bacon, Second Edition.
    A useful source for a symbolic interactionist approach to social psychology.
    fully illustrates the impact of culture.
Lyman, Stanford M. and Marvin B. Scott.
    1967   Territoriality: A Neglected Social Dimension. *Social Problems* 15:236–245.
    A definitive statement of a typology of human spacial arrangements. In addi-
    tion to describing classifications of territory, this article well illustrates varieties
    of boundary definition and boundary maintenance.

COMMUNITIES

Who reads Ferdinand Tönnies today?
Bell and Newby, 1972

INTRODUCTION

Both communities and organizations are macrosystems as contrasted with
the microsystems of persons, families, and small groups. Both are intermediate (or "mediating") systems between society and the small groupings in
which intimate affective transactions occur. Historically, sociology has had
difficulty defining and distinguishing among community, organization, and
society (Hillery, 1968). The major distinction between community and
organization that we have in mind is one made by Ferdinand Tönnies: "A
community is held together by feeling and sentiment, primarily, while an
organization is sustained by 'rational' considerations, usually explicit in
formal contracts, usually written" (Tönnies, 1957).

I. COMMUNITY AS SYSTEM

Probably the most difficult systems to define with precision are *community* and *small group* (which will be discussed in the next chapter). As
Heraud writes:

   . . . many difficulties have surrounded the meaning and use of the term
community,' not least of which has been the reluctance of sociologists to refine

61

the term in ways which would make it more useful either for the concerns of social policy or for actual sociological analysis. The term has reached a high level of use but a low level of meaning (Heraud, 1970:83–84).

Because the community is at the interface between society and microsystems, it is of concern to all social disciplines and professions. The family is a person's primary field of interaction during childhood; in adulthood, the other major field of interaction is community, or at least significant sectors of community. Such sectors include the financial, commercial, religious, educational, social, and legal institutions (among others) in which the person participates. French said of community that "at one and the same time it is an important building block of society, and it is society itself. It represents culture to the individual and as such shapes him, and it is subject to the will of the individual who as a citizen can enact changes in his community" (French, 1969:5). Notice the emphasis upon mutual causation here; the citizen and the community influence each other through mediation of family, small group, and organizations.

A. Kinds of Communities

Communities differ in several respects. First, Tönnies describes them as being held together by two sorts of bonds — gemeinschaft and gesellschaft. A gemeinschaft community is characterized by implicit bonds that relate all community members to the others. These bonds include common values and beliefs, mutual interdependence, respect, and a shared sense of status hierarchy. Rules regarding relationships are not formalized but rest in cultural traditions and complementary social expectations rather than written codes or contracts. An American Indian tribal community may be an example in that behavior is greatly influenced by tradition and culture; however, as tribes have "modernized," they, too, have become somewhat more formalized with Reservation Business Committees and parliamentary structures. Yet, there remains for many a gemeinschaft feeling of place. As for Roland Lussier, a sixth grader in Northern Minnesota:

> There is no place better than the Indian reservation. It's so beautiful, the land is covered with dark green pine trees and other kinds of trees. At dawn we can watch the sun, and we will see the beautiful colors around the sun. We are proud of our reservation and we thank God for giving it to us (Brill, 1974:56).

A gesellschaft community is characterized by bonds that are both formal and specific. Community members relate to one another through formally structured relations within community institutions such as work organizations, professions, and civic organizations (Nisbet, 1966).

A second way that communities differ from one another is in the degree of attachment to a specific location. This variable can also be used to determine distinct types of communities, but the reader should keep in mind that these categories, like all typologies, are ideal and not real. In reality, attachment to place or location is more or less present in all communities. Tönnies describes the following communities:

1. PLACE COMMUNITIES. Tönnies also calls this community a "locality"; it is also referred to as a *geographic* or *spatial* community. It is based upon a common habitat and ownership of adjacent (or nearby) properties. Examples of "place" community are neighborhoods, villages, towns, and cities.

2. NONPLACE COMMUNITIES. Tönnies also calls this community a "mind" community. This "implies only cooperation and coordinated action for a common goal," without reference to "place" (Hillery, 1968:77–78). Examples of nonplace communities include religious orders and professions. A spirited debate continues among sociologists as to whether "social networks" are nonplace communities (Bell and Newby, 1972: Chap. 6).

Beginning with J. A. Barnes' study of the social structure of the fishing community of Bremnes, Norway, researchers have found social networks a fruitful topic of study (Barnes, 1954). Barnes' definition of social network is still the most useful:

> Each person is, as it were, in touch with a number of other people, some of whom are in touch with each other and some of whom are not. Similarly each person has a number of friends, and these friends have their own friends; some of any one person's friends know each other, others do not. I find it convenient to talk of a social field of this kind as a NETWORK. The image I have is of a set of points some of which are joined by lines. The points of the image are people, or sometimes groups, and the lines indicate which people interact with each other (Barnes, 1954:127).

See Figure 6 for representative diagrams of Barnes' idea.

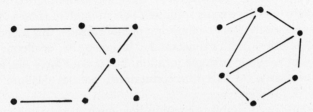

FIG. 6. Diagrams of unbounded networks.

The fact that it was a fishing village may have influenced Barnes' choice of the term NETwork rather than other possible terms, such as *web*. In Barnes' view, a network consists of the relationships between pairs of people. This is, of course, an atomistic view; some later network theorists have attempted to apply network concepts to larger social groupings with some success (e.g., Granovetter, 1977; J. Miller, 1978). Barnes' definition is perspectivistic; each person has an unique social network defined by the dyadic relationships the person has. In much of the current usage of the term social network, the term clearly is synonymous with nonplace community; it "implies only cooperation and coordinated action for a common goal, without reference to place." This is the sense in which it is used in discussing "networking" as a technique for changing the personal and work conditions of women (Kleiman, 1980; Welch, 1981).

"Network" is also a phenomenon observed by the late Virginia Hine of the University of Minnesota who studied social change. She noted the emergence of "segmented, polycephalous, ideological networks" (abbreviated to "SPIN"), which were loosely organized alliances with bonds based on strongly held ideology.

> She speculated that this was a new form of non-hierarchical organization, perhaps an unsuspected political model of a world desperately seeking less vertically-structured methods of governance. A SPIN, she noted, functions effectively, does not disintegrate in the face of opposition (indeed the bond gets stronger), and provides meaningful action that is also rich in shared relationships and devoid of subservence on anyone's part (*Tarrytown Newsletter*, 1982:4–5).

To the extent that they are stable and function as significant environments for their members, such networks clearly qualify as nonplace communities.

3. KINSHIP. Tönnies describes this third kind of community as *kinship*, or communities in which members have blood relationships. Barnes' definition of social network includes both the "networking," goal-oriented social system (which might also be viewed as a loose-knit organization) and kinship networks.

As mentioned, these categories are not exclusive. Nonplace communities and social networks have geographic ties, even though members may never convene in one location at one time and do not consider this aspect of their relationship to be primary or constant. For instance, the "academic community" does not reside in a single location, but it does have ties to college campuses. Similarly, the "scientific community" has ties to laboratories and other research facilities.

Other examples of nonplace communities, such as the barbering profession, are protected from intrusion by custom or law, as symbolized by the striped pole and a barber's license. Another example is the academic community's jealous protection of academic freedom, as when one professor went to jail rather than reveal his vote on giving another professor tenure. This case illustrates that academic freedom is a highly abstract and symbolic territory that some persons will defend with their liberty, if not their lives. The Polish labor union, Solidarity, is another example of non-place community for which people are prepared to risk imprisonment or die; in this case, of course, there is a strong element of place, the nation of Poland.

The press, or profession of journalism, another nonplace community or social network, is concerned about the public's right "to know." A dramatic illustration of this followed the killing in 1976 of an Arizona reporter, Don Bolles, whose car was rigged with a bomb. Reporters from across the country, some sponsored by their newspapers, others on their own, continued Bolles' investigation and secured information that resulted in convictions for Bolles' murder. That all of these territories (see Glossary, "Territoriality") can be disputed can be seen when legal action is taken against reporters who refuse to divulge their sources of information as happened to Daniel Schorr, former CBS (and now Cable News Network) TV reporter with the House Intelligence Committee's report on CIA activities. Another example is the 1982 bill that would make it illegal to publish the names of United States intelligence agents, even if the names already appear in public documents.

Racial and ethnic communities such as the "black community," La Raza, and "Indian Country," are nonplace communities. The black community is composed of blacks who share common identification in a cultural heritage, common interests in civil rights, and shared identity as exemplified by the slogan, "Black is beautiful." "Indian country" symbolizes both where American Indians now live, and the entirety of the continent which was theirs — a potent reminder to them of their heritage.

A third way in which communities differ is in the breadth of activities, interests, and needs that they encompass. The place community encompasses virtually all human interests and needs; the nonplace community is usually concerned with one, or a few, of these. Almost every kind of human activity (in one form or another) is to be found in Chicago, for example, while the nonplace "business community" or "academic community" concerns itself with a narrower range of interests and needs.

II. DEFINITION OF COMMUNITY

We suggest the following composite definition of community: *Community* is a population whose members consciously identify with each other. They may occupy common territory; they engage in common activities. They have some form of organization that provides for differentiation of functions, which allows the community to adapt to its environment, thereby meeting the needs of its components. Its components include the persons, groups, families, and organizations within its population and the institutions it forms to meet its needs. Its environment is the society within which it exists and to which it adapts, and other communities and organizations outside itself that impinge upon its functioning.

A. Energy Functions

1. FOR COMPONENTS/SUBSYSTEMS. The functions the community performs include the maintenance of a way of life or culture (in the second usage of "culture" in Chapter 3, this volume). Another important function is the satisfaction of common needs, interests, and ambitions. A striking example of the recognition of common interests and needs was Malcolm X's redefinition of the community to which he belonged. He found common interests and needs unexpectedly in a new community:

> That morning was when I first began to reappraise the "white man." It was when I first began to perceive that "white man," as commonly used, means complexion only secondarily; primarily it described attitudes and actions. In America, "white man" means specific attitudes and actions toward the black man, and toward all other non-white men. But in the Muslim world, I had seen that men with white complexions were more genuinely brotherly than anyone else had ever been.
>
> That morning was the start of a radical alteration in my whole outlook about "white" men (Malcolm X, 1966:333–334).

Further, the members of a community must be aware of its "we-ness" (French, 1969; Ross, 1955); in other words, there must be a social consciousness or "sense of community." This assists the community to meet the social identity needs of the persons who are its components. The community must provide for them "full opportunities for personal development through social experimentation. . . . This conception falls close to Erikson's views on ego identity and ego integrity as well as to Sullivan's emphasis on a full repertory of interpersonal relations"(Stein, 1960:335–336).

Erik Erikson, Harry Stack Sullivan, the social psychiatrist, and Karen Horney, psychoanalyst, recognized the importance of the social environment, including the community, in providing a medium for the evolution of the person. They are a distinct minority among psychoanalytic theorists in the importance they place upon the social environment. Stein elaborated, "A community must . . . provide its members with, at the least, meaningful sexual and work identities if it is to ensure its own continuity as well as the psychic integrity of its members" (Stein, 1960:266). Many communities during the 1980's are incapable of providing opportunities to develop work identities because of lack of jobs; if Erikson, Sullivan and Stein are correct, many of the persons in these communities will fail to develop ego integrity since they are prevented from viewing themselves not only as productive members of the community but also as worthwhile people individually. While some social theorists and policymakers accept this as an inherent risk in a capitalistic industrial society, others regard this as unjustified damage to the community as a system and to its members.

We do not yet know the effects of such failure by the societal system and the community system to provide adequately for its member's identity needs, although the effects of previous economic depressions are known to some degree. Some suggest that the effect may be to produce severely alienated individuals and groups who turn to authoritarian ideologies for security and as a means of participation in some form of community. Erich Fromm, Hannah Arendt, and other writers on "alienation" have stated strongly that such alienated groups are the breeding grounds for fascism (Arendt, 1962; Fromm, 1942, 1955; Giner, 1976:138–144).

Other components such as families, organizations, and groups must also be able to identify with, and find common cause with, the community's way of life in order that their energy may be used to meet the community's needs. The term, *common cause,* was adopted as the name of a national citizen's action group that explicitly recognizes the necessity to involve citizens and to draw upon their energies. This organization mobilizes energy in the form of funds and lobbying activity from its citizen – members to attain agreed-upon goals. It meets the definition of a system, specifically a social network, or nonplace community, in this respect.

Presthus emphasized these functions that the community performs for its components. He notes that there is

> . . . in every community a certain ongoing network of fairly stable subsystems, activated by social, economic, ethnic, religious, and friendship ties and claims. Such systems of interest, values, and power have desirable consequences for their members to the extent that they satisfy various human needs. In a sense, however, such subsystems are suprahuman, in that they tend to persist indefinitely and, more important, that their members may change but the underlying network of interrelated interests and power relations continues (Presthus, 1964:5).

2. FOR ENVIRONMENT/SUPRASYSTEMS. A community must also meet the needs of its environment in order to survive. It is clear from "central place" theory in geography and economics that place communities function as parts of hierarchical, relatively stable (perhaps less so during the current decade) economic and political systems, and that alterations in one community affect other parts of the region as well (Christaller, 1966; Dunn, 1980). The rise of Chicago ("that toddlin' town, the town that Billy Sunday could not shut down") as a major industrial and railroad center affected the commercial and social development of communities within its region. It became, as Carl Sandburg put it,

Hog Butcher for the World,
Tool Maker, Stacker of Wheat,
Player with Railroads and the Nation's Freight Handler. . . . (Sandburg,
1955:442–443).

Smaller communities nearby adapted, sometimes unwillingly, to Chicago's emergence as a trade center, both supplying and being supplied by Chicago's services and industries. Communities unsuited to adapt to new economic and transportation networks, or unable to compete with new centers of power, declined or ceased to exist. In the American West in recent years, "boom towns" have arisen as the demand for minerals or new sources for oil have increased; as noted elsewhere in this book, some have failed to prosper. Others have survived, some with serious social problems (Davenport and Davenport, 1982).

Religious communities, as examples of nonplace community, have also been confronted with the need to adapt to their environment. Within the Roman Catholic Church in recent years, some orders that formerly were relatively removed from society have become socially active, peforming less specifically religious tasks such as teaching and social services in prisons and hospitals. A few orders have disbanded as their members have returned to lay status, some members in order to marry, and others to carry on secular work as part of their religious commitment. The Roman Catholic "community," however, maintains some relatively clear boundaries: priests and nuns are still forbidden to marry, and procreation is still the purpose of marriage. The following news item illustrates the latter boundary:

PHOENIX, ARIZ.(AP)—The Roman Catholic Diocese of Phoenix has refused to marry a couple because the man is a quadriplegic unable to consummate the union, the church says. Jose Sosa, 28, and his fiancee, Barbara Albillar, 23, both of Mesa, are Catholics who want a church wedding. Sosa said the diocese's decision was a shock to both of them. Sosa said he didn't understand the church's decision and "I never thought there would be this sort of trouble". . . . Larry Bonvallet of Kankakee, Ill., after initial rebuffs in a publicized case, won approval for a Catholic wedding and was married in May. Church officials said they believed he might eventually be able to consummate the marriage. . . . Sosa and Albillar plan to be married in October in a civil ceremony if they are denied a church wedding (Iowa City PRESS-CITIZEN, July 5, 1982).

In another example of boundary-setting and adaptation for this community, the Pope banned priests from holding elective political office. As a result, Father Drinan of Massachusetts chose not to run for reelection to the U.S. House of Representatives in 1980.

Boundary maintenance and adaptation are crucial functions for the survival of communities. Between 1968 and 1973, approximately half a million people were involved in some kind of communal living. Approximately 30% of the communes survived that 5-year period, leaving about a thousand communes by 1975 (Gardner, 1978:240 ff.). Virtually none of the urban communes survived; the survivors were almost entirely rural, and were secular, rather than religious. By 1978, however, communal religious groups had increased and there were approximately the same number of urban, religious communes as rural, secular ones. Gardner stated that both types were adaptive to the societal environment (Gardner, 1978:247–251). The rural communes were the forerunners of a "back to the land" movement that reversed the historical United States trend toward urbanization. The urban religious groups offer sanctuary from a society often viewed as destructive.

> Leaving the old identity behind and reconstructing a new self are the basic themes uniting all these divergent organizations servicing the needs of the blissed-out and the blitzed-out. . . . Taken together both types are the inheritors of the commune movement's ideology of "working on yourself" as opposed to the student–radical ideology of "struggle against the system" (Gardner, 1978:248).

Both types have adapted to the environment by separating from it in some significant way, either geographically (place communities), or spiritually (nonplace communities). How successful they will be remains to be seen.

The history of utopian communities is replete with examples of those who attempted to isolate themselves from the social environment and thrive as closed systems, unsuccessfully. Without energy exchange with the surrounding environment, a system is certain to become entropic and die. Amish communities in Pennsylvania, Indiana, Iowa, and other states have survived by maintaining energy exchange with the environment in certain limited ways; this is an excellent illustration of boundaries that are relatively more closed than those of other communities but still open to exchanges of energy.

American Indian reservations are examples of communities that were excluded from the general society and suffered entropy. In recent years, economic and social development have opened the boundaries. Both American Indians and the general society have found it to their advantage to cross the boundaries. While white society may wish to remove the boundaries entirely (the so-called "assimilation" policy), American Indians have consciously encouraged maintenance of open, but clearly recognizable, cultural boundaries, especially during the past two decades. From a systems perspective, the assimilation policy was unworkable because it would have required only the Indian societies to accommodate (to change their schemas), after which white society would assimilate them. A systems perspective would indicate that mutual accommodation would be necessary, and each culture would have both to accommodate and assimilate.

In the past 20 years, some successful communes in the United States adapted to their environment, performing economic functions in the wider society and obtaining needed energy from other systems. Some cooperatives and communes begun during the 1960's and 1970's attempted "freak capitalism," producing and selling leather goods, ceramics, clothing, art, furniture, or vegetables to support the community. In some communes, such as Twin Oaks in Virginia, members alternated in taking employment in nearby cities for financial support of the community (Kinkade, 1973). The "Moonies" (Rev. Moon's Unification Church) have made conspicuous efforts to adapt to their environment by establishing a fishing industry that has enraged private, commercial fishermen on the east coast of the United States.

In general, the functions the community performs for its environment are the energy functions described in Chapter 1, II, giving, getting, and conserving energy. The community supplies energy to its environment and its components in the form of persons and products to be used by those systems. A community may supply students for higher education who become leaders while also supplying political support for organizations outside the community and taxes for state and national governments.

A large part of the debate about President Reagan's "New Federalism" concerns whether communities and states supply too much of their resources to their suprasystem, the federal government, leaving too little to meet the needs of the community's own components. President Reagan's answer is that, yes, too much has been taken by an overgrown federal bureaucracy. The position of many liberals is that only the federal government can be trusted to redistribute these resources equitably because communities and states are more vulnerable to pressure groups and more likely to deny resources to the powerless and disadvantaged components within communities and states. This liberal–conservative debate will continue for the foreseeable future; it illustrates well the need for an energy exchange, which meets the needs of each, between suprasystem, system, and components if all system levels are to function satisfactorily. A large part of the debate, also, of course, is over the definition of "satisfactory" functioning, and which functions should be performed at what system levels. It seems likely that the community system will be the arena in which a great deal of this controversy will occur during the 1980's and 1990's.

B. Aspects of Community System

1. EVOLUTIONARY ASPECTS. Lewis Mumford points out that the first cities were burial places to which wandering tribes returned at certain times to perform ceremonies that ensured the stability of the universe (Mumford, 1961:7). From that symbolic beginning, place communities have evolved to encompass all human needs and functions. Following Max Weber, Hans Paul Bahrdt contends that the city had its genesis in the market. Thus, a city is a settlement with a resident population that regularly satisfies economic

and social needs for energy exchange through the device of a local market (Warren, 1977:25ff.). Supposedly, Mumford's and Bahrdt's views could be reconciled by stating that cities began as locations that were sites of seasonal rituals, which became permanent market sites as agriculture grew.

The character of a particular community is determined by its relationships to other communities and the society within which it exists, by the characteristics of its components, and by its own preceding steady state. That is, it is a holon. B. F. Skinner's *Walden Two* (1948) describes a fictional utopia (copied by several real communities) that evolved into a complex, planned community. The Lynds' *Middletown* (Muncie, Indiana) evolved toward being a satellite in the regional system of New York City, because decisions about industries were increasingly made outside Middletown (Lynd and Lynd, 1929, 1937). Harry Caudill's *Night Comes to the Cumberlands* painfully illustrates the process by which rural Appalachian communities became the lowest level in a hierarchy of industrial power, subject to decisions made in Pittsburgh, Detroit, Washington, and New York (Caudill, 1963). Arthur Miller's play, *Death of a Salesman*, notes a similar phenomenon; Willy, the salesman, becomes increasingly distant from the central management of the company as it grows, and his contribution is forgotten as the company's activities expand. Further, his knowledge of the small towns in his territory is less and less valuable as the local community becomes less significant in mass marketing (A. Miller, 1955).

Doxiadis describes the evolution of large cities through five stages, differentiated by "kinetic fields," that is, the distance a person can travel within a certain span of time (J. G. Miller, 1972:117–118). His stages are:

A-level organization: The city encompasses 2 by 2 kilometers and has a population of no more than 50,000. No more than ten minutes are required to walk from the center to its periphery.

B-level organization: The city encompasses 6 by 6 kilometers and has a population of more than 50,000. Examples are capital cities of empires such as Rome, Constantinople, and Peking. Walking time in these cities at this stage of development was no more than half an hour; paved roads and horse-drawn carts moved people. Such cities were difficult to govern, slums grew, and mobs frequently controlled the city.

C-level organization: These cities depend upon subways or elevated trains to extend the "kinetic field." This is satisfactory only briefly, as cities evolve, and freeways are built to accommodate automobile traffic. It is entirely possible, of course, that cities may return to this mode of transportation, but if so, the largest cities would probably use high-speed subways to compensate for greater distances; San Francisco and Washington, D.C. are among the cities that have done this. Paris, Tokyo, and London are among older cities whose "Metro," elevated trains, or "tube" have provided rapid, efficient transportation for several decades.

D-level organization: This is the "modern" metropolitan city, beset by the myriad urban problems with which we are all too familiar. Again, transportation as described in C-level may be satisfactory, if it functions well. "The Warriors," a recent movie about a street gang, illustrates vividly both some of the social problems of a major city and the problems of mobility as the gang travels the subway confronting rival gangs at several stations before reaching their own "turf" and safety.

E-level organization: This is the megalopolis, the modern urban complex that comprises several cities with a total population of several million. In the United States, the so-called "BosWash" megalopolis from Boston to Washington, which is almost a single, continuous urban area, is an example. This urban level is marked by the pathology that remains from having failed to solve the problems at the D-level.

According to Miller, the "universal city" or "ecumenopolis" would be the ultimate city and would require highly centralized planning. In such a system, technology would solve the problems of transportation, distribution of energy supplies, and waste collection. How the problem of retaining a sense of community would be resolved is not clear. Others have suggested that our technology, most importantly the computer (like the one on which this chapter is being written), may allow us to continue participation in an advanced technological society while providing the advantages of decentralization in smaller communities.

The shape taken by cities of the future is being determined by experiences and crises in cities today. Many wonder whether the seeming exodus from cities to the suburbs is a permanent trend, especially given a long-term shortage in petroleum fuels. Others suggest radical solutions; the science fiction writer, Isaac Asimov, suggests underground cities may be the future; another science fiction writer fancifully suggests that whole cities may emigrate into space, like spaceships. Architect Paolo Soleri, creator of the futuristic community of Arcosanti in Arizona, suggests massive structures (resembling bee hives, in some respects, and similar to a "Buck Rogers" future) are the answer. Like other systems, cities are subject to multiple factors that influence growth and decline. A recent film, "Escape from New York," fantasizes about New York City's decline to barbarism, with Manhattan as a large prison sealed off from the rest of society.

In our nation's history, some communities have declined and others have died because of their inability to adapt to rapid change. Oliver Goldsmith's eighteenth-century poem, "The Deserted Village," illustrates that this began with the Industrial Revolution. Today, ghost towns that were formerly mining camps, small farming villages, or fishing villages attest to the alternative of disintegration for the community that does not have, or does not use, resources to adapt. Some communities like those just described have turned to tourism as a source of revenue (e.g., Central City, Colorado; Bayfield, Wisconsin; and Gatlinburg, Tennessee). Other examples of cities that have adapted to survive (in the sense of "steady state"; see Chapter 1, IV, "A. Steady State") include Iowa City, Iowa, first the state capital and then the site of the state university; and Duluth, Minnesota, a "boom town" dependent first upon lumber, then iron ore, grain, and coal.

The same principle of adaptation applies to nonplace communities. Certainly the history of Christian and Moslem sects or denominations illustrates the evolutionary process of such nonplace communities.

No clear pattern of evolution has been identified for communities other than cities. It seems likely that such communities parallel the evolution of groups or organizations to which they are similar.

2. STRUCTURAL ASPECTS. Included here are some systemic aspects of community that have a slower rate of change (see the earlier discussion of structure, behavior, and evolution in Chapter 1, IV, V and VI).

a. Boundaries. The boundaries that separate communities from larger and smaller social units — the so-called vertical hierarchy — are often difficult to establish precisely. The following quotation regarding Minnesota's Red Lake Reservation illustrates the point. As one drives the highways that enter the reservation, one encounters signs like this:

> Warning. This is Indian land. No trespassing. No fishing, hunting, camping, berry picking, peddling or soliciting without authorized permit from Red Lake Tribal Council Office. Violators and trespassers will be prosecuted under Federal Law 86-634 (Brill, 1974:22).

The sign indicates that the interactional boundary between the reservation and the federal government is an open one. The sign further indicates that the geographic boundary is relatively closed, but in reality is closed only in certain ways:

> Red Lakers are not isolated from the outside world. I am always amazed when someone asks me, "Can the Indians leave the reservation?" There are no fences around the reservation; the roads to Bemidji and other cities in the area are well traveled. . . . It is common for Red Lakers to drive to larger cities to shop in the supermarkets and discount stores; to bowl with the league on Tuesday and Thursday evenings; to play Bingo at the American Legion Club in Bemidji. Some commute to classes at Bemidji State College. In addition to the *Redlake Neighborhood Centers Newsletter* . . . many people subscribe to the *Bemidji Pioneer* and the *Minneapolis Tribune.* Television is popular and reception is generally good (Brill, 1974:22).

Their ancestors were wise in refusing to break up the reservation into smaller parcels that could be individually sold to outsiders; other reservations did, and many of the parcels were bought by whites. Red Lake continues as a "closed" (Indian-owned) reservation. Not all communities have been so fortunate in retaining their independence from the "outside world." Increasingly, as Warren (1963) and other writers (Lynd and Lynd, 1937; Stein, 1960) point out, communities are subordinate to larger, regional networks and to industrial and communications centers in their economic and social decisions. Within large communities, the internal structure may be composed of relatively autonomous bodies such as corporations that function as private independent governments (Bird, 1966: Chap. 10; Galbraith, 1968; Wright, 1979).

Boundaries within the community include those between institutions that differentiate tasks. These horizontal boundaries include, for example, the uniform worn and the choice of specific colors and tasks. Firefighters' gear is adapted to their task, but it also distinguishes them from police. What function does the bright, fire-red of the fire department's truck serve, especially since red is a low visibility color (many departments have chosen to use yellow, which is more visible)? Presumably the color says, "We fight fires. Don't ask us to baptize children with our hoses, to pick up garbage with our trucks, or to fight off mobs with our axes and poles!" Sometimes the boundaries between differentiated institutions are not so clear: Are parochial schools entitled to public funds? Should schools provide sex education? Should police conduct drug education programs? These continue to be controversial questions in many communities.

b. Institutions. Differentiation of functions by assigning them to specialized subsystems leads to the emergence of institutions within communities. Such institutions usually originate in several communities in slightly different forms. Since the community is a holon between society and "microsystems" (such as families and ethnic groups), it contains fundamental system processes such as J. G. Miller describes (J. Miller, 1978). In particular, the community performs basic systems functions such as social control through the church, school, and police; these institutions are prescribed in our culture. The form the institution takes in a particular community depends upon the community's components, previous steady state, and environment (an institution is a holon also). Our society prescribes that education shall be provided by formal schools, but the form of the school varies from community to community. It may be a one-room country school or an urban elementary school. It may be racially integrated or a private, all-white school; it may be single-sex or coed. The mode of instruction may be the Montessori method or the traditional "3 R's"; the instructional equipment may be slate blackboards or satellite television and computers.

Certain communities may evolve distinctive institutions. Pine Mountain Settlement School in Kentucky began the "Little School," a forerunner of the national Head Start program. Significant portions of the War on Poverty of the 1960's were modeled on the Mobilization for Youth program in New York City; hot lines and youth crisis centers originated in a number of cities at about the same time. Free, experimental schools of various kinds continue to spring up in communities across the country, and President Reagan's 1982 proposal to give tax breaks to private schools is a recognition of the role such institutions play in American education. Internationally, several Austrian communities are known for their Children's Villages, a unique response to the need to care for orphans. The process originates as a recognized need that is unmet by existing institutions; the community (or some influential component) differentiates a new institution to fill the need or modifies an existing institution to incorporate the new service. In some communities, hot lines are part of mental health clinics, and "crash pads" for runaways are maintained by churches.

Some institutions almost escape our notice because they exist in most communities, but their functions are overlooked. Examples are taverns or bars, e.g., Small's Bar which Malcolm X protected by turning himself in, an important institution in Harlem's social structure as were the night clubs Malcolm mentioned. Think of the bar as a setting for radio and television shows: "Archie Bunker's Place," "Cheers" (a show new in 1982; the bar is based upon an actual bar in Boston's Beacon Hill), "Duffy's Tavern," a staple of radio for many years, and Miss Kitty's bar in the long-running television series "Gunsmoke." The laundromat serves a socializing function in many neighborhoods. Restaurants serve a similar function (e.g., Leo's diner in "A Tree, A Rock, A Cloud;" it was evidently a place to socialize for cotton mill workers and transients, however "stingy" and inhospitable Leo was).

Community institutions pose special difficulties to social workers and other professionals acting as change agents. Institutions are systems and seek to maintain themselves. This may be done by modifying structure and function to better fulfill community needs (*morphogenesis*). However, as systems they also seek to remain the same (*morphostasis*). Thus, institutional provisions generally lag in meeting emergent community needs. As Thorstein Veblen wrote in 1899, "institutions are . . . adapted to past circumstances, and are therefore never in full accord with the requirements of the present. . . . This process of selective adaptation can never catch up with the progressively changing situation in which the community finds itself at any given time" (Boguslaw, 1965:150–151). Thus it is that we are always preparing for yesterday, believing it is tomorrow.

c. Social class and caste. Another important facet of community structure is social class. Studies of social stratification have substantiated social class or status groupings in various communities. Hollingshead's *Elmtown's Youth* is among the most ingenious of these studies and has been a fountainhead for others (Vidich and Bensman, 1958; Hollingshead, 1969). Some major differentiating characteristics found by researchers are income, lifestyle, and access to services. As noted in Chapter 3, communities differ

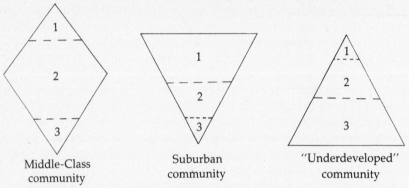

FIG. 7. Diagrams of class structure (1 = higher socioeconomic class; 2 = middle socioeconomic class; 3 = lower socioeconomic class).

in their cultures. Diagrams of class structure (or more accurately, socioeconomic status, usually) vary from a diamond-shaped structure, with most persons in the middle class, to an extreme pyramidal structure, with either very few poor in some wealthy suburban communities or very few wealthy in some Appalachian communities (Figure 7).

Another differentiation between communities may be that of caste. While most Americans deny it, caste status does exist in the United States if it is defined as an impermeable boundary, a status assigned by virtue of some characteristic beyond a person's control (e.g., skin color, sex, national origin, or age). Caste exists for some Mexican–Americans, Asian–Americans, and American Indians in many communities and for black Americans throughout the United States.

d. Social networks. We have placed this discussion of social networks between the sections on structural aspects and behavioral aspects of community systems because in reality it is difficult to describe social networks. There is an active debate among theorists of neighborhoods and urban subunits concerning whether neighborhoods and social networks are the same phenomenon. Some theorists maintain that neighborhoods (and by implication, communities in general) are simply social networks that have a base in a particular locality. Opposing theorists maintain that neighborhoods are not synonymous with social networks and have different dynamics. The opposing positions are similar to the distinctions between place and nonplace communities—that is, must a community (or a social network) be based in a particular location?

Social networks have become popular as a vehicle for "consciousness raising" among disadvantaged populations, such as women and racial minorities. Such networks emphasize awareness of commonality among the members and usually foster awareness of their disadvantaged status and understanding of the societal dynamics that underlie it. Further, the network provides support (often the networks are called "mutual support" groups) to members that consists of both emotional support and suggestions for immediate action. Rape support groups and feminist groups in general fit this description (Kleiman, 1980; Welch, 1981). The more organized the groups become and the more specific their goals (e.g., the National Organization for Women [N.O.W.]) the less they resemble social networks and the more they become formal organizations. Probably most "movements," including civil rights, antidraft, antinuclear, antiwar, right-to-life, and others could best be described as social networks even though many are very large and many are connected somewhat loosely with formal organizations that are dedicated to particular instrumental, limited goals of the movement.

Networks such as these can be highly useful to professional persons who are seeking support for a client for precisely the reasons previously mentioned. The client may need support, enlightenment, and guidance for specific action and may accept it best from a group with the same problems. Alcoholics Anonymous (A.A.) is probably the most successful of these social networks and one of the most dramatic. Members call each other at any time, day or night, for support, and it is given. In one instance, the then-Governor of Iowa, Harold Hughes, responded to late-night requests from other A.A. members; social networks often cross economic and social lines in their common identification as victims, or people with problems. Clearly, in these instances, social networks function as strong nonplace communities that perform functions for their members and for the environment. For the environment, they function as agents of change and at least as "escape valves" for their members if they do not accomplish personal or societal change.

3. BEHAVIORAL ASPECTS. These systemic characteristics tend to be of shorter duration than the structural characteristics discussed in the preceding section.

a. *Social control.* The overall purpose of social control is *to maintain the system, not necessarily to maintain the status quo.* Social control may be exerted by the entire community through its network of values and goals, which are embodied in one or several of its institutions. These institutions may act on behalf of the entire community or it may, as sometimes happens, act on behalf of some group or special interest. For example, blacks in ghettos complain that police do not act in their behalf to protect their property or lives but only to enforce order on behalf of white businesses and white property owners. The "web of urban institutions" that operates to enforce racial discrimination has been convincingly described and analyzed (see Knowles and Prewitt, 1969).

In nonplace communities, social control may be exerted by formal or informal sanctions. Amish men who secretly buy television sets may be banished from the community and not spoken to by other Amish people for months or years. In a professional community such as nursing or teaching, sanctions may include temporary loss of license or a public notice that the employer is blacklisted, which means that no member of the profession should work for that employer.

Social control is modified (but not necessarily lessened) by the overlapping memberships that community members have. Power structure and decision-making studies have revealed the interlocking positions held by some persons in the community (Domhoff, 1971). The same family may be represented on the public library board, the planning and zoning commission, the board of directors of a bank, and also may operate a large business. Such overlapping memberships may lessen the effect of centralized social control or may aggrandize it. The Lynds' 1929 study of Middletown indicates that whatever the formal arrangements might have been, the commercial leaders of the community (Muncie, Indiana) exerted a great deal of social control; the same has been found in most cities.

A related aspect of community, and one that has received increasing attention during the past 30 years, is that of "community power." Presthus comments:

> Simply put, individuals of similar interests combine to achieve their ends, and such combinations of interlaced values and interests form subsystems of power. The community is composed of a congeries or such subsystems, now co-operating, now competing, now engaged, now moribund, in terms of the rise and fall of local issues. Some subsystems are more powerful than others; some are transitory; others persist, one supposes, because the interests which they institutionalize are persistent (Presthus, 1964:6).

The classic and most frequently imitated study is Floyd Hunter's *Community Power Structure* (1953). Hunter's basic findings have not been refuted by subsequent studies. He found that the most powerful persons in the community were heads of large commercial enterprises, especially banking and finance; and that other leadership was composed of professional men and a few representatives of government and labor. Hunter found that within the group of those who were powerful, a relatively small number were "policymakers," or the "power elite" of the community. Other studies with a somewhat different focus by C. Wright Mills (1948, 1951), G. William Domhoff (1967, 1971, 1974), and others largely confirm the existence of a national power elite with bases in various communities. Domhoff details the activities of the power elite in the Bohemian Grove, a gathering place north of San Francisco (Domhoff, 1974). The dispute continues between "elite" theorists and "pluralist" theorists as to whether there is any single, dominant power group (see Banfield, 1961; Domhoff, 1967; Hunter,

1953; A. Rose, 1967; Silk and Silk, 1981). In part, the question is one of identifying the focal system since some theorists focused on the community and others on the national, societal system. Domhoff attempts to tie the two together with results that have been criticized with regard to methodology.

The process by which powerful persons exert control and how decisions are influenced is the subject of another group of studies, which overlaps the community power studies to some extent. These "decision-making" studies largely attend to specific cases and examine the factors that entered into critical decisions made by the communities studied. Hunter (1953), Dahl (1957), and Banfield (1961) each derived decision-making models that ranged from the bureaucratic, pyramid model in which decisions were made "at the top," to "mutual adaptation" models in which decisions were made by consensus in a relatively participatory, decentralized fashion. These two models have some relation, of course, to the argument between the "elite" and "pluralist" power theorists. In these decision-making studies, it was found that the political subsystems played important, but not necessarily dominant, roles. Decisions were made by informal or private subsystems differentiated by social class, organizational position, or by the kind of institution being represented. The informal decision-making structure was often as influential, or more so, than the formal (including political) structures.

b. Socialization. Socialization is essential to the life of a community. If new members are not socialized into the community to supply new energy *(negentropy)*, it becomes entropic. Some utopian communities (e.g., the United Society of Believers in Christ's Second Appearing [Shakers]) who were celibate have been unable to maintain themselves as members died, and present-day communes face a constant problem of attracting new members. Kephart (1976) notes an irony that although the commune espouses personal freedom, it must, like all systems, socialize its members to communal values and pursuits.

Enculturating the newcomer is often a community concern. The complaints of urban northerners that some Appalachian immigrants leave junk cars in the yard, throw their garbage out of the window, and tie clothes lines to their neighbor's houses point to the difficulty of socialization to an urban setting. Some communities have had to attempt to socialize deviant subcommunities (counter-culture communes) that reject established community values, specifically norms of productivity, health, and dress. In the face of such deviations, communities attempt to apply social control in the form of jail sentences, compulsory socialization (e.g., enforcing truancy laws or mandatory work programs for relief recipients), or expulsion. Expulsion took the form of "warning out" as early as the sixteenth century in England and was transferred to the United States. Persons likely to become recipients of public assistance were told to leave the county. In 1950, one of the authors was "warned out" of a county in a western state for being in a condition of limited means. This practice continued in some states as late as 1959, and one of the authors found people who had previously been warned out when he took over a caseload in 1960.

In the 1960's, Kabouters (literally, "elves"—equivalent to "hippies") slept in the central plaza of Amsterdam on the steps of a national monument. Their presence and habits offended many Dutch citizens, and in some respects presented health hazards (e.g., hepatitis). The law against sleeping on monuments was revived and enforced but to little avail. Eventually force was employed to expel the Kabouters. Socialization occurred as they became a political party and won seats on the city council, but socialization was incomplete. In order to reinforce the boundary between themselves and the rest of society, some Kabouters resigned from the council and thus avoided becoming part of "the system."

If deviance cannot be reduced or removed, communities may adapt to the deviant values by creating new institutions (as discussed earlier), just as public schools and settlement houses were created to socialize millions of immigrants from Europe and Project Headstart to "socialize" racial minorities in the 1960's.

There are less formal means of socialization; parades and Fourth of July celebrations socialize citizens into wider patriotic values. Formal ceremonies may mark induction to the community; the Jewish Bar Mitzvah, Christian baptism, freshman hazing, and naturalization ceremonies are examples. Such rites of passage symbolize the socialization of a person into a new status within the system. One example is drumming and singing in Chippewa Indian culture:

> A small boy may grow up standing at the edge of the drum circle. A circle of three or more intense, somber, sweating men. . . . The men are always serious. There are times, in the afternoon or early in the evening, when a young boy may be permitted to kneel between the men and beat on the metal edge of the drum with a stick. Then one day, when it is time, he will have the courage and the confidence to drum on the white surface, straighten his body, lean forward, and make the sound. It is time to become a man (Brill, 1974:82).

Social networks are probably highly significant in socialization in organizations and communities. Newcomers usually find that the most important task is to join a social network that reliably describes the norms, mores, and sanctions of the system. Everyone who has entered a new school, new job, new community, or who has changed status within a system can probably remember the process of finding such a network (or failing to find one).

As noted in Chapter 4, I, A, networks function primarily as sources of information and as efficient distributors of information. It has been demonstrated that nonmembers of networks have less information than members of the network about matters that are equally important to both. Networks are typically more fluid and have fewer fixed roles than groups, organizations, or communities; thus, it is easier to fit into a network and to both give and get energy (in the form of information). Networks often serve as "welcome wagons," assisting newcomers to find niches for themselves in new systems and to learn the "lay of the land." Frequently, information exchange is the primary (or sole) reason for the existence of a network, and network members abandon the group, or disband it, when their needs for information are more adequately met in the system they have joined. Networks are less demanding since they are partial and cannot offer either a full set of roles or complete roles. As illustrated in Chapter 6 on groups, centrality in the flow of information is often synonymous with leadership roles; thus, networks are often the "farm teams" or "out-of-town" debuts for more established systems. On occasion, a network functions as the embryo of a developing system in which network participants are the charter members.

c. Communication. Communication is a highly important aspect of community system behavior. Institutions such as churches and schools carry on some communication, but the major communications activities occur between persons face-to-face and by public media such as newspapers, television, and radio. In British, early American, and some Sioux communities, this function was performed by the town crier or its equivalent. Billboards, soapboxes, loudspeakers, sirens, pamphlets, and flyers are all means of communication used and controlled by segments of the community to impart symbols of the community's way of life. In contrast, bumper stickers, T-shirts, and citizens band radios tend to be communication devices used for individual expression.

> "The essence of community, as John Dewey suggested, is communication. For without communication there cannot be that interaction by which common meanings, common life, and common values are established" (Ross, 1975).

> "Communication has even more meaning in that a social system survives only as each significant component performs its particular specialty for the total system. In the social world this is not done by a unit isolating itself and following its own interests but by participating as expected in a network of relationships" (Sanders, 1958).

In both of the preceding quotations, it is evident that communication is energy exchange, without which systems disintegrate. In the broadest sense, communication is energy exchange—if information is viewed as potential energy.

Social networks, discussed earlier in this chapter, have communication as their major function. They have both instrumental (goal-oriented) and affective (emotional) functions, but networks perform primarily as conveyors of information, concerning instrumental and affective needs, rather than suppliers or intermediary systems themselves. That is, social networks identify groups, families, neighborhoods, or even communities within which primary needs can be met; but the networks themselves do not meet the needs. This distinction may seem petty, but it is necessary to clarify focal systems and whether or not something is a system. In this respect, a social network may be seen as an interlocking set of roles with relatively specific functions compared with some groups or communities that are broader in their functions. In other words, social networks resemble groups and communities in some respects while resembling organizations in other respects.

Components of the community system can monitor each other's performance and are provided with directives via feedback linkages such as newspaper reports of governmental meetings, public hearings on controversial issues, and elections. In some communities, such as Synanon, the utopian community of Oneida, and in communities in the People's Republic of China, specific times are set aside for mutual criticism by members (Kephart, 1976:69ff.). In some religious denominations and in A.A., testimonials serve a feedback function. Feedback was explicitly and formally sanctioned as part of social welfare programs under Title XX of the Social Security Act and as part of the Community Development Block Grant through low-income persons' membership on the governing boards. Community groups and client representatives had to be part of the process of program planning, and their views had to be acknowledged. This recently was changed substantially by revised guidelines under the Reagan administration.

C. Professions as Nonplace Communities

An established profession claims for itself and is recognized by society as responsible for a symbolic territory. Almost by definition, when a group carves out for itself a societal function or some part of the society's stock of ideas, it becomes sanctioned as a profession. When the societal function of instructing the young was delegated to and assumed by teachers, the next logical step was the formation and protection of territory by professional teachers' organizations. The same can be said of medicine, law, and the ministry, the three so-called "classic" professions. It can be said as well of the newer, developing professions of law enforcement, nursing, engineering, and social work. The following is a description of the emergence of a profession:

A domain of specialized knowledge must develop . . . which will furnish the theoretical underpinnings for the practice skills by which the profession expresses its function. In the absence of specialized knowledge at least the technical means — for example, techniques or skills whereby the professional is characterized and differentiated from the nonprofessional or layman — need to be specified (Boehm, 1965:641).

The major commonality among the professions is that they are formally sanctioned by society to bring about change that is beneficial to the society and its components, as well as to maintain the society. Despite their seeming conservatism on occasion, professions do regulate change as well as maintenance; for a profession to refuse to allow change would be deadly to a society and would probably signal that the profession would lose its societal sanction. Professional licensure symbolizes societal acceptance and sanction for a professional territory. Boehm made concrete the concept of professional territory: "Each profession has a specific or core function and in a sense holds a monopoly on this function. . . . However, each profession shares with all other professions in society what Hiltner has called a village green, a common area that is peripheral to each profession" (Boehm, 1965:642). Clearly, social work, psychiatry, nursing, education, and law enforcement, among other professions, share a "village green" that is socialization and social control.

Historically, social work has concerned itself more with change among microsystems (persons, families, and small groups) than with change among macrosystems (organizations, communities, and society). But it has dealt with societal and community change as well, although these have been the domains of other professional groups such as political scientists and sociologists. There are indications that social work is enlarging its territorial claims, and border disputes between professions within the same institution are common. Examples are social work and law within the juvenile court; social work and psychology in mental health institutions; and social work and educators in the schools. Clearly, there are boundary disputes between home economists and family counselors; between nurses and physicians' assistants; and between teachers, guidance counselors, and school psychologists.

Boehm points to other characteristics of community that distinguish a profession: a common system of values and ethics (way of life, or culture); a group identity that holds the allegiance of the members; and social control and socialization within the profession. All of these characterize professions as nonplace communities to the extent that they are true. However, in practice, professions sometimes fail to meet all these criteria (e.g., group identity or common values). The most accurate way to define a profession may well be to define it as a social network; that is, a set of interlocking roles organized for relatively specific goals that are set within expressly stated, idealized goals of "service to society" and the sanctity of the persons being served. Professions often lack a sense of "community" that is sufficient to mobilize their members to joint action. The professions usually resemble organizations as much as communities but lack the degree of social control typical of organizations. J. A. Barnes' definition, referred to earlier in this chapter, indicates that social networks may be the best way to describe professions. They are organized for specific purposes, with limited bonds between members, and largely depend upon affiliations between small numbers of members, who are loosely connected to some larger system.

CONCLUSION

Because the term carries many meanings, community is an elusive concept. Meanings range from the territorial community of Robert Park and the Chicago sociologists to the almost mystical "mind" community of more recent writers (Park 1952). Three critiques of the concept that are particularly germane to social work are those by Chatterjee and Koleski (1970), Meenaghan (1972), and Gusfield (1975), which review the literature of community and conclude that the concept of community is an evolving one. Each of the critiques concludes that community is a perspectivistic idea — that is, it is futile to attempt to understand a total community, but it is worthwhile to select issues or problems and then define community as it is relevant to these particular concerns. This stance is in agreement with our use of the concept of community in this book. We view community as a social system and, as such, perceive it from a particular perspective. To do this, it is necessary to have criteria for classifying patterns of relatedness as a system and then, further, to distinguish the community from family, group, or organization. These criteria come from the composite definition suggested earlier, that a community:

1. is a system intermediate between society and "microsystems"
2. has a consciously identified population characterized by a sense of belonging, that is, it is aware of itself and is part of its members' identities
3. is organized and engaged in common pursuits
4. has differentiation of functions
5. adapts to the environment through energy exchange
6. creates and maintains organizations and institutions to fulfill the needs of both subsystems and suprasystems

Further, its members may or may not occupy common physical space; and its boundaries may or may not coincide with the boundary of a political subdivision (city, town, or county). Communities can, and do, interlace through the overlapping memberships of their significant subsystems. For example, a nurse may be at the same time, a Minnesotan, an officer in the

Air Force, a Republican, a Roman Catholic, and a member of N.O.W. Each of these may signify a community to which she belongs. Membership in each of them may modify her beliefs and behavior in the others. As stated earlier, community is a vital system to humans, who require some sense of linkage, some sense of community in order to survive and flourish.

SUGGESTED READINGS

Bell, Colin, and Howard Newby.
   1972   *Community Studies: An Introduction to the Sociology of the Local Community.*
   New York: Praeger Publishers.
       A comprehensive survey of community theory up to 1972, which suggests promising leads for further theory.
Capelle, Ronald.
   1979   *Changing Human Systems.* Toronto: International Human Systems Institute.
       This text is a generalized overview of change techniques which is presented by level of system. Chapter Ten, "Community Change," pp. 167–182, suggests a way of selecting among techniques, but in rather sketchy fashion. You may be interested in reading this for ideas rather than as a course text.
Christenson, James A., and Jerry W. Robinson, Jr.
   1980   *Community Development in America.* Ames, Iowa: The Iowa State University Press.
       Beginning with a very brief review of the concept of community, this is a highly useful description of community development techniques and themes. It also examines in some detail the roles performed by community developers.
Davenport, Judith, and Joseph Davenport III.
   1982   "Utilizing the Social Network in Rural Communities," *Social Casework,* Volume 63, Number 2, February, 1982, pp. 106–113.
       This brief article describes the fundamentals of networking in communities and the role of the social worker.
Dunn, Edgar S.
   1980   *The Development of the U.S. Urban System, Vol. I.* Baltimore: The Johns Hopkins University Press, 1980.
       Chapter Two, "An Activity Network Image of Urban System Structure," pp. 17–33, is an excellent companion to this chapter. The entire book is compatible with the social systems view.
Gardner, Hugh.
   1978   *The Children of Prosperity: Thirteen Modern American Communes.* New York: St. Martin's Press.
       Insightful and incisive research into communes and their reason for existence. Concludes that the movement is far from dead, but notes that failure to transcend individualism doomed many of them.
Gusfield, Joseph R.
   1975   *Community: A Critical Response.* New York: Harper & Row.
       Together with Bell and Newby, above, this will bring community theory nearly up to date, with excellent critical reviews of each theory.
Hillery, George A., Jr.
   1968   *Communal Organizations: A Study of Local Societies.* Chicago: The University of Chicago.

A superb, exhaustive examination of the theory of the community. Should be read by anyone undertaking serious study of this system.

Kahn, Si.
  1982   *Organizing.* New York: McGraw-Hill.
  Although this is a "practice" text rather than human behavior theory, it gives the student a feel for the reality of "implementing change" in the real world of the community.

Kephart, William M.
  1976   *Extraordinary Groups: The Sociology of Unconventional Lifestyles.* New York: St. Martin's Press.
  An examination of six religiously based communities of historical significance and a quick look at modern communes. The author writes with verve and understanding.

Kinton, Jack, editor.
  1978   *American Communities Tomorrow.* Aurora, Illinois: Social Science Services and Resources.
  Interesting articles on neighborhoods. Donald I. Warren's chapter, "Neighborhood Theory: Loose Knit, Tight Knit and Unraveled," discusses neighborhoods and social networks.

Warren, Roland.
  1977   *New Perspectives on The American Community.* Rand McNally.
  Warren's thoughtful views on contemporary American communities and their futures.
  1963   *The Community in America.* Chicago: Rand McNally.
  A well-written general text on community. "The American Community as a Social System" (pp. 135–167) is particularly congruent with this chapter. We also recommend Warren's *Truth, Love and Social Change* (Chicago: Rand McNally, 1971).

LITERARY SOURCE

Steinbeck, John.
  1961   *The Winter of Our Discontent.* New York: The Viking Press.
  This novel sensitively conveys the interdependent ties of person and simple community in a New England town. The community has its foundations in ascribed status and allows for some movement by achievement, while its members seek to achieve individual goals.

ORGANIZATIONS

Our society is an organizational society. We are born in organizations, educated by organizations, and most of us spend much of our lives working for organizations. We spend much of our leisure time paying, playing, and praying in organizations. Most of us will die in an organization, and when the time comes for burial, the largest organization of all — the state — must grant official permission.

(Etzioni, 1964:1)

Careers in organizations — that is, careers as managers and other professionals — are the principal career opportunities for educated people. Nine out of ten youngsters who receive a college degree can expect to spend all of their working lives as managerial or other professional employees of institutions.

(Drucker, 1982:xii)

The fact that the United States is an organizational society was noted by such observers as De Tocqueville from virtually the day of its founding. However, human service professionals have been slow to recognize and take this into account in their appraisals of human behavior. Otto Pollak comments, "If ever this writer were asked to propose a further development of the theoretical underpinning of social work practice, he would put the emphasis on an integration of organization theory and psychoanalytic theories of personality development" (Pollak, 1968:52). While we do not attempt such a synthesis in this chapter, we do believe that the systems approach offers a greater opportunity to do so than any other theoretical approach.

The nature of organizations has been insufficiently understood, and even the most knowledgeable organization theorists readily admit that there is no single definitive theory. Miller writes:

> Organization theory is a field without a large body of empirically established fact. Like medicine before 1930, management science is based largely upon case studies. . . . Scholars in this area would also profit from an agreement . . . as to what are the basic subsystems common to all organizations. I suggest that comparisons with the other levels of living systems can provide this. A generally accepted taxonomy of types of organizations is also desirable, and general systems behavior theory may be able to provide it . . . (J. Miller, 1972:174).

In his 1978 encyclopedic book, *Living Systems,* Miller applies his framework to organizations to prove that

> General living systems theory can provide a unifying conceptual system for organization theory, including a definition which differentiates organizations from living systems at other levels, and identification of the chief subsystems of all organizations with their analogs at other levels. It can also provide a basis for understanding how organizations differ and for applying quantitative techniques and formal models to the study of organizations (J. Miller, 1978:597).

We agree with Miller's view, and believe that the systems approach provides the best opportunity to classify organizations and their subsystems. We must begin at the beginning, however, with a workable definition of *organization.* Probably Talcott Parsons's statement is clearer than most:

> Organizations are social units (or human groups) deliberately constructed to seek specific goals. Corporations, armies, schools, hospitals, churches, and prisons are included; tribes, classes, ethnic groups, friendship groups, and families are excluded. Organizations are characterized by: (1) divisions of labor, power, and communication responsibilities . . . ; (2) the presence of one or more power centers which control the concerted efforts of the organization and direct them toward its goals . . . ; (3) substitution of personnel . . . (Parsons, 1960:17).

This definition relies on specific examples in part because (using group theory terminology), the "formed" organization is very often difficult to distinguish from "natural" tribe, society, and community. The "natural" organization (if there is such, perhaps a family corporation would be an example) is difficult to distinguish from family or community. Parsons's definition states that differentiation, power, goals, and the interchangeability of persons for another are characteristic of organizations; each of these is true to some degree of societies and communities as well. Certainly some organizations are less characterized by these than are some societies and communities. Thus, the differences are not in the absence of these characteristics but rather the degree to which they are present and the form they take. We will expand on this at several points, particularly in the conclusion to this chapter. Consistent with Parsons' view, characteristics to be stressed in Section II of this chapter are goals, differentiation, power, control, leadership, and communication.

Another definition of organization that is concise and perhaps a bit cryptic is by C. Wright Mills: "An organization is a system of roles graded by authority" (Presthus, 1962:4). This definition implies that organizations have goal achievement as their primary reason to exist; it follows that persons are not expected to employ their full range of behaviors but only those that are necessary or useful to the purposes of the organization, that is, goal achievement. In other words, persons are to perform according to their assigned roles not according to their personal wishes (unless, of course, their personal wishes coincide with the needs of the organization, a situation deliberately sought by many organizations). Further, these roles must be coordinated so that they can combine to achieve the goals, that is, they must be differentiated, hierarchical, and have some functions taking priority over others (although the ranking in the hierarchy can change from one occasion to another).

Taken together, Parsons' and Mills' definitions indicate a relatively complete explanation of organizations that includes the following elements: (1) an organization is a social system that has the achievement of specific, explicit goals as its purpose. In order to accomplish this, its members must (2) confine themselves to a relatively narrow range of behaviors intended to fulfill this purpose. The members (3) exercise power over each other in the form of authority and hierarchical control to (4) assure compliance with the system's goals and adherence to the members' prescribed roles.

I. THEORIES OF ORGANIZATION

There are four major types of organization theory to which we add a fifth — systems.

A. The Classical Model

The classical model is sometimes called the "machine theory" because it "started with the assumption that the member of an organization was essentially a physiological unit" (Dubin, 1961, 1968:28). The organization was viewed as a machine with interchangeable parts and clearly identifi-

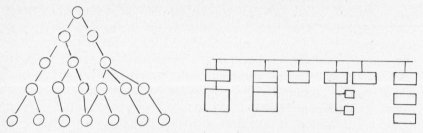

Fɪɢ. 8. Diagrams of the classical model.

able operations, and members were treated as cogs and gears in that machine. Principles of this formal organization include: (1) division of labor, with each unit performing specific tasks; (2) pyramid of control, with each unit subordinate to one above it in the hierarchy; and (3) unity of command, that is centralized control emanating from the top of the pyramid (see Fig. 8).

The emphasis is on mechanical regulation, control, and rationality of organization, the latter two being primary characteristics of this model. This has been the most visible model of organization, from the Roman army to the modern bureaucracy. The fact that this form of organization survived after thousands of years indicates how effective it can be at achieving goals and ensuring compliance. Henry Ford based his assembly line on the rationality of this model, saying of the giant industrial corporations, "It is clearly up to them now, as trustees, to see what they can do further in the way of making our systems fool-proof, malice-proof, and greed-proof. It is a mere matter of social engineering" (Flink, 1976:82–83). Social historian Lewis Mumford said that organizations arise from the human need to create regularity in the world (see the discussion in Chapter 3, II, "E. The Human Urge to Explain the World"), which he traced to earliest recorded history:

> Behind every later process of organization and mechanization one must . . . recognize primordial aptitudes, deeply engrained in the human organism—indeed, shared with many other species—for ritualizing behavior and finding satisfaction in a repetitive order that establishes a human connection with organic rhythms and cosmic event.
>
> Organization Man is the common link between the ancient and modern type of megamachine: that is perhaps why the specialized functionaries, with their supporting layer of slaves, conscripts and subjects—in short, the controllers and the controlled—have changed so little in the last five thousand years (Mumford, 1970:277).

This probably explains the inscription on the Great Pyramid of Egypt, presumably scratched by one of the original workmen, which says "Khufu is a drunk." Workers apparently resented their bureaucratic supervisors 4500 years ago, too.

B. The Human Relations Theory

The human relations theory arose partly in reaction to "machine" theory. It is exemplified by Elton Mayo, Kurt Lewin, and indirectly, John Dewey (Etzioni, 1964:32). It stresses the informal structure, and the emotional, nonrational motivations that operate in organizations. It emphasizes such processes as communication, participation, and leadership. Motivation of Japanese workers, or "Theory Z" is a variation of human relations theory in that it stresses increased productivity and decreased alienation due to greater participation and involvement in decisions by workers [see the discussion of Theory Z (Ouchi, 1981b) later in this chapter].

The best known studies issuing from the human relations theorists are the Hawthorne studies, including the Bank Wiring Room study (Mayo, 1945; Olmsted, 1959:25–32; Roethlisberger and Dickson, 1947). The results of these studies indicated conclusively that "machine theory" was inadequate to explain behavior in organizations; clearly, other factors besides rational, impersonal calculation determined the workers' production. In these studies, it was found that the highest motivation for one group of workers was neither money nor working conditions but rather what is now known as the "Hawthorne effect" — the fact that they were a special group being researched! The general conclusion that sets this theory apart from the "machine model" is that workers do not function as separate, distinct units but rather as members of groups to whose norms they adhere. The influence of the small group became readily apparent.

Later adaptations of human relations theory have employed Maslow's "hierarchy of needs" (discussed later in this chapter) to explain motivation and behavior in organizations. Herzberg's two-factor "hygiene" theory is another variation; in this view, workers have two hierarchies of needs, one of satisfaction and one of dissatisfaction (Herzberg, Mausner, and Snyderman, 1959). As Herzberg, Mausner and Snyderman describe it, "satisfaction" refers to the upper end of Maslow's scale, the worker's need for stimulation, and for self-fulfillment (Maslow's "self-actualization"). "Dissatisfaction" refers to the lower end of Maslow's scale, including the employee's "security" needs of pay, safety, and health and insurance coverage (the so-called "fringe benefits"). The worker can be "high" on one scale and "low" on the other, "high" on both, or "low" on both. That is, a worker can be highly satisfied and highly dissatisfied at the same time concerning different aspects of the work situation. Perhaps the pay and fringe benefits "package" is excellent, yet the employee is frustrated because there is little opportunity for creativity or career advancement, a frequent finding of studies on "worker alienation" (Work in America,

1973). Human Relations theory restored human, personal factors to the study of organizations.

C. Structuralist or Conflict Theory

The structuralists, who include Karl Marx and Max Weber, represent in some respects a synthesis of the two theories just discussed in that they recognize both formal and informal structures, and their interaction, as significant. They agree with the classical theorists that the attempt to achieve goals through rational, impersonal structure is useful and does not necessarily lead to unhappiness among workers. They also recognize a necessity for the organization to meet the human, personal needs of its components, as well.

The structuralists do not place primary emphasis upon the human, emotive factors, however. They stress the importance of the work setting and the influence of the technology used in the industry. This gave rise to the study of the "sociotechnical" aspects of industry, the interaction of persons with technology (often called *cybernetics*). Another difference between the structuralists and the "machine" theorists is that the former view organizations as open systems; that is, the structure of the organization varies according to the environment and the technology employed (Tausky, 1970:55–62). A pyramidal, bureaucratic structure will not fit every organization.

The major difference between the structuralists and the two previous theories is that the structuralists recognize the inevitability of conflict within the organization. Etzioni says, "The structuralist sees the organization as a large, complex social unit in which many social groups interact. . . . The various groups might cooperate in some spheres and compete in others, but they hardly are or can become one big happy family as Human Relations writers often imply" (Etzioni, 1964:41).

The structuralist view can be called a "conflict" or "tension" theory of organizations. This theory resembles a systems approach in that it recognizes components within the organization and recognizes that there is inevitably tension in the interaction between the components and the larger organizational system. Like systems theory and unlike the "machine" or human relations theories, structuralist theory does not view conflict as a problem, the resolution of which will restore equilibrium. Rather, conflict may lead to a new steady state (see the stages of groups in Chapter 6, II, A, "2. Stages"), and is thus an inherent characteristic of organizations. Indeed, one administrative or organizational development strategy may be to deliberately induce conflict in order to stimulate change. Lewis Coser (1964) cites positive effects of conflict—for example, that it may force a confrontation that leads to a test of power. The history of nearly any organization reveals successive tensions and conflicts whose resolution (or nonresolution) led to its present condition. Some of these conflicts can probably be viewed as "healthy" because they restored vitality or resolved issues that had retarded the organization's growth. Structuralist theory, then, portrays organizations more realistically than either the classical or human relations theories alone.

D. Neoclassical or Decision Theory

Etzioni calls neoclassical or decision theory the neoclassical school because it, too, is concerned with the achievement of rational decision-making whenever possible. This theory recognizes that there is, in addition to the horizontal differentiation by task, a vertical hierarchy or differentiation by "levels of decisions" that are made. This differentiation is made on the basis of power (i.e., whose decisions are binding upon whom). This theory distinguishes between policymaking and policy implementation (Barnard, 1968; March and Simon, 1968; H. A. Simon, 1945). In this theory, power consists of access to information that is sufficient to formulate policy, and the ability to get others to carry out the actions necessary to implement the policy. Perhaps most important is the qualification *whenever possible.* This school holds that human behavior in organizations is best described as "intendedly rational" (H. A. Simon, 1945:196). Thus, they recognize the nonrational aspects of decision-making in organizations. Also emphasized is *search behavior,* the concept that an organization does not seek endlessly for perfectly rational behavior but instead seeks satisfying solutions that are "reasonably good" or "acceptable" (Etzioni, 1964:30–31). If tension or conflict between components and the organization cannot be completely resolved to everyone's satisfaction (and it rarely or never is), the organization must find another "solution." The solution may be to coerce the component into agreement, or to modify the organization's behavior, or to arrive at a compromise that does not fully satisfy either but permits continued movement toward a mutual goal.

Neoclassical theory resembles systems theory in that it recognizes the inevitability of tension and conflict. It goes beyond human relations theory in stating that tension and conflict occur not only over personal factors but over the actions necessary to achieve the goals. That is, conflict is sometimes nonrational, but it is often rational and concerned with decision-making. Further, it recognizes the necessity for differentiation in order to make decisions that lead to task achievement. This does not imply that a fixed hierarchy is necessary, since the structure can change according to task, or does it imply that certain components must always be the decision-makers, since leadership may change according to task, also. It simply recognizes that people will "organize," that is, differentiate their efforts to achieve a task. It also recognizes that people will disagree about how to organize.

E. The Systems Model

Organization theorists have made various observations about organizations as systems. Gouldner describes the "natural-system model" including the following characteristics (Gouldner, 1961:394–395).

1. Organizations are "natural wholes"; the underlying model is organismic.

2. Structural changes are cumulative, unplanned, adaptive responses to threats to the equilibrium of the organization rather than purely rational, objective behavior.

3. While goal attainment is the fundamental reason for an organization's existence, it cannot be pursued to the exclusion of other functions of the organization. Goal attainment is only one of the important functions of the system.

March and Simon stress this organic analogy:

> A biological analogy is apt here, if we do not take it too literally or too seriously. Organizations are assemblages of interacting human beings and they are the largest assemblages in our society that have anything resembling a central coordinative system. Let us grant that these coordinative systems are not developed nearly to the extent of the central nervous system in higher biological organisms — that organisms are more earthworm than ape. Nevertheless, the high specificity of structure and coordination within organizations — as contrasted with the diffuse and variable relations *among* organizations and among unorganized individuals — marks off the individual organization as a sociological unit comparable in significance to the individual organism in biology (March and Simon, 1968:33).

Presthus emphasizes that large organizations are similar to society as a system in that they have specialization, hierarchy, and authority, and that they socialize their members in similar fashion (Presthus, 1962:94–95). This systems model, although not without faults, seems to avoid the pitfall of the earlier models. This systems model of organizations agrees with decision theory that the goal is not perfection. It goes one step further by stating that goal-seeking behavior is not necessarily the primary behavior of a system at all times since, as earlier stated, exclusive attention to goal attainment leads to neglect of other essential functions of the system. The systems model also stresses a wider context of decision-making and organizational behavior than is pictured in other theories. Like the structural theory, it takes into account environmental influences as well as the influences wielded by groups within the organization. Conflict is seemingly better explained by the systems model in that it recognizes the inevitability of conflict within and between components and subsystems, each of which holds to the legitimacy of its own goals. Miller states the systems point of view very well:

> No decision is entirely rational or satisfactory, a fact which can give administrators some solace. There is no perfect rational solution to most administrative problems. The higher the echelon, the truer this is of the issues which confront it. The dimensions along which many decisions must be made are incommensurable. Human lives are incommensurable with money. Money is incommensurable with time. Time is incommensurable with professional excellence. Yet all of these are in scarce supply to a given organization and trade-offs among them must be decided upon (J. G. Miller, 1972:79).

Thus the context and environment of any organization is complex, and is best portrayed by the systems model.

Control is also pictured differently in the systems model. It is, like goal attainment, exclusively pursued only to the detriment of other functions, and, at times, other functions do take precedence. The fact that power, control, and the influence of the environment may vary from one time to another requires us to use a flexible model of organization. The systems model has flexibility that allows for understanding variant forms of organization that do not fit the classical or "machine" model.

II. CHARACTERISTICS OF ORGANIZATIONAL SYSTEMS

Kahn claims that it is correct to identify the "job to be done," or goal achievement by organizations, as the function of the organization that takes precedence over any other function. He suggests that other activities that contribute to the overall functioning of the organization should be called "subfunctions" (A. Kahn, 1969:145). We disagree. Although it is goal achievement that justifies an organization's existence, other functions are necessary and at times take precedence.

A. Goal Direction

Parsons defines organizations as those systems that give primacy to goal attainment (Landsberger, 1961:215). While no system gives goal attainment primacy at all times, organizations are goal-directed to a greater degree than other systems. Miller emphasizes this in his definition of an organization as a "goal seeking system which has interacting goal-seeking subsystems with different goals arranged in a hierarchy" (J. G. Miller, 1972:5).

What is an organizational goal? Etzioni says that a goal is "a desired state of affairs which the organization attempts to realize" (Etzioni, 1964:6). In this sense, a goal may be expressed by an ideal or myth or by a rational, projected set of specific objectives — that is, it may be "maximum service to the patient" or "caseloads of 50, with short-term crisis intervention allowing attention to 50 percent more clients than at present" (Etzioni, 1964). The goal expressed by either statement is a desired future condition of the agency in which its declared purposes would be fulfilled. These goals guide the organization in its activity; they either legitimize or exclude certain specific actions undertaken or contemplated by the organization.

Etzioni's conception of goal is similar in some regards to the "ego ideal" of the person and to the self toward which one strives in Sartre's form of existentialism or Maslow's self-actualization. In fact, Argyris says that "research points up quite clearly that the importance of the organization as an organism worthy of self-actualization is now being recognized" (Argyris, 1968:83).

Two aspects of goal attainment should be distinguished. *Effectiveness* refers to the degree to which the organization achieves its goals; *efficiency* refers to the manner in which it is done, specifically the amount of energy and resources necessary to achieve a goal. The former is part of the GE and GI function of systems; the latter is part of the SE and SI functions. Efficiency in an organization requires reduction of conflict (or "friction," in slang) within the organization; thus some internal control of the utilization of energy is necessary for goal attainment. One example would be the coaches' encouragement of team spirit with its implied reduction of intra-squad animosities in a football team so that its points (or goals) may be scored.

As several theorists point out, goals are not static. Goals can be displaced (i.e., other goals can be substituted for them). The most frequent form of this is making ends of means. For example, efficiency in public welfare is purported to be a means to effective service to clients and society, but all too often efficiency in the form of having to account for every dollar spent becomes an end in itself. When this occurs, the completed forms become more important than the clients they represent — a frequent complaint of human service professionals in most kinds of organizations. Another example is the accusation by many university students that universities have displaced education with publication and research, resulting in lower-quality instruction.

Other forms of goal change are *succession,* in which an organization achieves its initial goals and establishes new ones, or the goal disappears and the organization turns to new goals. Examples of this include those private welfare agencies that began as adoption agencies in an era when there were more abandoned children than now and whose goals have become either the treatment of emotionally disturbed children or family treatment. Both Christmas Seals and the March of Dimes established new goals after attaining their original goals. There may also be goal *multiplication*. The Red Cross, which began as a service on the battlefield to soldiers, broadened its goals to include services to soldiers' widows and orphans, disaster relief, and visiting political prisoners. There are, of course, advantages and disadvantages to such goal multiplication. Among possible advantages are that synergy (see glossary) may increase the effectiveness of an organization, and recruitment may be easier because workers enjoy variety. Disadvantages include shortage of energy, or conflict between goals. An example of the latter may be the conflict between the social worker's concern for the unwed mother's future and the viewpoint of the social worker's agency which may oppose abortion.

B. Differentiation

Differentiation is probably more pronounced in organizations than in other social systems. Differentiation is the prime sociological characteristic of modernization according to Etzioni (1964:106). Modernization means essentially that modern society is a society of differentiated organizations.

> Differentiation . . . makes possible the formation of "artificial" social units, deliberately designed for the efficient service of (specific) functions. . . .
> Moreover, we now have secondary differentiation in each sphere—i.e., the emergence of subspecialties each with an organizational structure geared to its own needs. Thus the vocational high school is different from the academic high school, and a mass-production corporation differs from a small business (Etzioni, 1964:106–107).

Durkheim points out that differentiation of task within an organization is not all good. If workers do not see and understand the activities parallel to their own and are not horizontally related to it, they each become nothing but "an inert piece of machinery." They must "keep in constant relations with neighboring functions . . . not lose sight of [their] collaborators, that [the worker] acts upon them and reacts to them" (Durkheim, 1968:43); they are, then, not machines. Differentiation may lead to isolation of the components of an organization (e.g., in offices and factories where there is little exchange between clerical and professional staff or between workers and management).

C. Power and Control

In the definition of organizations attributed to Talcott Parsons discussed earlier in this chapter, the existence of one or more "power centers" that control the organization's efforts is acknowledged. Robert Bierstedt states this emphatically: "Power supports the fundamental order of society and the social organization within it, wherever there is order. Power stands behind every association and sustains its structure. Without power there is no organization and without power these is no order" (Bierstedt, 1961:246). Organizations must ensure compliance in achieving specific, narrow goals and therefore must apply some kind of control—the use of power. One characteristic of organizations as distinct from other systems is the explicitness of power; it is largely visible and institutionalized. What is power?

A widely used definition of power in political science is Robert Dahl's: "A has power over B to the extent that he can get B to do something B would not otherwise do" (Dahl, 1957:201–215). Similarly, Bierstedt says:

> Power is the ability to employ force, not its actual employment, the ability to apply sanctions, not their actual application. Power is the ability to introduce force into a social situation; it is the presentation of force. Unlike force, incidentally, power is always successful; when it is not successful it is not, or ceases to be, power. Power symbolizes the force which may be applied in any social situation and supports the authority which is applied. Power is thus neither force nor authority but, in a sense, their synthesis (Bierstedt, 1961:243).

What we mean by "force," in systems terms, is the application or deprivation of energy in order to affect the functioning of another system. Force should not be taken to mean only physical forces: moral force or Gandhi's Truth Force qualify as well. Since power is an energy function, it is finite; energy expended (through the GE or GI functions, for example) to influence the behavior of others may deplete the system's power potential.

We agree with Miller's terse definition: "In my conceptual system I use the word *power* as the ability of a system to elicit compliance from other systems" (J. Miller, 1972:66). We will define power, then, as the system's potential to achieve its goals by the application or deprivation of energy to another system or component so as to affect the functioning of that system or component. The degree of effectiveness of power depends upon the extent to which the "target" system is affected and the extent to which the goal is achieved. One example is the use of federal funds for Appalachian development. The goal was social and economic change; the result was an improved highway system and some new courthouses, which benefited the residents of the county seat towns and the politicians (in the opinion of one well-informed resident). A great deal of energy (funds and propaganda) was expended, but although there were some substantial achievements, they were not the ones originally intended. In this instance, the federal government's power to achieve its goals was shown to be minimal. If the federal government's covert goal was *political*, its power to achieve its goals through the political system of Appalachia was quite effective. Power must thus be measured by its objectives, not merely by the magnitude of its effects.

We consider power and control to be similar except that *control* suggests longer duration and wider influence over another system than does power. Further, power may have effects other than control. The application of power could release control. One example is education, which is the application of the teacher's and school's power so that the student is freer to perform the necessary tasks of adulthood (an idealistic view of education, we admit). Etzioni states the importance of control:

> The success of an organization is largely dependent upon its ability to maintain control of its participants. All social units control their members, but the problem of control in organizations is especially acute. Organizations as social units that serve specific purposes are artificial units. They are planned, deliberately structured; they constantly and self-consciously review their performances and restructure themselves accordingly (Etzioni, 1964:58).

The objective of power and control is *compliance*, the cooperation of a system or component in achieving the goals of the system that applies power and control. Dessler suggests that "there are two basic aspects of organizations (their *structure*, and how *compliance* is ensured) that organization theorists have focused on. . . ." (1980:7). Organization theorists and managers of organizations perhaps devote more attention to compliance than to any other aspect of organizations; how to assure the desired results? The problem of compliance is apparent in the following example, reported from Vietnam by correspondents Horst Faas and Peter Arnett:

> A reporter was present at a hamlet burned down by the U.S. Army's 1st Air Cavalry Division in 1967. Investigation showed that the order from the division headquarters to the brigade was: "On no occasion must hamlets be burned down."
> The brigade radioed the battalion: "Do not burn any hamlets unless you are absolutely convinced that the Viet Cong are in them."
> The battalion radioed the infantry company at the scene: "If you think there are any Viet Cong in the hamlet, burn it down."
> The company commander ordered his troops: "Burn down that hamlet" (J. Miller, 1972:69).

Implicit in this effort to control is the expectation at each level that some control must be exerted in order to achieve compliance at the next lower echelon; but with each descending level, the latitude allowed was enlarged. Miller suggests that such distortions might have accounted for the My Lai massacre of Vietnamese civilians in 1968, which resulted in trial and conviction of some military personnel and a review of the manner in which such orders were given.

An example of the opposite form of control, in which latitude is reduced at each lower level, is described by a former General Motors executive:

With such closed-mindedness at the top, a guiding precept of management soon developed. "Thou shalt not contradict the boss." Ideas in this kind of a system flowed from the top down, and not in the reverse direction. The man on top, whether he was a plant manager, department head or divisional general manager, was the final word. Each executive in turn supported the decisions of his boss right up the ladder. The chairman, of course, in this system had the final say on everything unless he parcelled out power to those around him (Wright, 1979:46).

There are three forms of control, as Etzioni describes them: (1) physical control; (2) material rewards (such as goods and services); and (3) symbolic rewards (Etzioni, 1964:47–59). Elsewhere, Etzioni describes three kinds of organizations based upon the form of control used by each: (1) coercive organizations, which use threat and punishment, resulting in alienation among the members of the organization; (2) remunerative organizations, which provide material rewards, in which the members calculate the benefits they will receive; and (3) normative organizations, which use moral involvement and social acceptance as means of control, which tend to encourage high levels of commitment to the organization by its members (House, 1975:74–78). The latter, symbolic or normative rewards, are in many ways the most significant because one's sense of who one is and what value one has is derived from symbolic interaction with others (as noted in Chapter 3, II, "C. Language"). Symbolic rewards are most likely to be used by the systems with the least physical control or material rewards—religious institutions are the prime examples. In this light, nursing, social work, or education can be regarded as means of social control; through the deliberate use of symbols, they assist organizations such as schools, hospitals, prisons, or the military in securing compliance (the SI and GI functions).

Organizations whose primary purpose is social control are examples of what has come to be termed *total institutions*, a phrase coined by Erving Goffman in his classic work, *Asylums* (1973). He describes a total institution as an organized agency of society in which a large number of like-situated individuals, cut off from the larger society for an appreciable length of time, together lead a formally administered round of life. This is descriptive of such organizations as prisons, mental hospitals, the military, and, in some respects, public and private education. These systems are composed of two groups variously called staff and patients, guards and inmates, keepers and kept, or faculty and students.

Generally, the purpose of a total institution is to socialize or resocialize the population with which it works. This is done by the staff through a two-step process designed to change the "structure of self" of their charges. The process begins by changing the person through external definition. Elements of this usually include (1) divesting the person of socially defining symbols and characteristics (e.g., the "bald" haircut in army basic training and personal clothing); (2) using clothing to symbolize distinction between inmates and staff (e.g., separate uniforms for guards and inmates and "street clothing" for the administrators or hospital gowns for patients, as opposed to the green or white clothing of the medical staff); and (3) severing links with outside systems that tend to support and validate previous self-identity. Thus, depersonalization and dehumanization are often the initial phase of experience within a total institution. Once a new, imposed definition has been established, the second step in the process is to see that the definition is internalized by the inmate (or patient, or prisoner, or student), thus changing that person's "selfhood" or self-image. The objective of power and control, again, is to ensure compliance with the organization's goals.

D. Leadership

Leadership may be either formal or informal, and it includes power and control used to achieve organizational ends and make means effective. *Command* is defined as the use of power to insure compliance, and *leadership* is defined as a "continually creative function involving constant appraisal;" the distinction is really that between power and authority, or "authority of position" and "authority of leadership" (Dubin, 1961:350). "Authority of position depended upon centrality in the organization's communications system—it was determined by a structural decision— while authority of leadership was dependent upon the superiority of the leader" (Zalenznik and Jardim, 1967:217). In other words, command derives from the organizational position, from the role and status, while leadership derives from the personal characteristics of the leader. But leadership is not solely dependent upon these personal qualities; it also depends upon the context (the environment) in which it occurs.

> No single set of personal traits essential to the performance of managerial jobs has yet been established to the general satisfaction of psychologists and personnel experts. Different combinations of qualities may carry different men equally far. The qualities needed depend to some extent on the nature of the job and of the organizational environment in which the job is placed (Gordon and Howell, 1968:165).

This illustrates the mutual, multicausation that is part of systems thinking. Leadership also depends upon the relationships the leader has with those being led; the leader is limited by this interdependency. In fact, some research indicates that the higher the organizational position, the more the leader complies with the organization's norms. Barnard observed, "If a system once accepted destroys that mutual adaptation of behavior of leaders and followers—either because it reaches ineffective decisions, or destroys leadership or divides followers—then disorganization, schism, rebellion, or conformance to a new system ensues" (Barnard, 1968:357).

Robert Townsend, former president of Avis ("We Try Harder"), commented that a leader can permit conflict within the organization

> . . . up to a point. A good manager doesn't try to eliminate conflict; he tries to keep it from wasting the energies of his people. . . .
>
> If you're the boss and your people fight you openly when they think you're wrong—that's healthy. If your men fight each other openly in your presence for what they believe in—that's healthy. But keep all the conflict eyeball to eyeball (Townsend, 1970:39).

Again, if systems are untended, entropy results; conflict can energize.

It should be added here that leadership, like power, is not only hierarchical but horizontal. Leadership occurs at all levels; groups operate within organizations and leadership emerges from these. In some organizations, such emergence of leadership at lower levels is deliberately cultivated; the usual manner in which this is done is to decentralize the decision making. In essence, this is the concept behind moves to decentralize the decisions of government and return initiatives to lower levels—state, city, and county governments. Presidents Reagan and Carter have been among the most prominent advocates of such decentralization and of dismantling of federal governmental organizations. Mechanisms for accomplishing this include revenue sharing and block grants to the states, which supposedly will require leadership by the states.

III. STRUCTURE: THE BUREAUCRATIC SITUATION

The term *bureaucratic situation* is borrowed from Presthus, who used it to describe the total environment provided by large organizations (Presthus, 1962:4). We use it in the same sense, knowing that not all organizations are characterized by what is usually referred to derogatorily as bureaucracy. Bureaucracy is a phenomenon contemporary with industrialization and its primary theorist is Max Weber. Weber's primary concern is power: the distribution of power, control of power, legitimation and uses of power, and the satisfaction derived from membership in the organization. It is clear from Weber's writings that organizational structure is intended to permit and regulate the exercise of power. The principles of bureaucracy as Weber describes them are:

1. a clear-cut division of labor corresponding to a high degree of specialization of tasks;

2. a hierarchy of office in which each officeholder or employee is under the control and supervision of a higher one;

3. a consistent system of abstract rules in which tasks must be performed to assure coordination through uniformity of work results;

4. impartiality in the conduct of the office;

5. career employment within the organization; and

6. machine-like efficiency (Pollak, 1968:51).

These are, of course, characteristics of the classical or machine model of organizations, as well. To these should be added that,

7. ideally, positions are filled by persons fully trained and experienced to the degree required by that office; and

8. transactions are reported in writing and carefully checked and filed (Washburne, 1964:41–42).

The following memos (Figures 9 and 10) are illustrations of extreme applications of some of these principles, especially the first and the last. Note the usage of systems analysis jargon in the second (1982) memo. Note also that one memo is from a governmental organization and one from a private organization; neither the public nor the private sector has a monopoly on bureaucratization.

These principles are intended to protect the integrity of the offices and the officeholders at all levels; like the feudal contract between lord and vassal, which spelled out mutual obligations, these bureaucratic prescriptions detailed the rules for interactions. Blau said that "authority is strictly circumscribed and confined to those directives that are relevant for official operations. The use of status prerogatives to extend the power of control over subordinates beyond these limits does not constitute the legitimate exercise of bureaucratic authority" (Blau, 1956:29). It is not so easy to limit the power of one's superiors in bureaucracy, however. We have the examples of Nazi Germany, Soviet Russia, and Watergate to remind us of the potential abuses of bureaucratic power. In the case of Watergate, bureaucratic power was also employed to bring justice: the power of legislative committees, the Department of Justice, and the courts.

Such rationality as is demanded by rules and regulations is, as the human relations school pointed out, unrealistic. There are limits to rationality—"the capacity for self-denial which the rational organization requires cannot be developed within it; it depends upon the more encompassing social relationships that exist in the traditional family or charismatic movement" (Etzioni, 1964:53). There must be a basic commitment to the organization that is only partially rational. It inevitably involves emotive factors such as loyalty and sentiments about the worth of the organization and about oneself as part of it. Such commitments, values and feelings do not originate with the organization; they must begin in other systems.

Persons in modern society must learn to shift constantly between systems to release the tension that they experience in one system during their stay in another system. Thus, tension at work is discharged at home, while

Memo of the Month

DEPARTMENT OF THE AIR FORCE
HEADQUARTERS AIR FORCE LOGISTICS COMMAND
WRIGHT-PATTERSON AIR FORCE BASE, OHIO, 45433

REPLY TO
ATTN OF MMWC

SUBJECT: SAC/Plattsburg C/R B3264-0140/C3271-1630/D3289-3687, FSN 8820-188-3880, Dog Patrol, Explosive (Your ltr, 17 Oct 73)

TO: WRAMA/MMSEB

1. Recommend clarification of the Plattsburg request, the FSNs used, WRAMA's comments, and FSNs in the TA.

2. There will be a tendency towards confusion unless more or more explicit information is given. AFLC cannot identify any FSN to Dog Detection - Explosive or as WRAMA puts it in 17 Oct 73 letter, Patrol Dog/Explosive. We cannot determine whether they want a dog or an explosive. TA 538 lists FSN 8820-435-9005 as a Dog-Patrol which may be an animal to ferret out narcotics or explosives.

3. Plattsburg started out with a request for FSN 8820-243-7542 which is related to narcotics (a/w 538C) not explosives. The FSN was supplanted with 8820-188-3880. TA 538 and TA 002 list 8820-128-2880. Was there an error? Is 188-3880 a new number? Is 188-3880 a dog to sniff out explosives? Also what does Plattsburg really want: Dog-Explosive or Dog-Narcotics? Why has an exchange been offered in your 17 Oct letter?

4. Please review this whole thing for AFLC. Clarification is in order and a change to TA 538 for better identification seems in order.

FOR THE COMMANDER

charles K. Pickell

CHARLES K. PICKELL
Aerospace Equipment Division
Office of DCS/Material Management

FIG. 9. Reprinted with permission from *The Washington Monthly*, copyright 1977. (The Washington Monthly Co., 2712 Ontario Road, N.W., Washington, D.C. 20009.)

Memo of the Month

BANK OF AMERICA

FROM: IOS-Development Support Services #3445
      San Francisco Headquarters

  TO: IOS Staff

DATE: August 31, 1982

SUBJECT: Pacific Gateway Move Task Force

The attached matrix indicates the Move Task Force Representatives for Pacific
Gateway. The following diagram illustrates the recommended approach for
information/questions to flow in order to ensure all your requirements/needs
are met:

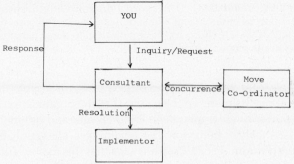

The "Consultant" role is to screen all inquires/requests for feasibility. The
"Implementor" role is to provide back-up to the "Consultant" and to ensure
plans are carried out for day one move in service and thereafter. The "Move
Coordinator" role is to review all updates/concerns and act as primary
interface with all non-IOS departments, e.g.EB-Administration & Premises.

Bruce Lee
Ext. 2-6847
Senior Systems Analyst
(Move Coordinator)

cc: Kathy Stout
    Valerie Pinkert
    Fran Farmer
    Felix Canari
    Roger McClure

1v/2116f

FIG. 10. Reprinted with permission from *The Washington Monthly,* November,
1982. (The Washington Monthly Co., 2712 Ontario Road, N.W., Washington,
D.C. 20009.)

tensions at home are discharged in a social club or at work, for example.
Work organizations that demand rationality are particularly demanding
and require tension discharge in other, more communal systems such as
family, church, or other informal setting (the bar, the bowling league, or
with coffee companions or fishing buddies).

Many writers have described the effects of bureaucratic organizations on
the personalities of their members. Some have suggested a *bureaucratic
personality.* Etzioni describes the features of this personality: it (*a*) is accus-

tomed to shifting between social units, especially the family and the organization; (*b*) has high tolerance for frustration and the ability to defer gratification; and (*c*) has the urge to achieve material and symbolic rewards (achievement orientation). Etizioni adds this note about the relationship between organizations and other systems:

> The major credit for this convergence of personality and organizational requirements . . . must go to the modern family and the modern educational system, both of which produce the type of person who will make a good organization man. The middle-class stress on the values of punctuality, neatness, integrity, consistency, the accent on conformity, and above all achievement, are the foundation. . . . The organization's effectiveness . . . is due more to the social environment which provides the "right" kind of participants than to any deliberate efforts by the organization to shape personalities according to its needs (Etzioni, 1964:110).

The organization values the kind of personality that puts the organization's goals above its own. To the extent that the organization can enforce this, it has power over its members. Erich Fromm and others have shown that this is unhealthy behavior that encourages alienation because it is manipulative (Fromm, 1962). Presthus says that this may result in "a subtle corrosion of integrity" (Presthus, 1962:18). We refer the reader here to Erikson's conception of integrity (Erikson, 1968:139) discussed in Chapter 8, II, "F. Conservation of Identity."

Currently, much attention is being given to the dehumanizing influences of our institutions and organizations. In the effort to structure large-scale human interactions along lines of efficiency, objectivity, and merit, the needs of individual human beings have been relegated to the background. Alienation, referred to at various points in this book, is an end product of dehumanization. The other consequences are many and increasingly visible in shoddy products and inadequate services.

> I can just look at a car and see all kinds of things wrong with it. You can't do that because you didn't see how it was made. I can look at a car underneath the paint. It's like x-ray vision. They put that trim in, they call it. The paint and all those little pretties that you pay for. Whenever we make a mistake, we always say, "Don't worry about it, some dingaling'll buy it" (Laughs.) (Terkel, 1975:229).

Classical organization theory assumes that rational behavior on the part of workers prevents alienation. Human relations theory perceives alienation as inevitable. This is similar to entropy, in that organizations will degenerate into randomness and disorganization if the member's personal needs are not tended to. Both the structuralists and decision system theorists seem to suggest that some degree of alienation is inevitable. The source of alienation is disputed by various writers, however. In a thoughtful book, Robert Agger maintains that the source of alienation is the *belief* that a person can be split between their roles in work organizations and their roles in everyday life. He says that this belief

> . . . is misleading because the conventional wisdom is wrong which implies that when a total person moves from everyday-life into institutional space (say, into working, economic institutional space) the person somehow loses totality by putting on certain clothing or a uniform and becoming known by a job classification or organizational title. For every man and woman the world of work, the week of work, the wages in kind or in other symbolic payment are a vital part of their lives. When at work or anyplace else, the person remains total despite the practices that surround him or her, practices often designed to give people a machinelike sense of identity or even a sense of being components or cogs in a machine (Agger, 1978:100).

Agger advocates restructuring institutions (including work organizations) in ways that recognize the wholeness of persons.

Perhaps the most damning indictment of modern organizations is a book by Scott and Hart, both professors in a school of business administration. They say that "We believe that the most significant source of the subversion of the individual right to 'life, liberty and the pursuit of happiness' is the modern organization, with its supporting technologies and behavioral sciences" (Scott and Hart, 1980:ix). They maintain that

> Outrageous as it may seem, the fact is that a new value system dominates America. The organizational imperative, while originally a subset within the context of the overarching social value system, has now become the dominant force in the homogenization of organizational America, displacing the more individualistic values of the past (Scott and Hart, 1980:52).

They protest the image of the individual which they believe dominates management's thinking:

> It is a vision of individuals who are innately malleable and, thus, completely susceptible to techniques of education, development, and control through the modification of the environment and mind (Scott and Hart, 1980:59).

They point to the theories of B. F. Skinner and other behaviorists as reinforcing this view of compliant workers. Further, they claim that individuals have surrendered their autonomy to the organization. This is consistent with the viewpoint of one of the authors of this book, who labeled corporate domination "the new feudalism" several years ago. Scott and Hart sound the alarm:

> What is new is that the organizational imperative does not require the fanaticism so common to mass movements; in the popular parlance, one should be a cool "gamesman". . . . But one central feature of mass movements is present: the substitution of the collective absolute for personal values" (Scott and Hart, 1980:64).

If these authors are to be believed, we face a crisis in the degree to which organizations are responsive to the needs of the human beings within them and the degree to which these persons are manipulated for the good of the organization.

A. Burnout

Many theorists and organizational specialists have studied the phenomenon of *burnout* among professionals and members of organizations. Burnout has been defined as

> . . . a debilitating psychological condition brought on by unrelieved work stress, which results in:
>
> 1. depleted energy reserves;
> 2. lowered resistance to illness;
> 3. increased dissatisfaction and pessimism;
> 4. increased absenteeism and inefficiency at work (Veninga and Spradley, 1981:6–7).

Burnout may be considered a particular form of alienation. Clearly burnout is a serious and, in some cases, life-threatening condition. Studies indicate that such work-related stress affects 80% of business executives, 66% of teachers and secretaries, 44% of garment workers, and 38% of farmers (Veninga and Spradley, 1981:12). Women are highly vulnerable to burnout because they are (*a*) frequently in tedious jobs with little chance for advancement; (*b*) lacking in leisure time because of family responsibilities, and (*c*) isolated and lonely because of demands upon their time, which limit opportunities for social contacts (Veninga and Spradley, 1981:12–13).

Veninga and Spradley identified five stages of burnout, beginning with an initial period of satisfaction with the job ("the honeymoon"), followed by a second stage in which the characteristics previously listed (energy depletion, etc.) begin to be evident. The worker is not necessarily aware of the symptoms in this stage. In a third stage, the symptoms become chronic and begin to interfere with the person's functioning at work and at home. In a fourth stage, *crisis,* the worker becomes obsessed with the problem and burnout dominates his or her life. In a fifth stage ("hitting the wall"), if the worker progresses that far, the worker cannot function on the job and his or her life deteriorates in significant ways (Veninga and Spradley, 1981:38– 39). There is no inevitable progression through the stages. People have highly individual patterns, sometimes moving in and out of burnout depending upon their own resources and the resources available to them from the environment and as they find ways to relieve the chronic stress contained in the job. Change can come about, in true systemic fashion, by altering the job, the environment, or the person's perception of the job or themselves. At times, however, the only possible change is to exit the job.

One means of altering the job and the environment that Veninga and Spradley do not explicitly mention is *networking*, mentioned in Chapter 4, I, C, 2, d "Social Networks." A worker may find other workers experiencing similar problems, and they may be able, through group action, to provide mutual support or, even further, to effect change in the job situation. The recent movie, "Nine to Five," showed not only some hilarious means of achieving change (including tying up the boss as a prisoner) but also some serious efforts at reduction of burnout including "flextime" (allowing workers to vary their hours), more individualization of work space ("flexiplace"), and day care for employees' children. Usually, efforts to humanize organizations take the form of decentralization: less emphasis on specialization by workers, reducing units to smaller scale, or restructuring decision-making processes to allow employees to have more influence in determining their own fates and that of the organization.

IV. EVOLUTIONARY ASPECTS

Are there realistic alternatives to large-scale bureaucracies? For large numbers of people in a technological society, there may not be. Some organizations have attempted other forms of decentralized structures with autonomous work groups that allow freedom and control to line workers (Bennis, 1969; Illich, 1973; McGregor, 1960; Ouchi, 1981b). Such attempts have drawn heavily upon research done subsequently to World War II by the Tavistock Institute in England. These studies indicate that greater productivity and reduced alienation are best achieved by autonomous work groups. Other efforts have focused on redesigning jobs ("job enrichment," "job enlargement") and restructuring to permit greater self-determination by workers. In rare instances, United States companies have permitted workers to participate in management decisions. In Europe, this is known as "co-determination" or "industrial democracy." Worker participation in management is required by law in West Germany.

A popular concept in management recently has been "Theory Z," an organizational style derived from Japanese corporations. As management expert Peter Drucker points out, the ideas underlying Theory Z were originated by United States companies two or three decades earlier and adapted by the Japanese. It is now being used by Hewlett-Packard, IBM, Dayton-Hudson, Eli Lilly, Rockwell International, Buick Motor Company, and Westinghouse, among others. William G. Ouchi, who coined the phrase "Theory Z management," said that there are several lessons to be learned from this style of management:

1. *Trust,* between management and workers, which encourages sacrifice in the belief that eventually the employee will receive rewards
2. *Subtlety,* the recognition that human relationships are far too complex and changing to be captured by bureaucratic rules or labor contracts
3. *Intimacy,* the expression of caring and support among those at the workplace, certainly not a common experience in United States industries

Ouchi maintains trust, subtlety, and intimacy at the workplace lead to greater productivity in which everyone shares. Ouchi says of Americans:

> We resist the idea that there can or should be a close familiarity with people in the workplace. "Personal feelings have no place at work," is the common feeling. . . . In the Japanese example, we find a successful industrial society in which intimacy occurs in the place of work as well as in other settings. The Japanese example forces us to reconsider our deeply-held beliefs about the proper sources of intimacy in society (Ouchi, 1981b:9).

Trust is fostered by companies' commitment to lifetime employment for each employee; in case of recession, companies aggressively look for new markets or new products while workers perform other duties (including janitorial services) until the financial situation becomes better, meanwhile keeping their jobs. The "groupness" of the work situation is encouraged by workers sharing space without walls; interaction is not only encouraged, it is demanded. Permanence of employment and group feeling result in absence of (or at least lessened) alienation, since "people committed to long-term relationships with one another have strong commitments to behave responsibly and equitably towards one another" (Ouchi, 1981b:34). Ouchi remarks elsewhere that this kind of organization resembles a clan with a strong sense of community (Ouchi, 1981b:415).

Decision-making is also a group process governed by consensus. It apparently is disturbing to Westerners who are accustomed to more authoritarian decision making and who perceive the Japanese as slow to decide and their decision process difficult to fathom. The Japanese reply that it may take longer to arrive at consensus, but that once achieved, it is quicker to implement with little dissatisfaction with the decision. Ouchi says

> . . . intimacy, trust and understanding grow where individuals are linked to
> one another through multiple bonds in a wholistic relationship. . . . The
> Japanese show clear evidence that wholism in industrial life is possible (Ouchi,
> 1981b:54–55).

And further that

> it is a consent culture, a community of equals who cooperate with one another
> to reach common goals. Rather than relying exclusively upon hierarchy and
> monitoring to direct behavior, it relies also upon commitment and trust (Ouchi,
> 1981b:83).

"Humanization" or improving the "quality of work life" are complex
undertakings, involving recognition of more facets of the person than
simply his or her role as a production unit in the industrial system.
Paradoxically, it well may require the person to give up some freedom and
independence to assume new obligations of mutuality with management
and other workers. Toffler suggests that we are witnessing the breakdown
of bureaucracy and that it will be supplanted by "Ad-hocracy" (Toffler,
1970:124–151). Adhocracy denotes an organizational scheme congruent
with an era of accelerated change, wherein people are brought together to
accomplish a specific task and disband once that task is accomplished.

According to one of Miller's hypotheses, increasing size generates
greater variety of subsystems: "In general, the more components a system
has, the more echelons it has" (J. Miller, 1978:92). He comments that
organizations, unlike organisms or some groups such as a nuclear family,
may outlast the lives of the original members. Because organizations can
replace components and learn from experience, it may be true that the
longer an organization lives, the better its chance for survival (J. Miller,
1972:130). Miller further comments that old organizations are resistant to
change (see the discussion of "schemas" in the section on Piaget (Chapter 8,
I, B, 1, "c. Schemas"), but that research is so far inconclusive. John Z. De
Lorean's exposé of practices at General Motors would indicate that at least
one major corporation finds it very difficult to change its ways:

> The system is so rigid now that I do not think an innovative thinker like Alfred
> P. Sloan, Jr. could qualify for a job in the upper ranks of General Motors. Even
> if he did, he wouldn't have the freedom necessary to operate effectively there. I
> do think that my fall from favor and subsequent departure from General
> Motors posits the inability of the system of management to blend and accom-
> modate. The rigidity of the system would not tolerate my successful alternative
> to the standard way of doing business. Even though I was working for the
> ultimate good of the corporation, I was not permitted to make a contribution
> (Wright, 1979:280).

In October 1982, De Lorean was apprehended and charged with illegal traffic in drugs, which was presumably his means to contribute to "the ultimate good of the corporation," in this case his own De Lorean automobile corporation.

The pace of change in an organization is nearly always controversial. The last three presidential elections, for example, indicated public dissatisfaction with the speed of change in the federal bureaucracy; racial reforms were occurring too quickly for some, but tax reforms were occurring too slowly. Centralization of power in the executive branch was feared by many, who cited revenue sharing as organizational decentralization and by others who cited control of prices and wages as organizational centralization. The 1976 and 1980 elections have been interpreted as a "mandate" against centralized federal bureaucracy.

One reason for the mixed nature of organizational change is the rapid diversification and expansion of major corporations during the past generation. Examples include the purchase of luxury hotels in London and purchase of corporate stock by Arab petroleum interests and other international oil companies, which presently dominate the international economic scene. Management expert Peter Drucker said of the new multinational corporation that

> It does not fit the traditional organization structure of the multinational corporation, with a central top management to which management of subsidiaries reports. It requires, rather, a systems approach, in which one body coordinates autonomous managements that do not report to one another (Drucker, 1982:191).
>
> A major requirement is the ability and willingness to adapt to different cultures and to work with people of different habits and traditions. [It] is not only transnational, rather than multinational; it is, above all, transcultural. And it is an idea whose time has come (Drucker, 1982:192).

Thoughtful analyses (including some by science fiction writers, notably Isaac Asimov in the *Foundation* series) suggest that the governments of the future may not be nation–states. Instead, international conglomerates may rule, and in some cases, more rationally. It may well be that unless governments become equally adaptable, other organizations may absorb what we now recognize as "governmental" functions. The United Nations recognizes the insufficiency of information on multinationals and their activities and is attempting to formulate a code of ethics for multinational enterprises. Many such corporations have voluntarily subscribed to the "Sullivan Rules" concerning opportunities of citizens of Third World countries to be trained and employed by multinationals located in their countries.

While the future of organizations is unclear and events seem mixed in their implications, Miller may be correct when he states that organizations increase their potential for survival the longer they exist. The most successful organizations seem to be those that can adapt rapidly to changing environments — altering goals and functions (as when the March of Dimes took on new research targets after polio was controlled) or altering structure (as many corporations do when acquiring or divesting subsidiary companies according to their financial, research, or market needs).

Not only commercial organizations will be subject to the necessity of change. Miller suggests that persons may work for more than one organization; that part of one's time will be spent at one organization, part at another. This is a counterpart to Toffler's "modular" relationships between persons (J. Miller, 1972; Toffler, 1970). Such "plugging in" would permit fairly rapid modification of organizational structures and require greater professional identification beyond the particular organization that employs the professional. In fact, a significant number of professionals are presently related to two or more organizations, serving as consultants or part-time service workers. Many of these are regular employees of one organization and "moonlight" or act in consultant roles with other organizations. It seems likely that this will become more common. Knowledge of organizations and how to work with, or within, them is essential to effective professional practice for all human service professionals.

SUGGESTED READINGS

Barnet, Richard and Ronald E. Muller.
  1974   *Global Reach*. New York: Simon and Schuster.
      A detailed examination of the extension of corporations through out the world. The material is useful for large-scale examples of organizational principles, and the trade-offs between increasing size and concern for smaller-scale systems.
Beer, Stafford.
  1981   "Death Is Equifinal," *Behavioral Science*, Volume 26, pp. 185–196.
      A provocative general systems statement about what is amiss with modern organizations. He suggests that only a systems perspective will enable the relinquishing of worthless models of organizational behavior.
Dessler, Gary.
  1980   *Organization Theory*. Englewood Cliffs, N.J.: Prentice-Hall.
      This is an excellent introductory text. Chapters 1, 2, and 3 together make up a thorough review of older and contemporary theories of organization.
Domhoff, G. William.
  1971   *The Higher Circles*. New York: Vintage Books.
      One of the most thought-provoking studies of power structure. It presents a strong argument for the existence of a power elite in our society.
Etzioni, Amitai.
  1964   *Modern Organizations*. Englewood Cliffs, N.J.: Prentice-Hall.
      An excellent, concise examination of theories of organizations and processes.

Hasenfeld, Yeheshkel.
   1983   *Human Services Organizations.* Englewood Cliffs, N.J.: Prentice-Hall.
   This is the most useful text for a course on human services organizations. It is
   comprehensive, up-to-date, and thought-provoking. One of the authors used it
   as a text, and found it to be excellent. It would benefit from a more explicit
   usage of systems ideas, but it is entirely compatible with our approach.
Kimberly, John R., and Robert H. Miles and Associates.
   1981   *The Organizational Life Cycle.*
   This is a seminal book, exploring new ground in organizational theory. The
   authors propound a biological or systems view of organizations while explicitly
   stating its limitations. Ouchi's chapter on organizational failure is perhaps the
   most relevant and suggestive of systems ideas. Miles' chapter on research is
   highly valuable as an update on the field.
Lauffer, Armand, et al.
   1977   *Understanding Your Social Agency.* Beverly Hills, California: Sage Publications, Inc.
   This little paperback is an excellent way to introduce students to a systems view
   of social agencies. It is a slightly different set of systems ideas from ours, but the
   two books are compatible.
Miller, James G.
   1978   *Living Systems.* New York: McGraw-Hill.
   Chapter 10, "The Organization," pp. 595–745. Again, very productive of
   stimulating ideas, for the serious student of systems.
Ouchi, William G.
   1981   *Theory Z: How American Business Can Meet the Japanese Challenge.* Reading, Massachusetts: Addison-Wesley.
   The originator of "Theory Z" makes a compelling case that U.S. companies
   should adopt the Japanese style and structure.
Veninga, Robert L., and James P. Spradley.
   1981   *The Work-Stress Connection.* Boston: Little, Brown.
   Comprehensive discussion of burnout. Suggests means to reduce or eliminate
   work-related stress.
Wright, J. Patrick.
   1979   *On a Clear Day You Can See General Motors,* New York, Avon Books.
   This revealing look at a major corporation contains an abundance of case
   examples of systems ideas.

GROUPS

Nothing is harder to stop than a freely and fully
united band of human beings.
— Milton Mayer, *On Liberty: Man* vs. *The State*

It is within the group that the power, basic and
immense, human beings have over one another
occurs; the power of acceptance or rejection.
— Gisela Konopka, *Social Group Work*

INTRODUCTION

The social group is a critical system to each person and, in particular, to the
helping professions. As an arena of social interaction, the group has the
potential to provide for a range of human needs that include:

1. A need to belong and to be accepted
2. A need to be validated through feedback processes
3. A need to share common experiences with others
4. Opportunities to work with others on common tasks

The human group is a social system that has received, and deserves,
extensive investigation. The term, *group*, includes those patterns of association and activity in which persons engage most of their "selves" from day to
day. It is a holon composed of individuals and small constellations of
persons, and it is a component of its environment. A group is more than
simply an aggregate of individuals; it has a unique wholeness of its own. As
Lewin phrased it, "The whole is *different from* the sum of its parts; it has
definite properties of its own" (Marrow, 1969:170 [Emphasis ours]). (Note
that the words "different from," not "more than," are used.) Thus the
human group is a system disinguishable from its environment, having the

115

characteristics and functions of a system and providing the connectiveness between its components and its environment. Like other social systems, groups are characterized by energy exchange. The term, *synergy*, originated by anthropologist Ruth Benedict, was used by psychologist Abraham Maslow to apply to groups; the following passage illustrates Hampden-Turner's use of Maslow's idea and illustrates the diffusion of systems ideas through various disciplines.

> Synergy involves the resolution of the selfish/unselfish dichotomy by making the enhancement of the Other the precondition or result of personal enhancement. . . . Further evidence for synergy came from the supervisors' reports on their work groups. There was a substantial increase in groups which reached decisions by mutual agreement and in reports that 'differences in opinion are directly confronted and discussed to productive solutions' (Golembiewski and Blumberg, 1970:51–52).

Since the discussion of groups in this chapter is from a social systems viewpoint, a cluster of persons can be considered a group only if it fulfills certain specific criteria of systems. Donald Campbell suggests that rather than starting with the assumptions that aggregations are systems, it is advisable to subject such aggregates to empirical examination to see whether they do in fact have the properties of systems. If the subject of such examination is not found to possess such properties, that is, cannot be established to be a holon, then the analysis should properly be carried out at the next lower level (Campbell, 1958). Thus, a group with *a high level* of systems properties might be analyzed largely with group concepts; *a moderate level* with group and individual concepts; and *a low level* with individual concepts. In other words, a gathering together of persons does not make a group. The expression "the group jelled" conveys a point in time or process when an aggregate of persons became an entity, a group, distinguishable from its environment, and different from the sum of its parts. This leads to the question: What are the significant properties of a group as system or entity? The remainder of this chapter addresses this question.

I. DIMENSIONS OF GROUPS

There are as many kinds of groups as there are group leaders, observers, and therapists (and perhaps members, since each has a personal perspective on the group). Rather than attempt a comprehensive taxonomy, we will discuss a few important dimensions that have been used to classify groups. These dimensions are polarities. Any given group, at any given time, theoretically could be placed at some point on each continuum.

A. *Instrumental versus Expressive*

Drawn from Parsons' formulation, this continuum is similar to others that are frequently used: "task vs. sentiment," "goal achievement vs. group maintenance," "task-oriented vs. group oriented," and "guidance behavior vs. sociable behavior" (Olmsted, 1959:135; Parsons, 1964b:79–88). The distinction is usually understood as being between a particular, articulated, time-limited objective and a diffuse, unarticulated, enduring, and supportive group climate. Further, the distinction is usually taken to imply that a "goal" or "task" is adaptive, that is, related to the environment, whereas "expressive" or "sentiment" is related to interactions among components of the group. It seems to us that the distinction is best understood as a distinction between two steady states toward which the group could evolve. The first steady state is one in which some fairly clear, specific objective has been accomplished with specific results for "vertical" relations (Warren, 1963:161). The other state is one in which the objectives are fairly diffuse and nonspecific, with the general result of integration of components (i.e., "horizontal" relations) (Warren, 1963:161–162). Consequently, "instrumental versus expressive" activities or orientations are intended to move the group toward one of these two steady states. Probably "adaptive versus integrative" would be more accurate. Bales agreed with this: "The social system, in its organization . . . tends to swing or falter back and forth between these two theoretical poles; optimum adaptation to the outer situation at the cost of internal malintegration, or optimum internal integration at the cost of maladaptation to the situation" (Weisman, 1963:87). Bales identified this as the "equilibrium problem" (Hare, 1976:93).

These are polarities and are not mutually exclusive: The "adaptive" steady state focuses *more* attention on goals and tasks but also deals with integration, although to a lesser extent. The "integrative" steady state, similarly, does not exclude some adaptive activity. For example, the United States Supreme Court must spend some time mediating between the justices' personal feelings at times (Woodward and Armstrong, 1981). A sensitivity group must make decisions about meeting dates and when termination should occur. Reginald Rose's play *Twelve Angry Men* illustrates the successive steady states of a jury as it alternately focuses upon the court's demand for a verdict and the members' needs (R. Rose, 1955).

It is this variability that makes the group difficult to characterize in contrast to the family, which is predominantly integrative, and the organization, which is predominantly adaptive. The community is largely made up of groups and shares their indeterminate character; indeed, it is sometimes difficult to distinguish between communities and groups. We suggest this guideline: *The greater the breadth of influence upon its members and the more diffuse its goals, the more the group resembles a community.*

To the extent that groups are aimed toward specific goals, they resemble organizations. In fact, many such groups are probably components of organizations and may be considered as such with accuracy. These examples clearly demonstrate that groups range widely in character. Some resemble families or communities and some resemble organizations in their position on the "instrumental versus expressive" continuum. Northen (1969:189ff.) comments that problem solving in groups is a major emphasis at a certain stage of group development; at that stage, perhaps, all groups move toward the instrumental end of the polarity.

B. Primary versus Secondary

Olmsted equates this polarity with "instrumental versus expressive," calling the poles "primary – expressive" versus "secondary – instrumental" (Olmsted, 1959:133). This is logical, and we agree with this usage, but some further precision is advisable. A group may be essentially expressive or integrative but be of minor significance to the members. The afternoon (or morning) coffee klatch is a good example. It is predominantly expressive. If it is important to its members, it is clearly a primary group; but if it has little importance to them, it should be considered secondary. One criterion, then, is the breadth of influence the group has upon its members and particularly its influence upon their affective functioning. Another way of saying this is that if members react to each other more as role occupants than as persons, it is a secondary group. As these roles become more formalized, the group becomes more goal-specific and narrows its range of influence, thus, the closer the secondary group comes to being an organization.

C. Narcissistic versus Generative

This polarity is similar to Parsons' polarities of "self versus collectivity" and "particularism versus universalism" (Parsons, 1964b:58 – 67). The polarity is self gratification of one or more members versus wider commitment to the group's goals. Mills notes that this dimension is similar to Freud's pleasure and reality principles, to Erikson's concept of "generativity," and to Redl's typology of authority relationships (T. Mills, 1967:120 – 122).

The importance of this dimension of groups is that it explains the ability or inability of some groups to survive. Mills states that in narcissistic groups, "no provision is made for internal and external adjustment as protections against threat or the realities of the passage of time. . . . They tend to be rigidly structured. . . . Their principle of organization is narcissism, which in itself opposes the social arrangements necessary for resolution of the critical issues of their system" (T. Mills, 1967:121). In other words, they violate the principle that no function can be concentrated on to the exclusion of other functions. Evolutionary capacity is nullified by inability to change structure (i.e., a closed, morphostatic system results). A "generative" system, like a generative person, is engaged in mutually constructive interchange with its environment (see Erikson's seventh stage in Chapter 8, II, "E. Perpetuation and Sharing of Indentity").

These dimensions used to classify groups indicate that groups share important properties of systems: adaptation, integration, goal-seeking, structural maintenance, and structural change.

II. ASPECTS OF GROUP AS SYSTEM

A. Evolutionary Aspects

Analysis of any specific group requires much attention to its evolution — more so, perhaps, than with any other system except family. This is true because groups and families are more dependent upon particular persons than other systems and are thus more likely to be affected by changes in personnel than other systems. Organizations, in fact, are usually deliberately designed to minimize dependence upon individual persons. Because groups are susceptible to these factors, the formation and disintegration of a group are more likely to occur during a single member's lifetime than other systems; it is thus more subject to observation and analysis.

Accordingly, in literature about groups, less attention has been given to structure and more to "process" and to problem solving as a significant aspect of process. Because of this, the balance or steady state of the group has received most attention in research. In group work practice, it has been almost a dogma that all aspects of groups are subordinate to the maintenance of steady state. In our discussion of other systems, we have had to establish that they are systems and to establish that *steady state* is a valid term to apply to them. With groups, the problem is the converse; so much has been research and written on the group as a system and on group "equilibrium" or steady state in particular, that the task is to establish that any other aspect of the system is of equal importance.

1. STEADY STATE

The group is like an organism — a biological organism. It forms, grows, and reaches a state of maturity. It begins with a set of constituent elements — individuals with certain personalities, certain needs, ideas, potentialities, limitations — and in the course of development evolves a particular pattern of behavior, a set of indigenous norms, a body of beliefs, a set of values, and so on. Parts become differentiated, each assuming special functions in relation to other parts and the whole. . . . As a group approaches maturity it becomes more complex, more differentiated, more interdependent, and more integrated (T. Mills, 1967:13).

This is a detailed way to describe a group's steady state. More general ways are to describe its "identity," or its "culture." Mills describes groups as having some of the same qualities as Erikson describes in persons. Groups have "personality," similar to the personalities of individuals, according to some writers (J. Miller, 1978:543; Shaw, 1981:19–20). This personality was labeled "syntality" by R. B. Cattell as early as 1948. Syntality is defined as "the personality of the group, or, more precisely, as any effect that the group has as a totality. . . . Syntality traits are inferred from the external behavior of the group and may include such behaviors as decision making, aggressive acts, and the like" (Shaw, 1981:20).

Olmsted observes that groups have "micro-cultures":

> Each group has a sub-culture of its own, a selected and modified version of some parts of the larger culture. The significance of these subcultures lies not so much in what they add to the larger culture as in the fact that without its own culture no group would be more than a plurality, a congeries of individuals. The common meanings, the definitions of the situation, the norms of belief and behavior—all these go to make up the culture of the group (Olmsted, 1959:84).

a. Norms and consensus. A group establishes norms through consensus. Northen's definition of *norm* is:

> a generalization concerning an expected standard of behavior in any matter of consequence to the group. It incorporates a value judgment. It is a rule or standard to which the members of a group are expected to adhere. . . . A set of norms introduces a certain amount of regularity and predictability into the group's functioning (Northen, 1969:33–34).

"Regularity and predictability" are obviously relevant to steady state. Sherif explores the concept of group norm and finds that when individuals are placed in groups, the individual norms tend to converge into a group norm (Cartwright and Zander, 1960:23–25). This was illustrated in the Bank Wiring Observation Room study in which workers had explicit expectations about the production norms and pressured others to conform (Roethlisberger and Dickson, 1947). Another example was Shils' finding that soldiers observed group norms about supporting their "buddies" (T. Mills, 1967:4n.). As Bill Mauldin states in *Up Front*, combat units "have a sort of family complex."

> New men in outfits have to work their way in slowly, but they are eventually accepted. Sometimes they have to change their way of living. An introvert or recluse is not going to last long in combat without friends, so he learns to come out of his shell. Once he has "arrived" he is pretty proud of his clique, and he in turn is chilly toward outsiders (Cartwright and Zander, 1960:165).

The norm is cooperation; the underlying consensus is survival.

Consensus is "the degree of agreement regarding goals, norms, roles, and other aspects of the group" (Shepherd, 1964:25). When this agreement is carried further into mutual satisfaction of important needs by the group members, it is "symbiotic" (Cartwright and Zander, 1960:81). When such agreements and need satisfactions operate to bind members to the group, it has "attractiveness" or "valence," and the result is *cohesiveness* of the group. Such cohesiveness gives rise to *solidarity*, which is

> the stabilized mutual responsibility of each toward the other to regard himself as part of the other, as the sharer of a common fate, and as a person who is under obligation to cooperate with the other in the satisfaction of the other's individual needs as if they were one's own (Bales, 1950:61).

The Polish worker's union, Solidarity, obviously includes this meaning in its name. Another term for this is *group bond*. Grace Coyle describes group bond as having three levels:

1. conscious purpose, for example sociability or friendship;
2. assumed or unavowed objectives, such as achievement or status, ego expansion, courtship (especially among adolescents), and class rise;
3. unconscious purpose, including sanctioned release of aggression, escape from reality, and sublimation of erotic impulses (Coyle, 1948: Chap. 4).

The narcissistic group, as Mills describes it, is most likely to have a bond at the unconscious level.

Consensus and cohesiveness, then, are *expressive, integrative,* and *primary* aspects of the group.

b. Goal direction. The other component of steady state that should be discussed is goal direction or goal pursuit (T. Mills, 1967:108). In contrast to consensus and cohesiveness, goal attainment is instrumental, adaptive, and secondary. Northen uses the term *purpose,* saying that "every group has a purpose for being. Purpose means any ultimate aim, end, or intention; objective or goal usually refers to a specific end that is instrumental to the purpose" (Northen, 1969:19). Her discussion of these terms leads us to conclude that "purposes" mean those goals the suprasystem assigns to the group; while "goals" mean those ends sought by the group itself. We prefer to use the term *goals* for both to maintain consistency within the systems framework.

Locomotion is the name given to the group goal pursuit by Kurt Lewin and the Group Dynamics theorists: "The concept of locomotion may be interpreted as Group Dynamics' chief intellectual device for dealing with task- or problem-oriented activity in the group. It is generally treated as a characteristic of groups rather than individuals; group process is thus represented as a movement toward (or away from) the group's agenda" (Olmsted, 1959:115). Locomotion means that groups move within an environment or field to achieve goals that are mutually defined by the group and its relevant environment. Goal-directed behavior has effects on group consensus and cohesiveness. It may disrupt earlier expressive, integrative norms and force members to choose between instrumental and expressive behaviors. In some instances, groups may disband because of the divergence.

2. STAGES OF EVOLUTION. Several formulations of group evolution have been presented by group theorists. We present here a brief sketch outlining a general evolutionary process in groups. Weisman summarizes one such evolutionary view.

> 1. The group adapts to its environment; in response to this adaptive behavior, members develop activities, sentiments, and interactions. These adaptive components are the group's external system.
> 2. The group develops activities, sentiments, and interactions beyond the necessary adaptive behavior, through its goal-oriented behavior; these become the internal system.
> 3. As the internal system elaborates, it develops bond, cohesiveness, norms, roles, and statuses.
> 4. In feedback fashion, adaptation is affected by the environment and the developing internal system.
> 5. The group, in turn, modifies the functioning of its members (Weisman, 1963:87).

Homans carries this further and describes the development of the internal system as a process of "elaboration." At some point, a countertrend occurs in which members' behaviors and sentiments become more alike. Homans describes this as "standardization" and, as we show later in Table II, this is a form of social control (Homans, 1950:109–110, 119–121). If social control or adaptive and integrative functions fail, the group may disintegrate or merge into other units. For example, a task force may dissolve and each member return to his own department or organization; or a friendship group may merge into a large group, such as a church group or fraternal group.

We synthesize a scheme of group evolution from several sources (including Garland, 1965; T. Mills, 1967; Sarri and Galinsky, 1967; Trecker, 1955; Tropp, 1976; and Shaw, 1981). The scheme focuses on the internal development of the group; little reference is made to the environment. Thus the scheme is abstracted from reality, since the environment has profound influence on groups. Table II presents the scheme in abbreviated form. An excellent scheme of group development has been presented by Bennis and

Shepard; it is compatible with our scheme here but based on somewhat different theoretical premises (Bennis and Shepard, 1956).

In our survey of literature on group evolution, three major phases with several subphases seem to emerge. A fourth phase may or may not occur. If it does, the result is a loop back to some earlier stage and subsequent redevelopment of the group, or the result may be disintegration or termination. None of these phases is presented here as discrete or absolute. This is a *highly general synthesis* that—to refer again to the introduction of this book—corresponds to reality of groups in the same manner that a map corresponds to mud, rocks, and clear running water.

a. Phase I: E pluribus unum. During the first major phase, exploration of each other occurs among the members. The activity of the members in this phase is similar to the "inclusion" stage identified by William Schutz: "In the inclusion stage, the member confronts questions dealing with his individual membership in the group. He asks: Do I want to be part of this group and do the other members want me to be part of it? Who else is here? Should I become intensely involved or marginally involved? Can I trust my real self to the others?" (Galper, 1970:72). Such questions are answered by probing each other. Levine (1979) describes the earliest stage as the "parallel" stage (like the "parallel play" of young children). In this phase, each member relates primarily to the leader rather than to one other. Eventually (in successful groups), members agree to tolerate each other's thoughts, feelings, and behaviors although there may be some reluctance initially. Such tolerance permits open discussion of the group's emerging culture—as we define it in Chapter 3 (See "Introduction") "the way we do things."

As members give assent to, and sanction for, group "we-ness," they accommodate (in Piaget's terminology) to each other; in systems terminology they approach a steady state.

Carl Rogers identifies and describes the phases of encounter groups. His phases are similar to our intentions here. Rogers describes "patterns or stages," the first five of which fit within our first major stage. His first five stages include (1) "milling around"; (2) "resistance to personal expression"; (3) "description of past feelings"; (4) "expression of negative feelings"; and (5) expression of personal feelings (C. Rogers, 1970:15–20). Evident in Rogers' stages are the characteristics shown in Phase I of our scheme. Discussion of symbols and meanings may take the form of tentative exploration of what structure is possible, what "freedom" means in this group, and how others interpret what the leader says. The interpretation that members arrive at determines the group's *valence* or attractiveness. Members begin to share their *life space* (Lewin's term) to permit others to enter their interactional, personal territory, their "bubbles."

b. Phase II: The control phase. In this second major phase, the emphasis shifts, as Schutz describes it, from "inclusion" to the "control" stage. "In

TABLE II. Synthesis of stages of group evolution

Phases	Cognitive aspects	Affective aspects	Behavioral aspects
I. E pluribus unum			
Components' goals predominate	Discussion of symbols, meanings	Checking for feelings, values of others; "valence"	Observes behavior of others; tentative participation
Affiliation (approach–avoidance)	Attempt to find common meanings, symbols	Expression of feelings	Interaction and reaction in overt behavior; territory shared
Commitment [a]	Limited agreement on symbols, meanings, norms	Development of group bond; satisfaction of individual's feelings; group values emerge	Beginning of modification of behavior to conform; mutual accommodation; locomotion
II. Control phase			
Group goals predominate	Internalization of developing group culture; accommodation of schemas	Same as cognitive	Roles defined and agreed to
Socialization	Standardization; acceptance of group views; subordination of idiosyncratic views	Subordination of idiosyncratic feelings; reinforcement of those that "match" others'	Group prescription of behavior; reduction of deviance; differentiation of roles and territories
Social control [a]	Enforcement of group views; codes and stated purposes; "right thinking" and developed symbol systems	Enforcement of group values; statements expressing solidarity and allegiance; traditions	Rituals, offices, hierarchy
Stability (internal)			
Group goal direction (external) [a]	Problem solving; decision making; thought exclusively focused on goal and means to achieve it; "brainstorming"	Elevation of values that support goal; devotion to them, excluding other values, both personal and group	Focus on specific group goal; sacrifice and joint effort
Intimacy; cohesiveness	Exchange with each other to the exclusion of nonmembers; "private" group views, beliefs, actions	Devotion to each other, to exclusion of ties with "outsiders"	Group rituals and culture concretized and protected

124

III. *Conflict phase* Components' goals predominate	Dissensus on norms, goals, evaluations; selectiveness of evidence used against group members	Disaffection; return (or maintaining) to predominance of individuals' sentiments; "hidden-agenda" predominates	Antagonistic behavior; violation of roles, territories, boundaries; violation of rituals, hierarchy

Loop to earlier phase or move to terminal phase

IV. *Terminal phase* Disintegration (subgroups or complete disassociation)	Maintenance of divergent views; ideological combat	Hostility; defensiveness; feelings of betrayal, anger	Alliances; power struggles; "splitting" from the group; "betrayal" to outsiders

OR

Termination (planned or by agreement)	Reinforcement of belief of worth of group; attempt to analyze "meaning" of the group	Feelings of guilt, rejection because of termination; warmth toward other members	Open communication about termination; displays of sentiment; approach or "flight" behaviors

---

a Arrows indicate that these subphases may be reversed in sequence.

125

the control stage he asks: Now that I have decided to be a member of the group, what power will I have in it? Who is in charge and how do I find this out? What does the group want of me?" (Galper, 1970:72).

One text describes a stage following the preliminary testing of each other by members, a stage in which members are engaging in productive, mutual activity. This stage is called the "working stage" and has the following characteristics:

> This stage is characterized by a here-and-now focus. . . . Members are also willing to have direct and meaningful interactions with one another, including confrontations. Conflict in the group is recognized, and members have learned that they need not run away from it. . . .
>
> Communication in the group is characterized by a free give-and-take among the members. . . . In many ways, the group has almost become an orchestra in that individual members listen to each other and do productive work together. . . .
>
> Self-disclosure is the norm and is seen as appropriate. . . .
>
> Members gain knowledge of how their behavior affects others from the ongoing feedback they receive. They tend to be more trusting of the feedback and suggestions they receive from other members. . . .
>
> Group cohesion is increased during the working phase. The members have worked together to develop a trusting community, and they respect and care for each other. This sense of community encourages members to explore themselves on a deeper level than is typically true in the beginning stages of the group (Corey, Corey, Callanan, and Russell, 1982:91–93).

Rogers' stages 6–10 are not applicable to all types of groups but illustrate evolution in encounter groups. In these stages, immediate interpersonal feelings are disclosed, a "healing capacity" develops, members, therefore, are willing to risk, resulting in self-acceptance and change; "facades" begin to be discarded, and the individual receives feedback, both positive and negative. Rogers describes in stages 6–10 the elements that we include in the subphase, "socialization," in Table II. Members have taken the group norms "to heart"—they have internalized them. They have begun to sort out roles of "facilitator" (not always the group leader), "conciliator," and so forth. They "heal" each other and restrain other members who violate the group norm of "caring" for each other. Those members who express "caring" or negative feelings interact within the group's norms of behavior. Intimacy and cohesiveness are achieved as thoughts and feelings, and behaviors are expressed among themselves that do not include others outside the group. The notable disparity between our scheme and Rogers' is that Rogers deals little with group goal direction. This is understandable since Rogers' encounter groups are oriented toward relatively diffuse goals, with the achievement of goals outside the group process itself being of minor importance.

c. Phase III: Conflict phase. Phase III can occur at any point in group process; it does not necessarily follow Phases I or II. When it occurs, however, it is a crisis in the life of the group; the group will either loop back to an earlier stage (similar to regression in individuals) to resolve the issue or resolve the issue in some fashion so that it can proceed (analogous to Erikson's description of the resolution of growth crises).

Rogers describes well some of the most intense encounters that can take place in groups, in his stages 11 through 15.

> *Confrontation.* There are times when the term feedback is far too mild to describe the interactions that take place. . . .
> *Norma:* (loud sigh). . . . Any real woman I know wouldn't have acted as you have this week, and particularly what you said this afternoon. That was so *crass*!! It just made me want to puke, right there!!! And—I'm just *shaking* I'm so mad at you—I don't think you've been real once this week!. . . . I'm so infuriated that I *want to come over and beat the hell out of you*!! (Rogers; 1970:31–32).

Here it is apparent that the group Rogers describes could have disintegrated or reverted to an earlier stage. Positive resolution can occur, however. Rogers describes one manner in which it can occur and the results:

> *The basic encounter.* . . . This appears to be one of the most central, intense, and change-producing aspects of group experience . . . "When a negative feeling was fully expressed to another, the relationship grew and the negative feeling was replaced by a deep acceptance for the other. . . ." (Rogers, 1970).

It is apparent from this description that this is compatible with Schutz's term for a stage following *inclusion* and *control,* the stage of *affection.*

If such positive outcomes as Rogers and Schutz describe are not forthcoming, however, conflict may result in disintegration and termination. Lewis Coser raised the rhetorical question, "if conflict unites, what tears apart?" His answer was that "not all conflicts are positively functional for the relationship, but only those that concern goals, values, or interests that do not contradict the basic assumptions upon which the relation is founded" (Coser, 1964:73,80). It could be assumed, then, that if members of one of the groups Rogers describes did not take the healing role or offer mutual support, the conflict would indeed concern the basic function of encounter groups (i.e., to provide an experience of confrontation and caring). The group would terminate, in all likelihood, or break up into subgroups as indicated in the disintegration subphase of our Phase III.

Northen describes several efforts to resolve conflict that include:

. . . *elimination,* that is forcing the withdrawal of the opposing individual or subgroup, sometimes in subtle ways. In *subjugation,* or domination, the strongest members force others to accept their points of view. . . . Through the means of *compromise* . . . each of the factions . . . give up something to safeguard the common area of interest. . . . . An individual or subgroup may form an *alliance.* . . . Finally, through *integration,* a group may arrive at a solution that is both satisfying to each member and more productive and creative than any contending suggestion (Northen, 1969:42–43).

The latter is an example of synergy, of course, and very close to the sense in which we mean *integration* as a basic system function. Ødd Ramsoy, a Norwegian sociologist, investigated the conflict inherent between system and subsystem in social groups (Ramsoy, 1962). He observed that a group as an entity must be tending toward adaptation and integration. The members thus always face the dilemma of making choices that favor system, suprasystem, or subsystem. He postulated that conflict between part and whole decreases as the integrative problems of the common inclusive system outweigh each subsystem's adaptive problems and goal problems. Ramsoy, as others before him (including Coser, 1964), concluded that *conflict can be reduced through concentration on a supraordinate problem.* This occurs most readily when the problem is an external threat. In the presence of a stranger, there are no subgroups. Conflict then may provide the occasion for a redressing of the necessary balance between adaptation and integration. As an outcome of group process, it means that components (group members individually) and system (the entire group) may have both satisfied needs and goals in synergistic fashion. That, indeed, is the height of achievement in the evolution of any system.

B. Structural Aspects

1. BOUNDARY AND AUTONOMY. As with all systems, the boundaries of a group are determined by the group and its components through interaction among the members and with the environment. Persons define themselves as members and are defined by others as being members of the group (boundaries are reinforced both internally and externally). For example, segregation by race or sex is usually prescribed by society, whereas separation into religious denominations is largely a matter of choice in most societies (though not all, certainly).

Groups have greater or lesser degrees of autonomy from their environment. A delinquent group such as Whyte's Norton gang was relatively autonomous from its environment with few direct controls or supports (W. Whyte, 1955). The group of workers in the Bank Wiring study was much less autonomous, being subject to a high degree of control by the organization (Roethlisberger and Dickson, 1947). The boundaries of both groups were clear; the Norton gang's boundary was much less permeable. Another example of permeability is Mauldin's description of combat units cited earlier in this chapter. A group, as any other system, must have discernible, locatable boundaries in order to exist.

2. DIFFERENTIATION, HIERARCHY, AND ROLE. As previously noted, differentiation of roles occurs as part of elaboration in the evolution of groups. These roles are ranked by the group according to both their adaptive and integrative usefulness. In addition, the person filling the role is evaluated; members of the group may respond to either the role or the person, or to both. As noted, in secondary groups, members tend to respond more to roles than to persons. When such rankings reach a consensus among the group members, the group may be said to be stratified (Bales, 1950:77).

Some roles become standardized within the group and persist regardless of the person occupying the role: Some roles are common to most groups. Some examples are: the *scapegoat,* who serves as the recipient of group hostility; the *clown* or *joker* (Hare, 1976:146), who may be either the butt of humor or the donor and who serves an important expressive function; the *peacemaker,* to whom the group turns for conflict reduction, an important integrative or social control function; the *idol,* who sets some moral or social standard for the group; and the *critic,* "who is idealistic and argumentative" (Hare, 1976:148).

The role that has been the subject of most research is leadership in its various forms. The two most commonly identified forms are the *task* (instrumental or adaptive) *leader* and the *social–emotional* (expressive or integrative) *leader* (Olmsted, 1959:69). The latter is sometimes called the sentiment leader. In his study of groups, Homans observes several rules for leadership:

1. The leader will maintain his own position.
2. The leader will live up to the norms of his group. The higher the degree of conformity, the higher will be the member's rank.
3. The leader will not give orders that will not be obeyed; he would "lose face" if he did so.
4. In giving orders, the leader will use established channels.
5. The leader will listen.
6. The leader will know himself (Homans, 1950:425–440).

While this seems to be a recipe for leadership, the steps describe common expectations for the leader role:

"The fact is that leadership in a group may be at one time abrupt, forceful, centralized, with all communications originating with the leader, and at another time slow, relaxed, dispersed, with much communication back and forth between leader and followers. Each mode is acceptable, appropriate and authoritative, but each in different circumstances" (Homans, 1950:419).

In other words, interaction between the leader and the group members and between the group and its environment determine which form of leadership is most functional for the group system at any particular time. The leadership role need not, and usually does not, reside in only one person. Leadership tasks are usually, if not always, distributed among the members. Perhaps leadership is best defined as "the set of functions through which the group coordinates the efforts of individuals" (Katz and Bender, 1976: 117).

C. Behavioral Aspects

1. ADAPTATION. Adaptation has been discussed under the section on steady state, this chapter. It remains here only to restate that all group behavior has some bearing upon securing and expending energy externally (SE and GE functions), whether explicitly designed to do so or not. As Homans puts it, "adaptation is the name we give to the prallelism between what successful operations on the environment may require and what the organism itself creates. Adaptation is as characteristic of the group as it is of other organisms" (Homans, 1950:155). Berrien, in his discussion of groups as systems, states that adaptation is fundamental in that systems must "produce some service or product acceptable to another social system" (Berrien, 1971:120); Parsons would undoubtedly agree, but we repeat that a system could not concentrate upon adaptation to the exclusion of integration.

An important component of adaptation is leadership, as already mentioned, but specifically, the problem-solving and decision-making activities inherent in the leadership role. These components have received much attention in research on groups and in research on organizations, in particular. As noted earlier, problem-solving has received prime attention in social group work practice. Mills prefers to refer to task leadership and decision-making in the wider context of

> an *executive system;* i.e., the set of all executive orientations and processes as they are distributed and organized among and performed by group members. Any member, regardless of position or office, who performs executive functions . . . participates in the executive system. . . .
>
> The executive system is the group's center for assessment of itself and its situations, for arrangement and rearrangement of its internal and external relations, for decision-making and for learning, and for "learning how to learn" through acting and assessing the consequences of action. . . . The executive system is partly independent, autonomous center where information about the role-systems . . . is processed (T. Mills, 1967:93).

More accurately, it is an executive *subsystem* that primarily serves the function of goal attainment. It should be noted that this is isomorphic to the "ego functions" of the personality system. Miller refers to the "decider" subsystem that must exist in any system (J. Miller, 1978).

2. SOCIALIZATION. Socialization is, of course, integrative behavior within the group intended to furnish energy to the group and to reduce the likelihood of conflict. The attractiveness or valence of the group is based upon the various levels of goals discussed earlier.

The use of small groups to facilitate socialization is widespread [e.g., the pledge group in the sorority, the basic training unit in the military, groups to prepare schizophrenic persons for employment (Epstein, 1982:211–212), and to resocialize former cult members (Goldberg and Goldberg, 1982)]. Much like the family, the small group can readily serve as a transition into wider systems. Socialization into the group itself is based upon some match between the person's needs and the group's offering; a good example is the frequent use of groups by adolescents for security, opportunities to meet friends, and to learn the cultures of both youth and adult life stages.

According to Kelman, the process of socialization may be of three kinds:

1. compliance, in which the person conforms without believing or accepting the group's view;
2. identification, in which the person adopts the group's view through making the group part of his own identity; or
3. internalization, in which the group's view is adopted because it "solves a problem for him." The group's views agrees with his own (Shepherd, 1964:48–50).

In this process, the person may engage in various "games" (as Eric Berne calls them in Transactional Analysis) or role strategies aimed at achieving his ends (Berne, 1966; Goffman, 1961). The adaptation of the person and the integrative behavior of the system must reach some mutually acceptable bargain, or the process of socialization will fail.

3. SOCIAL CONTROL AND SOCIAL CONFLICT. The process of standardization is related to social control. Among other ways, a group achieves consensus or steady state by shaping its members' behaviors in certain ways. The application of sanctions in one form or another is social control. As noted earlier, social control is exercised by the entire group through various means. The major means of control is energy applied to, or withheld from, a member. One example is the traditional Roberts' Rules in formal meetings; if members do not conform to its usage, they may not be recognized (i.e., allowed any verbal interchange with the entire group) or may be ejected from the group. An extreme example would be forcing group members to accept certain roles such as worker, hunter, or mate in order to survive. A more subtle example is that junior members of the United States Senate are expected to "be seen but not heard"; and in many offices, women staff

members are expected to make coffee for the entire staff. The play *Twelve Angry Men* (R. Rose, 1955) illustrates the various forms social control can take in a group, from threat of violence to ridicule and "putting down" a member.

An important part of social control in groups is conflict and the management of conflict.

> Group experience *is* conflict. . . . a response to the reality that there is a shortage of what people need and want. . . . To organize, a group must coordinate one part with another, and in doing so must limit the freedom of some parts. . . . And further, groups accept and reward some members more fully than others, and this inequality creates yet another type of conflict. . . . Change, which occurs at every moment, is determined both in direction and in quality by the manner in which conflicts are resolved. Response to conflict determines the new state of the system (T. Mills, 1967:14–15).

As noted earlier, probably the most complete state of the dimensions and uses of conflict in groups is found in Coser's *The Functions of Social Conflict* (1964).

4. COMMUNICATION. Communication is a basic process in groups. We have previously defined communication as "transfer of meaning or energy" by any means. According to this definition, virtually all group activity could be considered communication, rendering the term so broad as to be meaningless. Rather, we mean communication intended to accomplish adaptation, integration, social control, or goal attainment (in other words, the SE, SI, GI, and GE functions) for the sytem.

Bales' Interaction Process Analysis theory of groups is based upon the analysis of units of communication into a few categories, such as "shows solidarity," "shows tension release," "disagrees," and "shows antagonism." Tabulating the number of units exchanged during a given time and their distribution by categories allows some index of group process to be derived. This has been a popular means of group analysis (Bales, 1950).

Other theorists, especially those with backgrounds in information theory, have focused upon communication as the basic process in groups. Satir's conjoint family therapy and Berne's transactional analysis both focus upon communication. Small group communication has become a field of study in its own right, with a rapidly increasing body of literature (see, e.g., Bormann and Bormann, 1980; Hare, 1976:260–271; Mabry and Barnes, 1980; Shaw, 1981:150–161). Bavelas published studies of communication networks in groups in 1948 followed by Leavitt in 1951 (Hare, 1976:166–267; Mabry and Barnes, 1980:136). They describe basic variations in these networks, including the following diagrams (Figure 11) (Shaw, 1981:152).

Being in a central position (in all but the "circle") in the network was clearly associated with the leadership role, because of access to more

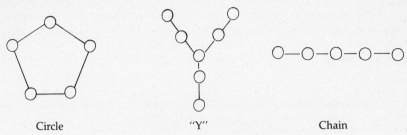

FIG. 11. Diagrams of communication networks.

information than others; that is, one powerful element of leadership is control of communication between the members (Hare, 1976:300). Frequently, the purpose of such communication is to allow the group members to improve their communication skills within the group and then transfer these skills to other systems. One example is a group of single, pregnant young women and their parents. This group provided

> . . . the means whereby families may learn new, more appropriate communication behavior. . . . In some instances, family members learn how to communicate better when the therapists and the group decode messages that are sent and inappropriately received in a family system. In other instances, good communication among the therapists in the group's presence serves as a positive model (Papademetriou, 1971:88).

III. SOME USES OF GROUPS

Small groups are distinctive among the social systems examined in this book in that a group system can be created for particular purposes by human service professionals (as could an organization, although this occurs less frequently). Groups can be created for purposes of therapy, self-actualization, support, problem solving, goal achievement, or to influence larger systems as in community organization and social action.

A. Human Potential Groups

Human potential groups are organized to further the purposes of their members through provision of "intensive group experience" over a limited time span. Examples include T-groups, sensory awareness groups, encounter groups, sensitivity training groups, and marathon groups.

As to the dimensions of groups earlier discussed, human potential groups tend to focus on expressive functions. These groups are structured to emphasize feelings and interpersonal transactions. The norms include mutuality of support, openness, and disclosure. The group's powers of acceptance and validation are employed. However, it is essential that group leaders be competent to deal with the hazards of intensive group experience.

> A study by Yalom and Lieberman found that 16 of 130 undergraduates who completed encounter groups (of 209 who began) could be considered "casualties"—defined as an enduring, significant, negative outcome . . . caused by their participation in the group." This was a careful study, using selected, supposedly competent leaders, representing most major therapeutic ideologies (Kovel, 1976:168).

B. Therapeutic Groups

Therapeutic groups are structured to serve as vehicles for persons struggling with intrapsychic concerns. Often the group is open-ended and long-term, with members cycling in and out. In describing the efficacy of the therapeutic group, Kovel says:

> . . . in a therapeutic situation an individual's problems often become clearer when expressed in a context of interaction with, or in reaction to, several others. Sometimes behavior in the group stimulates or surfaces problems which an individual has not dealt with in his interviews with a therapist (Kovel, 1976:52).

Therapeutic groups usually have an expressive focus with leaders clearly differentiated from the group. Socialization and communication are emphasized. Group process may be subordinated at times to the need of an individual.

C. Self-Help Groups

In recent years, there has been a phenomenal increase in the incidence of persons who come together around a common concern. Self-help groups exist for virtually every personal concern. Sharing experiences and ways of coping are the vehicles for mutuality of help—self and other, helping and accepting help. Professional direction is usually not wanted, although in some circumstances, a professional helper may convene a group or sponsor it. The focus is either on participants working on a kind of personal problem they share with the other group members *or* joining together to influence external systems to provide resources or recognize members' needs and rights (e.g., a Welfare Rights group). Although some self-help groups may be largely task-oriented, sentiment is an ever-present factor. Katz and Bender (1976:37–38) provide this classification of self-help groups:

1. Groups that are primarily focused on self-fulfillment or personal growth" (so-called "therapeutic" groups)

2. "Groups that are primarily focused on social advocacy" (e.g., Welfare Rights groups)

3. "Groups whose primary function is to create alternative patterns for living" (e.g., Women's Liberation and Gay Liberation)

4. "Outcast haven" or "rock-bottom" groups (close supervision in a sheltered environment by "peers or persons who have successfully grappled with similar problems . . . .")

Some self-help groups are spawned locally, whereas others are national organizations with local face-to-face chapters. Alcoholics Anonymous and Weight Watchers fit the cultural penchant for mobility. A member who migrates to a different geographic locale can immediately affiliate with a local chapter in her/his community. Vattano describes self-help groups that "are primarily concerned with the failures and inadequacies of the environment and social institutions" (Vattano, 1972:13). Notable examples are welfare rights groups, gay rights groups, tenant associations, and the Guardian Angels (a "vigilante" group that became an organization). Such groups evolve their own leadership in order to pursue specific goals, often the protection of civil rights.

CONCLUSION

It seems clear from the wealth of research on groups that groups do share the common properties of systems. Furthermore, it is apparent that most group theory is based in systemic thinking. Since group experiences are both natural and essential to social living, purposeful use of groups offers opportunity for people to come together to pursue mutual interests and goals. Those who work in human services must understand group phenomena and develop competence in working with groups in order to use wisely the fundamental and immense power contained in the human group.

SUGGESTED READINGS

Alissi, Albert S.
   1980   *Perspectives on Social Group Work Practice.* New York: Free Press.
      A reader, this book includes historical, classic material on social work group work and current critiques. Highly informative regarding social work's use of the group.
Durkin, James E.
   1981   *Living Groups: Group Psychotherapy and General System Theory.* New York: Brunner/Mazel.
      This is the best example of the attempt to reconcile the systems approach with psychoanalytic and other group treatment theories. Highly useful for the practitioner or teacher looking for stimulating ideas. Includes some case examples of the fit between the two bodies of thought.

Hare, A. Paul.
  1976   *Handbook of Small Group Research.* New York: The Free Press.
          This is the definitive collection of information regarding small groups. Most
          useful for anyone wishing a mass of detail for formulation of theory.
Johnson, David W., and Frank P. Johnson.
  1982   *Joining Together: Group Theory and Group Skills.* Englewood Cliffs, N.J.:
          Prentice-Hall.
          This book is truly impressive in its comprehensiveness and its inclusion of
          examples and exercises. Perhaps too large for a supplementary text, but it
          contains a wealth of material for students. A delight to read.
Katz, Alfred H., and Eugene I. Bender.
  1976   *The Strength In US.* New York: New Viewpoints.
          This reader pulls together material on a range of self-help groups, with cri-
          tiques on the functions of self-help groups in various societies.
Marrow, Alfred J.
  1969   *The Practical Theorist: The Life and Work of Kurt Lewin.* New York: Basic
          Books.
          A biography of Lewin written by a former student and colleague. This traces
          the evolution of Group Dynamics from its roots in Gestalt holism to the
          development of training groups.
Miller, James Grier.
  1978   *Living Systems.* New York: McGraw-Hill.
          We refer here to Chapter nine, "The Group," pp. 515–593. Useful for exam-
          ples of processes in groups. It is Miller's massive application of systems
          processes to groups. It is useful as an example of the length to which a systems
          theorist may go in elaborating the ideas. Useful to the serious student.
Roberts, Robert W., and Helen Northen, eds.
  1976   *Theories of Social Work with Groups.* New York: Columbia University Press.
          Excellent sections on historical development and thoughtful evaluation of
          current status of group work theories. They demonstrate explicitly that a
          systems approach is fundamental to virtually all theories of group work.
Shaw, Marvin E.
  1981   *Group Dynamics: The Psychology of Small Group Behavior.* New York:
          McGraw-Hill.
          A readable and comprehensive text. It includes re-views of the major theories
          in the field. Perhaps too large to be used as a supplementary text, but it could be
          used well as the primary text in a course on groups, or students could be
          assigned selected readings from it. The discussion of "syntality" (pp. 19–22) is
          valuable.

LITERARY SOURCES

Golding, William.
  1959   *Lord of the Flies.* New York: Capricorn Books, Putnam.
Rose, Reginald.
  1955   *Twelve Angry Men.* Chicago: Dramatics Publications Co.
          A play about the interactive processes among jurors deliberating a capital case.
          Dramatically illustrates the shifts between individual and group goals; demon-
          strates that a group is indeed different from the sum of its parts. Can readily be
          used for role playing. The film, rated by the late Henry Fonda as his best (and
          we agree), is also available.

FAMILIES

All happy families resemble each other; each unhappy family is unhappy in its own way
                                    Leo Tolstoy, *Anna Karenina*

INTRODUCTION

A separate chapter is devoted to the family as a social system since the family is the single social unit in human society inextricably interwoven with all other systems. As noted in Chapter 3, I, "B. The Family as a Human Universal," the family assumes, or is delegated, primary responsibility for socialization into the culture and thus is charged with major responsibility to insure the survival of humankind.

> The family is the *primal* group in which *learning how to learn* begins. The child is taught how to learn before anybody is aware of teaching, and the learning of the child how to learn teaches the parents how to teach as well. And all this occurs long before the child has ever learned the word "why?" This nonse-quential experience is biologically important. We need to learn new ways of learning, of developing our senses to take in new information (Brodey, 1977:64).

Because the family can and should be viewed as a special instance of the small group, most of Chapter 7 is applicable to family. In every phase of the person's life cycle, family is of central importance in definition of social expectations and in provisions of the resources necessary for growth.

The approach to the family in this chapter is consistent with the systems model presented earlier. We construe the family as holon with attention to the system itself, its components, and its significant environment. Family fulfills the requirements for designation as a human system. The singular "family" is used in this book to designate this level of system. The chapter is entitled "Families" to emphasize the plurality of family forms. Much of the confusion attendant to "family analysis," "family impact," and the study of "family policy" derives from the use of the singular "family" and its implication of a norm or modal form.

I. APPROACHES TO FAMILY ANALYSIS

We will forego until later in this chapter the dubious pleasures of establishing our definition of family in favor of a brief examination of a few selected approaches to understanding the family. Our intent here is to summarize only those approaches we find most congruent with the purposes of this book.

A. The Family as a System of Roles

The family as a system of roles is an important theme in the literature of family analysis. Roles are conceived as embodying the cultural expectations for behavior, and the family is the arena wherein these roles are learned and carried out. Goode, a sociologist, begins his textbook on the family:

> In all known societies, almost everyone lives his life enmeshed in a network of family rights and obligations called role relations. A person is made aware of his role relations through a long period of socialization during his childhood, a process in which he learns how others in his family expect him to behave, and in which he himself comes to feel this is both the right and desirable way to act (Goode, 1964:1).

In psychoanalytic thought, the resolution of the oedipal conflict is dependent upon the existence of appropriate role models and the assumption by the child of the appropriate roles. Lidz, a psychiatrist, states: "The family is recognized as a biologically required social institution that mediates between the biological and cultural directives of personality formation, and a social system in which the child assimilates the basic instrumentalities, institutions, and role attributions that are essential to his adaptation and integration" (Lidz, 1963:75–76).

Feldman and Scherz, social workers, write:

> The family operates through roles that shift and alter during the course of the family's life. Roles can be explicit or instrumental; they can be implicit or

emotional. . . . The healthy family carries out explicit and implicit roles appropriately according to age, competence and needs during all the different stages of family life. The disturbed family experiences serious difficulty in the management of roles (Feldman and Scherz, 1967:67).

The family system of roles must be examined, then, both structurally and functionally. Parsons' earlier formulation of the family as social system differentiated between instrumental and expressive role functions on a sexual axis; that is, the male – father role as breadwinner and adapter to the environment, the female – mother role as social and emotional provider. In his critique of Parsons' view, Rodman stresses the fluidity of the distribution of the instrumental and expressive roles within the changing American family (Rodman, 1966:262 – 287). In another study, Billingsley (1968) pictures the fluidity of roles in the black family as a source of strength. Black families are able to function effectively in a frequently hostile environment by shifting roles (mother or children as breadwinners when father is unable to find work). They also incorporate extended family or neighbors. The role of the "aunt" in black families is well known (e.g., Ella's role in *The Autobiography of Malcolm X* [1966] or Stack, 1974).

Rodman cites evidence from Parsons' writings to support his conclusion that the female role in general has broadened from the "pseudo-occupation" of a domestic pattern to include role choices of "career pattern," "glamour pattern," and "good companion pattern"; and that society sanctions a feminine role combining these role patterns (see Margaret Adams' comment on this later in this chapter). Parsons and others have held that the masculine instrumental role has also shifted because of the changes in occupational roles. The family business or family farm formerly located and consolidated the instrumental functions in the father and reinforced his paternal authority; the father's modern organizational membership diffuses and dissipates this authority. It should be noted that in the United States, as of March 1980, 50.3% of married women were working. "Interestingly, the rates are even higher for married women who have children. In 1979 no fewer than 59.1 percent with children six to seventeen were in the labor force, as were 43.2 percent who had at least one child under six" (Hacker, 1982). Of single-parent mothers that hold jobs, 60% usually work full-time (Bohen and Viveros-Long, 1981).

The family as determinant and perpetuator of role expectations has long been at issue. In 1902, Engels argued that the family is a bourgeois device designed to enslave women: "The modern individual family is founded on the open or concealed domestic slavery of the wife" (Engels, 1902:65). More recently, C. Wright Mills states in the same vein: "In so far as the family as an institution turns women into darling little slaves and men into their chief providers and unweaned dependents, the problem of a satisfactory marriage remains incapable of purely private solution."

The role system perspective on the family, especially the dysfunctional family, is a dominant one in social work literature (Feldman and Scherz, 1967; Perlman, 1968). Far more attention is devoted to adult–family roles as necessary to family integrity and functioning than to child–family roles, although the purposes of adult–family roles as explicated are largely parental. Certainly the "normal" family roles are emphasized in the literature of child development. Feminist literature is particularly concerned with liberation from traditional role constraints for women, and frequently for men as well.

Viewed from a role perspective, contemporary work provisions such as flexitime, flexiplace, and maternity/paternity leaves are designed to relieve role stresses and strains and to accommodate shifts in family structure and role allocations.

B. The Family as Cause or Effect

The family as cause or effect is a second major approach. As Nimkoff explains, the family can be seen either as "dependent" variable or as "independent" variable (Nimkoff, 1965:37–73). In the former instance, the family is responsive to the demands and dictates of the larger social systems. It adapts, or more precisely, accommodates to the goal requirements of the society within which it exists. The nuclear, mobile family emerges because of the requisites of the economy; it relinquishes its functions to other social institutions due to pressures exerted upon it by its environment. The government influences by prescriptions and proscriptions (e.g., compulsory school attendance, abortion laws, and court decisions that place the "welfare of the child" above the rights of the parents). The family is seen as existing to fulfill the cultural dictates of its society as that society seeks to perpetuate itself.

The family as independent variable is seen to be cause rather than effect. The family initiates change, and society accommodates to these changes. Examples of this dynamic are infrequently cited in the literature on family. One example is sociologist Elise Boulding's view that

> the family is a potentially powerful contributor to the generation of alternative images of the future. During the "quiet" periods of history—the times of relative stability, when few demands are made on the adaptive capacities of individuals or groups—and also in periods of severe repression, the futures-creating capacities of the family may remain undeveloped. In periods of rapid social change, when each age group represented in the household has experienced critically different stimuli and pressures from the larger society, the futures-creating family is held together by strong social bonds (Boulding, 1972:188).

In this sense of creating alternatives, the family is independent variable. It generates social change, according to Boulding, in that the family is a "play community"; play may be one means by which culture is created, and thereby alternative societal futures may be imagined. Clearly, the position of the family as the system interfacing between individual and society allows it to perform this function.

The controversy over abortion laws exemplifies the family initiating change requiring social accommodation, in that family planning, in order to liberate the parents and maintain living standards, requires that society provides sanction and means for birth control. The 1973 Supreme Court decision gave legal sanction to abortion as a method of birth control. Subsequent court decisions and federal legislation have severely restricted access to abortion for poor people.

Although few family theorists opt for either extreme, dependent or independent variable, most do see the family as determined by societal changes rather than the reverse. A typical position is expressed by Goode:

> Because of its emphasis on performance, such a system (industrialization) requires that a person be permitted to rise or fall, and to move about wherever the job market is best. A lesser emphasis on land ownership also increases the ease of mobility. The conjugal family is neolocal (each couple sets up its own household), and its kinship network is not strong, thus putting fewer barriers than other family systems in the way of class or geographic mobility. In these ways the conjugal family system "fits" the needs of industrialization (Goode, 1964:108).

Our opinion is, of course, that the family is both independent and dependent variable, since it is a holon (for a notable example, see Sennett, 1974). The mutual causal interactions between families and society can be seen in all aspects of living. For example, shifts in family structure and roles that are responsive to changes in employment patterns lead to marketplace accommodations. Both females and males are employed increasingly outside the home. Employment hours vary, influencing time available to shop, prepare, and serve meals, and for family dining. All of the following could be construed as societal adaptations to such family changes:

1. Extension of hours in which commercial and retail establishments conduct their business (particularly in shopping malls)
2. Marketing of increased varieties of frozen prepared foods
3. Fast-food restaurants that generally portray workers or families in their advertising
4. Technological developments to enable faster food preparation (e.g., microwave ovens and food processors)
5. Large-scale development and production of synthetic fabrics marketed as "wash and wear" (the often maligned polyester sharply reduces the time necessary to maintain clean clothing)

C. The Family as Evolving System

The family as evolving system is a dual approach to family inquiry. One focus is on the developmental cycle of *a* family, while the other is a focus on the evolutionary cycle of *the* family as a social institution.

Various attempts have been made to delineate the developmental stages in the life cycle of a family. Nye and Berardo describe some of these and combine them to illustrate their compatibility (Nye and Berardo, 1968:198–222; see especially Table 1, pp. 208–209). The general direction taken in conceiving of the family life cycle is from the point of marriage, to and through expansion stages, to and through contraction stages. The more thorough formulations of family stages attempt to account for the related growth tasks for all family members, not just the children. These formulations are grounded in assumptions of a nuclear unit, childbearing, and a marriage that will continue until the death of a spouse. Thus, these postulated family stages are, in fact, applicable to only a limited number of actual families.

Elise Boulding describes the evolution of *a* family:

> Family life is a swiftly moving series of identity crises as members of various ages are socialized into new roles. At the same time, the image of the family as a whole, as conceived by each family member, is subject to the same set of identity crises. The pre-schooler may face the crisis of becoming a kindergartener at the same time that his parents face the crisis of narrowing horizons that hits adults in their late twenties when the future no longer seems wide open, and his grandparents face the crisis of retirement. The teenager trying to decide whether to enter one of the many subcultures and counter-cultures open to him may have parents who face both the empty-nest crisis of unrealized aspirations as the zenith of career activities is passed, and grandparents who face the crisis of no longer having sufficient health to live independently in their own apartment (Boulding, 1972:186).

This is, of course, similar to the role-system approach to the family system but suggests a cyclical process through which a family passes.

Carle Zimmerman is acknowledged as the best known advocate of a cyclical theory of *the* family. He begins with the premise that the family and society constantly interact and cause changes, each in the other. Other social institutions (particularly the church and government) vie with the family for control of the family members. Drawing on historical data, Zimmerman proposes a three-phase family typology and suggests it is a repetitive cycle.

> 1. "Trustee" family—the living members are trustees of the family name, family property, and family blood. The family itself is immortal, there is no conception of individual rights, and individual welfare is ever subordinate to the family group.

2. "Domestic" family — an intermediate type that evolves from the trustee family. As the state gains in power, family control over its members is weakened. The state shares this power and control with the family and creates the concept of individual rights to be maintained against family authority.

3. "Atomistic" family — the power and scope of family authority is reduced to an absolute minimum and the state becomes essentially an organization in the sense that the family no longer mediates between its members and society (Leslie, 1967:223–230).

Zimmerman judges the present-day American family to be well into the third phase, the "atomic age" in yet another sense. Zimmerman does not find the "present decay of the family" unique. He documents similar family dissolution just prior to the fall of Greek and Roman civilizations. Since the family is the primary humanizing force in human life

[modern] inhumanity lies close, in a basic causal sense to the decay of the family system. Indeed the familial decline may well be the primary causal agent in the sapping of the universal capacity for human sympathy. Juvenal held this opinion when he wrote of "the decline in the capacity to weep". . . . The conseqence then of a declining family system is that controls of society come more into the hands of men who, in the words of Bacon, have no "hostages to fortune," and who do not possess judgments biased by an immersion in fundamental humanism (Zimmerman, 1947:77).

Zimmerman deplores the popular view of the family as ever evolving to higher and better forms. He recommends open recognition and understanding of the current state of family decline and hopes that a "creative minority" will come forward to reassert the values of familism.

D. The Structural Approach

The structural approach to the family has received the attention of a host of investigators. In fact, any attempt at family analysis addresses itself to certain family forms and excludes others.

The majority of Western observers of the family accept the two-generation nuclear family as the norm. This is particularly true of those interested in the child-rearing aspects of the family. The "normal" family is seen to be composed of two parents and their minor children. Voiland and associates note "the rise of prominence of the family of procreation — father, mother, children — as an independent unit. This primary family group has, indeed, become the structural norm of our culture. There are many manifestations of this fact" (Voiland and Associates, 1962:46–47). It is this family structure that serves as the basis for societal policy in support of the family (e.g., welfare and tax structure). It should be noted this family composition is not found in the majority of families in the United States.

Parsons has characterized the present-day American family as "the isolated nuclear family," isolated especially residentially and economically from the extended family. He sees this as a natural consequence of the specialization and differentiation of the complex social system of America today. He does qualify the degree of isolation. "I think it very important indeed, that there is much accumulating evidence that the extended family is an exceedingly important resource to fall back on in case of emergency or trouble, for financial support and for emotional support and help in planning and all sorts of things of that kind" (Parsons, 1964a:17). More recent evidence confirms that indeed the extended family maintains its importance in times of need. The composition of an extended family may well go beyond the bounds of those related by blood or marriage (see Roberts and Northen, 1976:318–319, for a discussion of family network, or Stack, 1974 p. 31 ff.). During the economic hard times of the early 1980's, adult children and their children are returning to the homes of their families of orientation (the "nest" contracts and expands in keeping with the state of the economy).

Billingsley draws on the formulations of Parsons, Bales, and Shils to establish a typology of forms for categorizing black family structures. The refinements he introduces through his three categories and twelve types have broad applicability (Billingsley, 1968:15–21).

1. The *nuclear* family includes three types; the incipient, consisting only of the marital pair; the simple, consisting of the marital pair and minor children; and the attenuated, containing only one parent and minor children.

2. The *extended* family includes types wherein other relatives are added to the nuclear household.

3. The *augmented* family includes types of family situations wherein unrelated family members are incorporated into the household.

Boulding classifies the second and third types, extended and augmented, under the heading "expanded family" in order to "emphasize the commonality between the biologically related extended family and the household as a voluntary association" (Boulding, 1972:188). She places all family forms on a continuum from one isolated householder to a cluster of persons either biologically or voluntarily associated. She correctly points out that there is no hard and fast line between the expanded family and the "intentional community" (i.e., a community organized for specific social or ideological purposes). Given the variety of social experimentation being attempted today, such an elastic definition of family is very useful.

The study of kinship networks and relationships, particularly in the work of social anthropologists, has yielded additional insights into the variety of family forms. Raymond Firth comments:

The study of kinship is a perennial theme for the social anthropologist. An understanding of the kinship system in any society is essential as clues to the working of some of the most fundamental relationships—sexual, marital, economic in that society. It also may be of prime importance in the process of socialization, in developing patterns of reaction to authority and in providing important symbols for the moral evaluation of conduct (Nye and Berardo, 1968:19).

Rodman discusses kinship responsibilities in the United States and concludes that in many respects, this is a neglected dimension in family studies (Rodman, 1966:179–185). Cultural guidelines for determination of allegiance to kinsmen are ambiguous and often conflicting. Although the nuclear family norm would seem to dictate primary kin responsibility to spouse and children, conflicting claims do arise. The parent of today in an isolated nuclear family might have been the child of yesterday in a closely tied extended or nuclear family. For such a person, the transfer of allegiance and emotional involvement from the family of orientation to the family of procreation may be a monumental task, as indicated by frequent letters to "Dear Abby" from wives and mothers-in-law about the son/husband's responsibilities to each. The unenviable status of the aged in our society and the guilt felt by their adult children are products of this dilemma. The unenforceable "relative responsibility" laws in public welfare are another reflection of this situation.

Alternative family forms are increasingly being suggested as possible substitutions for traditional ones, especially to replace the nuclear family norm. Presently there is seen emerging a new family form most easily termed, *living together.* Moore (1958) argues that the family in any of its traditional forms is dysfunctional in modern industrial society.

E. The Functional Approach

There is another dominant theme in family studies. Usually, functions are looked at in tandem with family structures in acknowledgment of the fact that these two aspects cannot readily be separated, not even for purposes of objective study. There are inherent difficulties in functional analysis of family, not unlike the problems in looking at the functions of any other social system. The pitfall is, of course, to reason circularly that a pattern or value is "functional" to the given system and the proof of functionality is found in the fact of its existence.

The family is generally acknowledged to exist universally to perform certain functions necessary to the survival of the species. Generally, these functions are enumerated as procreation and child rearing, implying that the family has major responsibility for these societal imperatives. Beyond this level of generality, there are divergent ways of describing and explaining family functions and the relationships of these to the broader social systems.

Parsons applies his functional prerequisites of goal attainment, pattern maintenance, integration, and adaptation to the family system. As stated earlier, he stresses the instrumental and expressive role functions within the family constellation and how these are allocated to the family members, especially on the sexual axis. He accounts for the changing functions of the modern family through emphasizing the system characteristics of differentiation and specialization. As the macrosystem becomes increasingly complex, the family as a component system becomes increasingly specialized in the functions it performs for both the larger system and the family components. Parsons says that "when two functions, previously embedded in the same structure, are subsequently performed by two newly differentiated structures, they can *both* be fulfilled more intensively and with a greater degree of freedom" (Rodman, 196:264). The core functions remaining in the family are the maintenance of the household and the intimate personal relations of the members of the household, including child rearing and socialization into affective networks.

As specialized institutional arrangements evolve to provide for socialization of children into the culture, the family relinquishes functions and becomes increasingly specialized. This relinquishment of family functions particularly affects women, leading to the broadening of the female role. Margaret Adams, a social worker, comments on the transfer of "nurturant" roles for women from the family to professions. She describes the process by which women are channeled into social work, nursing, teaching, secretarial work, and certain other professions, as "the compassion trap." She says:

> the proliferation of the helping professions into a complex array of welfare services took many of the more highly specialized aspects of the nurturing and protective functions out of the home. . . . In addition, when one or both parents were out of the home for a substantial part of the day, they had to delegate their acculturating functions. Thus the synthesizing role traditionally discharged by women in the home was translated to a wider sphere and spread its influence through a broader range of activities. Instead of (or in addition to) keeping the family intact and maximally functional, women became involved in housekeeping tasks on behalf of society at large and assumed responsibility for keeping its operation viable (Adams, 1971:72).

Christopher Lasch deplores the transfer of nurturance and parenting from the family to the burgeoning professional experts (Lasch, 1979b). He, as Parsons previously, notes the emergence of specialized peer groupings that evidently have assumed functions previously performed by the family. These peer groups differentiate on the axis of age. Examples include the aged, adolescents, and young adults. Kenneth Keniston has proposed a "new" stage of life that occurs outside the context of either a family of orientation or a family of procreation.

> We are witnessing today the emergence on a mass scale of a previously unrecognized stage of life, a stage that intervenes between adolescence and adulthood. I propose to call this stage of life the stage of youth. . . . What characterizes a growing minority of postadolescents today is that they have not settled the questions whose answers once defined adulthood: questions of relationship to the existing society, questions of vocation, questions of social role and life-style (Keniston, 1970:634–635).

The youthful followers of Reverend Sun Yung Moon (disparagingly referred to as "Moonies") may well be a manifestation of this new life phase. Those who have received the most notoriety because of their parents' efforts to regain their allegiance have been in their twenties, opting for a vocation devoid of any kind of family connection.

This "youth" stage is clearly related to Erikson's sixth stage, that of intimacy versus isolation (see Chapter 8, II, "E. Perpetuation and Sharing of Identity"). If the family is not sufficient in assisting young adults in resolving this crisis, then they must look to other institutions or create new ones; or, conceivably, simply fail to resolve the crisis in massive numbers.

Feldman and Scherz take the position that the rapid changes accompanying technology and industrialization have disrupted the traditional family functions that provided for the survival and socialization needs of its members. Other institutionalized provisions must then be created to substitute for or augment the family.

> Thus, schools supplement learning conducted within the family; clinics, hospitals, rest homes and other facilities provide health care; foster care is available for children and adults who cannot be provided with needed care at home; family counseling is extended when marital discord or parent-child relationships indicate the need for the intervention of an outside authority; juvenile courts and correctional institutions assist with severe problems needing control (Feldman and Scherz, 1967:53).

This functional position is congruent with Zimmerman's description of the atomistic family form.

Lidz finds the family performs three sets of discrete but interrelated functions (Lidz, 1963:44–46). For the children, the family provides physical care and nurturance and at the same time directs their personality development. For the spouses, it furnishes the means to personal fulfillment and stability. For society, the family takes responsibility for enculturating new members. Lidz suggests "it is possible that these functions which are fundamental to human adaptation cannot be fulfilled separately at all and must be fused in the family" (Lidz, 1963:45).

Magorah Maruyama finds the extent of family function specialization alarming. He coined the term *monopolarization* to describe the state of affairs wherein the child's relationship to adults is confined to a mother or a father, or more precisely, to one set of parents (Maruyama, 1966:133). Monopolarization is seen as a metassumption of theories of personality and of many Western philosophies. The totality of children's relationships to their parents sets narrow parameters for development and invests undue responsibility in the parents.

Maruyama recommends dilution of this relationship through increased interfamily contacts and integration of persons who are not in the family circuit. This could be accomplished through the formation of voluntary adult – child communities without any necessity of major reforms in family structure (Maruyama, 1966:147). However, many communes have deliberately attempted to create alternative family structures. One writer reports that "today's communes seek a family warmth and intimacy, to become extended families. A 50-person commune in California, for example, called itself 'The Lynch Family,' a New Mexico commune 'The Chosen Family,' a New York City group simply 'The Family'" (Kanter, 1970:54). Kanter also points out that exclusivity of parenting was avoided in successful nineteenth-century communes by separating children from their parents, creating a "family of the whole" (Kanter, 1970:55; Kephart, 1976:91ff.).

II. A HUMAN SYSTEMS VIEW OF FAMILIES

The family has come to be viewed as a system by many observers. Perhaps most notable among these in their relevance to this book are family therapists. One of the outstanding researchers of family therapy, Jay Haley, says:

> What family therapists most have in common they also share with a number of behavioral scientists in the world today: There is an increasing awareness that psychiatric problems are social problems which involve the total ecological system. There is a concern with, and an attempt to change, what happens with the family and also the interlocking systems of the family and the social institutions in which the family is embedded. The fragmentation of the individual into parts, or the family into parts is being abandoned, and there is a growing consensus that a new ecological framework defines problems in new ways and calls for new ways in therapy (Sager and Kaplan, 1972:270).

For purposes of the following discussion, we will treat the family as a social system (holon) possessing the characteristics of a social system but distinguishable from other social systems by its goals, functions, and climate of feeling. The family is defined both by its members and by the culture and community within which it exists. Lidz's functional viewpoint, referred to earlier, points to the functions performed by the family as system, subsystem, and suprasystem. The family provides the opportunity for intimate social interaction for all of its members. It is also the base of personal security for all its members.

To begin with, any discussion of family structure must necessarily start from the perspective of some individual. The inclusions and exclusions of the family system must be from some particular perspective. If that perspective is the legal status of a person for inheritance purposes, it is quite different from a perspective for purposes of establishing who are the members of a household.

A family then is to be construed as patterns of relatedness as they converge in a person. These patterns may be identical to those of another family member or they could be unique to this one person. Those relationships of the person that can be classified as family relationships will be delineated within the remainder of this chapter. The characteristics of family will be grouped under the familiar headings of structure, behavior, and evolution. For consistency, we will use the subtopics introduced in Chapter 1.

A. Structural Characteristics

As with any social system, *organization* is of prime concern. Family organization is distinguishable from other systems by its high level of intrarelatedness. Since it is the smallest social and interpersonal system, there is an intensity of interdependence among its components.

The effectiveness of family organization is the extent to which its goals are fulfilled — the goals of its members and the goals of society. If societal goals are not fulfilled, the family may be dissolved by legal decree, as when children are removed or divorces granted. This action does not necessarily dissolve the family as an interacting system. Malcolm X clearly describes the difference. After his family was dispersed by the court, "separated though we were, all of us maintained fairly close touch around Lansing — in school and out — whenever we could get together. Despite the artificially created separation and distance between us, we still remained very close in our feelings toward each other" (Malcolm X, 1966:22).

Society, the family, and its members may all share familial goals of economic independence, intimacy, and affection but be in conflict about the priorities to be assigned to each of these goals. These conflicts may occur when people find it necessary to leave familiar territory to find employment. A Kentuckian told this story to one of the authors:

A man died and was being shown around Heaven by St. Peter. Off in one corner of Heaven they saw a group of people with suitcases. The man asked who these people were and St. Peter replied, "Oh, they're from Kentucky; they go home on weekends."

In order to achieve goals, the family must, through its organization, secure and conserve energy from both internal and external sources. The members of the family must contribute energy for the family system as well as import energy for their individual purposes. The following dialogue between the mother and sons (about the father–husband) is illustrative of this dependence of the family upon energy from its members and from the environment. It is from the play, *Death of a Salesman*.

LINDA: No, a lot of people think he's lost his—balance. But you don't have to be very smart to know what his trouble is. The man is exhausted.
HAPPY: Sure!
LINDA: A small man can be just as exhausted as a great man. He works for a company thirty-six years this March, opens up unheard-of territories to their trademark, and now in his old age they take his salary away.
HAPPY: (Indignantly): I didn't know that, Mom.
LINDA: You never asked, my dear! Now that you get your spending money someplace else you don't trouble your mind with him.
HAPPY: But I gave you money last—
LINDA: Christmas time, fifty dollars! To fix the hot water heater it cost ninety-seven fifty! For five weeks he's been on straight commission, like a beginner, an unknown!
BIFF: Those ungrateful bastards!
LINDA: Are they any worse than his sons? (A. Miller, 1955:56–57)

The *boundary* of a family is behavioral and is evidenced by the intensity and frequency of interaction among its components. The intensity of sentiment interchanges is especially distinctive as compared to other small groups. It is within the interactional boundaries of the family that the member participates in a particularly *close network of feelings, both positive and negative*, with a minimal sense of needing to put up a front. The common expression, "I feel at home," conveys something of this feeling of freedom to be oneself.

This exchange between Martha and George from *Who's Afraid of Virginia Woolf* illustrates closeness through negative feeling.

MARTHA: You've really screwed up, George.
GEORGE: Oh, for God's sake, Martha!
MARTHA: I mean it . . . you really have.
GEORGE: You can sit there in that chair of yours, you can sit there with the gin running out of your mouth, and you can humiliate me, you can tear me apart . . . ALL NIGHT . . . and that's perfectly all right . . . that's O.K. . . .
MARTHA: YOU CAN STAND IT!
GEORGE: I CANNOT STAND IT!
MARTHA: YOU CAN STAND IT!! YOU MARRIED ME FOR IT!!
GEORGE: That is a desperately sick lie.
MARTHA: DON'T YOU KNOW IT, EVEN YET? (Albee, 1963:152–153)

Family boundaries change as members come and go. Extended kin, close friends and neighbors, or foster children may be absorbed within the boundary of a given family. Even physical presence is not the measure of participation within family boundaries. A person may be related by birth or marriage and living in the same household, yet not be within family boundaries and not part of the interactional network, the bond that coheres. On the other hand, the family member in the hospital, away at school or military service, or incarcerated may well remain within the family boundary as just defined. Again a quotation from Malcolm X is illustrative. Malcolm describes his activities:

> I'm rarely at home more than half of any week; I have been away as much as five months. I never get a chance to take her anywhere, and I know she likes to be with her husband. She is used to my calling her from airports anywhere from Boston to San Francisco, or Miami to Seattle, or here lately, cabling her from Cairo, Accra, or the Holy City of Mecca. Once on the long-distance telephone, Betty told me in beautiful phrasing the way she thinks. She said, "You are present when you are away" (Malcolm X, 1966:233).

Maintenance of family boundary occurs on both sides of the boundary. The family frequently excludes nonmembers ("It's a family argument"; "the family vacation"). Society supports family boundaries through assigning the family priority on occasions highly charged with sentiment (weddings, funerals, and religious holidays). Cultures decree special occasions to reinforce family sentiment and interchange, such as Mother's Day and Father's Day. Business organizations permit employees leave for illness of immediate family members and for funerals of members of the extended family. Colleges and universities also recognize and support family boundaries of sentiment through allowing students to absent themselves for such family occasions. One student of our acquaintance mourned three grandmothers in the span of one semester!

As is true of all social systems, families require exchanges across boundaries. Monopolarization referred to earlier in this chapter expresses concern that the specialized nuclear family tends toward entropy because of insufficient sentiment exchanges with its environment.

Other concepts applicable to the family are *differentiation* and *specialization*. We have already alluded to the fact that the family has become a highly specialized cultural component uniquely responsible for meeting the security and sentiment needs of its members. The narrowing of family functions can be understood as a result of differentiation within modern society. Other institutions such as social welfare services that provide income maintenance, health care, emotional support, and day care have emerged to specialize in functions previously fulfilled by the extended family.

Within the family, differentiation and specialization are reflected in role allocations. So that the family can meet societal expectations and continue as an economic household, particular family members are breadwinners by mutual consent of the family members. Differential role expectations are commonly determined by age and sex, but these are uniquely refined in each family system. A particular family may reposit much of its unresolved or unacknowledged tensions in one family member, who then specializes as the "problem" family member. The concept of the family scapegoat is a case in point. Vogel and Bell elucidate the conditions that lead to a child becoming the family scapegoat.

> The parents are fraught with internal conflicts and ambivalence but each consciously expressed only one side of the ambivalence thus forming a set of overt polarization and mutual avoidance. A marriage cannot survive under these conditions so an appropriate object is selected to symbolize the conflicts and draw off the tension. The emotional disturbance of the child is simply the effect of internalizing the conflicting demands placed upon the child by his parents. In the short run he receives rewards from his family when he accepts his special role. The scapegoating mechanism may be functional for the family group through enabling its continued existence but be dysfunctional for the child's development and his adaptation outside the family (Vogel and Bell, 1960:382–397).

Another aspect of family structure is its *territoriality*. Family territory has both a spacial and behavioral dimension. The concept of home territory is notably descriptive of family territory since the occupants have a profound sense of "place" and belongingness (Lyman and Scott, 1967). The family consolidates around and finds its identity through achieving and maintaining territory. Behavioral territory was earlier described in the discussion of boundary; it is the interactional territory of feeling-closeness. Physically, the family also occupies territory. The architect, the contractor, the city planner, the mail carrier, indeed the garbage collector, all exist as societally supported occupations to serve and maintain the family within its spacial territory. This territory is signified by the house or apartment number; it may be further marked by posts, fences, and hedges.

The family territory may encompass a village, town, or neighborhood. "In ancient imagery, the center of his territory is a man's 'house,' be it a home or a farm, a firm or a family, a dynasty or a church; and his 'city' marks the boundary of all the houses associated with his" (Erikson, 1969:176). Society requests and requires families to be territorially based, to be oriented in space. Society's primary means of establishing social identifications are the answers to two questions: "Name?" "Address?" Or, less formally, "Where are you from?" which actually means "What was the place of your family of origin?" This societal concern with family territoriality is clearly expressed in the following quotation. "Show me a man who cares no more for one place than another, and I will show you in that same person one who loves nothing but himself. Beware of those who are homeless by choice" (Southey, 1959:508). Similarly, groups of people who are not identified with a particular or specified "home territory" (e.g., gypsies, Bedouins, and migrant workers) are viewed with suspicion by others.

B. Behavioral Aspects

Social control and *socialization* are characteristic functions of the family. The family is always a subsystem of its society and, as such, participates in the socialization processes of that society. It would be defensible to classify all socially defined dysfunctional families as failing to meet the requirements for socialization of its members. Socialization as used here may be defined as "the process by which the young human being acquires the values and knowledge of his group and learns the social roles appropriate to his position in it" (Goode, 1964:10). A central task of the family is to assure that its members are sufficiently acculturated to participate in the other societal subsystems that enable attainment of societal goals. For example, Project Headstart was instituted to supplement families that were not fulfilling this expectation as societally defined — to socialize the children and, if necessary, the parents as well.

Furthermore, the family is expected to control its members in order to prevent them from engaging in deviant behavior which seriously interferes with attainment of the system's goals. Witness the recurring idea that parents should be held accountable for the delinquent behavior of their children and legal efforts to enforce this parental responsibility.

Billingsley emphasizes the fact that the socialization charge is doubly difficult for the black family. In addition to the pressures that affect all families in America, the black family must cope with three additional facts of life:

> a. the peculiar historical development;
> b. the caste-like qualities in the American stratification system which relegates all Negroes to inferior status; and
> c. the social class and economic systems which keep most Negroes in the lower social classes.
>
> The American Negro family must teach its young members not only how to be human, but also how to be black in a white society (Billingsley, 1968:28).

No doubt the breadth of the socialization job allocated to the family has narrowed as some aspects have been assumed by other social institutions, particularly the school, but the primacy of family influence in personality development remains relatively intact.

Communication is increasingly emphasized as both the keystone of family interaction and the key to understanding family dynamics. All family behavior is influenced by its style and effectiveness of communication. Communication is here used to denote the exchange of meaningful symbols, vocal and gestural. It refers to the transfer of energy to accomplish system goals. The discussion of communication in Chapter 1 applies exactly to the family system.

A family can be seen to have a characteristic communication style. These characteristic patterns of interaction operate within the boundaries of the family and in transactions with external systems. Don Jackson has emphasized that the "redundancy principle" operates in family life. "The family will interact in repetitious sequences in all areas of its life, though some areas may highlight these repetitions (or patterns) more quickly and systematically than do other areas" (Jackson, 1970:121). Brodey offers that, "Each family has its own particular game, its rules and regulations. It has its rules of status, its rules of power, its techniques of movement" (Brodey, 1977:41–42). Humberto Maturana's employed the concept of *autopoiesis* (meaning self-creation or self-production) to suggest that a family, as any other system, strives to continue its existence; its characteristic processes serve to so maintain itself. Change must also contribute to survival of a system's identity (Maturana and Varela, 1980). An individual family then has a unique combination of communication patterns that strongly influences the behavior of its members.

The concentration of a few writers on body language has extended the reservoir of concepts capable of exploring family communication patterns (Birdwhistell, 1970; Hall, 1961; Scheflen, 1972). Communication practices are especially crucial to any understanding of family because of the importance and intensity of feeling exchange.

Communication in the family is extremely complex and subtle because of the number of functions served by the family. One energy exchange can convey any number of meanings. An example is a parent's directive to a child to do what the teacher says. Included in this could be several messages:

1. You *ought* to obey authority (to meet societal expectations)
2. But you *ought not* to be required to submit to unjust orders (to meet the child's needs)
3. Nevertheless, do what the teacher tells you to do (to avoid conflict with the environment)
4. Keep out of trouble (and avoid conflict between parent and teacher, that is, between family system and environment)
5. Because if you don't, you'll get it from me (meet parents' needs in order to satisfy the child's need for security)

The child is expected to understand and respond to all these messages.

Some critics of traditional patterns of marriage have advocated *open marriage* and have emphasized communication in such a marriage, using communication in a broad sense as we have used it here. An open marriage is described as one in which synergy results from free energy exchange between partners and between them and their social environment. Similarly, we suggest that a synergistic family may exist, one in which members communicate (verbally and nonverbally) in such fashion as to stimulate and support one another. This generation of energy permits members to become fuller individuals and, at the same time, enables the family to become richer and supportive for its members.

Adaptation is an essential family function. Family is a system of accommodation to social change. Because the family has consistently had the capacity to change its structure and function to adapt to marked changes in its environment, it has survived wars, industrial and technological revolutions, and traumatic disruptions in social conditions that made traditional patterns of coping obsolete. The family calls upon the energies of its components and exchanges energies with its significant environmental systems.

Another necessary adaptive mode of the family is its assimilation of exterior stress as experienced by its members. Although other social institutions such as religious and fraternal organizations also fulfill this function, the family is expected to be the primary system wherein one can relax (unwind), cast off externally adaptable role behaviors, and be oneself. If a family cannot so assimilate stress and enable a person to be oneself, or if a person cannot allow this to happen, substitutes must be found. Perhaps the emergence of sensitivity and support groups is a replacement for a defunct family function.

A family is considered maladaptive when it cannot adapt to the changing demands placed upon it by its environment and its members. If it is too unchanging (morphostasis) and devotes an undue proportion of its available energies to maintenance of existing structures, it will not be able to cope with external requirements and the individual development of its members. In essence, it maintains its previous functions and is thus dysfunctional. If, on the other hand, it is in a constantly unstable state of transition, it does not furnish the degree of stability its members require for repair of ego insults and for the chance to merely be oneself in an atmosphere of feeling-closeness. This leads to the final system aspects of the family.

C. Evolutionary Aspects

Steady state is characteristic of the family system, which needs to be simultaneously changing and remaining the same. The family exists through its life cycle with ever-changing requirements from its members and from society. The well-adapted marital pair, for example, must modify its mode of functioning with the advent of its first child. A family may

operate to its satisfaction and to that of society while the offspring are
dependent, but run aground when the children need emancipation from
their family of orientation. As Pitrim Sorokin points out, "any system
changes incessantly during its existence: among all its properties something
new is incessantly introduced and something old is incessantly lost from
moment to moment of its existence. In this sense any sociocultural process
is ever new and unrepeated" (Rodman, 1966:253).

The steady state of a family is maintained in various ways. James Framo
describes a family in therapy:

> Family therapy observations have revealed how the symptoms of one member
> often serve useful and necessary functions for the others, how the underlying
> system reciprocity is revealed by symptoms appearing in a previously asymp-
> tomatic member when the symptomatic one improves, and how a marriage
> may rupture when the symptoms which had been built into the relationship
> are no longer present (Sager and Kaplan, 1972:288–289).

He says further:

> Generally speaking, symptoms are maintained or reduced to the extent that
> they serve relationship system functions and are an integral component of a
> bonding force in the relationships. . . . Of course, changes occur in people
> and in symptoms in circumstances other than formal psychotherapy, most
> often when the context changes, that is, when the symptoms no longer have
> meaning in a given relationship system in time (Sager and Kaplan, 1972:294).

Haley aptly describes some of the morphostatic operations within the
family, such as "mutual secondary gain," "monitoring," "open sharing,"
"scapegoating," and "vicarious participation." These occur in a "circular
feedback system. Interpersonal conflict affects intrapsychic conflict, and
vice versa" (Sager and Kaplan, 1972:304).

All that was said about steady state in Chapter 1 applies to the family.
Often the family in crisis is in a situation of disruptive transition from one
form of steady state to another. At such times, a family may be more open to
use of energies from outside its own system, more amenable to interventive
efforts. Erikson's definition of crisis applies to families as well as individuals
(see Chapter 8, I, A, 1, "C. The Idea of Crisis").

A family tends to function so as to eliminate pain rather than change to
foster well-being of itself and its members (Friedman, 1971). It is not easy to
achieve a sense of family as a system — as an entity in its own right, more
than the sum of its members. Our cultural emphasis on the individual as the
most significant entity makes it difficult to conceive of the family as other
than molder, background, or environment. Paradoxically, we, at the same
time, categorize families as good or bad as measured by the social performance of their members. This leads to the pernicious doctrine that all
problematic or antisocial behavior is rooted in the family in a cause and

effect relationship. Of course, there is an element of truth in that belief, but as society blames its families, it is denying its part in personal and social dysfunction. In the past, the "broken home" has been especially maligned. This process is similar to family scapegoating, wherein a family member is loaded with the responsibility for family pain and dysfunction. Thus is the family both scapegoating and scapegoated.

The human services professions must and are beginning to come to appreciate the special systemic qualities of family. Tolstoy's observation that all happy families resemble each other and each unhappy family is unhappy in its own way suggests that the resemblance may be more apparent than real. Perhaps each happy family, too, is happy in its own way. Each family is like others in having rules, games (games meaning sequences of events governed by rules), secrets, and ghosts. Each family is unique in that its rules, games, secrets, and ghosts are its own.

Often work with families is best construed as aiding a family to discover what its unique patterns are and how they operate.

SUMMARY

The family is a critical human system. It serves unique, yet constantly changing, purposes for its subsystems (family members and combinations of family members) and suprasystems (society and parts of society). *A social system view of the family provides a skeletal frame that can include, but not substitute for, the various perspectives on the family that have been offered.* Each of these perspectives is valuable in its contribution to a particular aspect of the family.

We suggest that the family is best defined from the viewpoint of the person within it. The definition should include those relationships that are "family" to that person (i.e., a person's family are those with whom the person interacts and performs the family functions within the given society). In many crucial ways, the family is the principal intersection between the culture and the individuals within the culture, the point of most interaction and change. While discrete aspects of the family may each be better explained by one of the family theories we have examined, a systems view best explains the changes the family undergoes and the relationships that are cause and effect of those changes.

In recent years, family issues have been largely perceived as women's issues, and this has enabled the broadening of marital and parental role expectations for both women and men. Family issues have also entered more fully into the political realm, making it possible for politicians to insert themselves and their beliefs into family concerns (especially family planning and abortion). Legislating family matters diminishes the tolerance for pluralism of family forms and functions. The fiasco of the 1979–1980

White House Conference on Families illustrates the hazards of politicizing the family. As Gilbert Steiner observes, "diversity of family styles and traditionalism in family style peacefully coexist only as long as neither one gains actual or symbolic advantage over the other. Planning for a White House Conference ruptured the peace between the two" (Steiner, 1981:45).

What does the future hold for families in the United States? We would only predict that in the future, a wider range of family forms will be sanctioned, and the definition of roles in families will be on axes other than primarily the sexual one. Since families are interdependent parts of the fabric of society, they will continue to influence and be influenced by changes in other social institutions. We anticipate families will continue to have their unique position at the point where persons and culture meet.

SUGGESTED READINGS

Ackerman, Nathan W.
  1958   *The Psychodynamics of Family Living: Diagnosis and Treatment of Family Relationships.* New York: Basic Books.
     A readable, interesting psychoanalytic approach to family diagnoses and treatment. Possibly the first attempt to shift the focus of attention from the individual to the family.
Billingsley, Andrew.
  1968   *Black Families in White America.* Englewood Cliffs, N.J.: Spectrum.
     A systems approach to the family that has been used as the small-map text for this chapter. Billingsley has drawn on experience of blacks to supplement and revise sociological analyses of the family.
Brodey, Warren M.
  1977   *Family Dance: Building Positive Relationships Through Family Therapy.* Garden City, N.Y.: Anchor Books.
     A brief, readable explication of a pragmatic approach to working with families. Excellent incorporation of nonverbal material.
Califano, Joseph A., Jr.
  1981   *Governing America.* New York: Simon and Schuster.
     An obviously biased, informative explanation of political aspects of family issues during the first years of the Carter administration.
Cottle, Thomas J.
  1974   *A Family Album: Portraits of Intimacy and Kinship.* New York: Harper Colophon.
     A series of vignettes of people living their lives in families.
Friedman, Edwin H.
  1971   Family Systems Thinking and a New View of Man. *Central Conference of American Rabbis Journal,* 28(1).
     A provocative essay, drawing heavily on the author's practice.
Goode, William J.
  1964   *The Family.* Englewood Cliffs, N.J.: Prentice-Hall.
     A basic family text, excellent for an overview. This could well serve as the small-map text for this chapter for students who have not had previous family studies.

Jackson, Don.
    1970   The Study of the Family. In *Family Process*, Nathan W. Ackerman, ed. New York: Basic Books.
    An approach to understanding the family, drawing heavily on social systems concepts.
Nye, F. Ivan, and Felix M. Berardo.
    1968   *Emerging Conceptual Frameworks in Family Analysis.* New York: Macmillan.
    An ambitious attempt to summarize various perspectives for viewing the family system. Especially useful is Chapter 2, "The Anthropological Approach to the Study of the Family." Also includes the systems perspective.
Sager, Clifford, and Helen Singer Kaplan.
    1972   *Progress in Group and Family Therapy.* New York: Brunner/Mazel.
    Oriented to systems approach, which Chapter 1, "Analytic Group Therapy and General Systems Theory" by Helen E. Durkin makes explicit. Excellent; current experience and research. Much on applications of systems models. Many case examples.
Sennett, Richard.
    1974   *Families Against the City.* New York: Vintage Books.
    A former student of Erik Erikson, Sennett studied the relationship of family and community in the microcosm of a Chicago suburb. This history reveals the intimate relationship in an unusually vivid and detailed manner.
Watzlawick, Paul, Janet Helmick Beavin, and Don D. Jackson.
    1967   *Pragmatics of Human Communication: A Study of Interactional Patterns, Pathologies, and Paradoxes.* New York: W. W. Norton and Company, Inc.
    An excellent text dealing with systemic communication in a family context. The analysis of communication patterning in the play "Who's Afraid of Virginia Woolf?" is especially interesting.

LITERARY SOURCES

Anderson, Robert Woodruff.
    1968   *I Never Sang for My Father.* New York: Random House.
    Portrays a relatively closed family system and the affects such closure has on the children as they deal with becoming adults. The film version is excellent.
Guest, Judith.
    1976   *Ordinary People.* New York: Viking.
    A family coping with the aftermath of tragedy. Also available as a movie.
Olsen, Tillie.
    1976   *Tell Me a Riddle.* New York: Dell/Laurel Edition.
    A small collection of short stories commenting with sensitivity and insight on common human experiences within a context of culture and family.
Salinger, J.D.
    1961   *Franny and Zooey.* Boston: Little, Brown.
    The interior of a family of particular interest.
Zindel, Paul.
    1970   *The Effect of Gamma Rays on Man-in-the-Moon Marigolds.* New York: Harper and Row.
    A Pulitizer Prize winning play about the daily tribulations of a family with complex rules, games and ghosts. The film version is especially well presented.

THE PERSON

I. THEORETICAL APPROACHES

This chapter deals with the individual person as a human system and introduces concepts of human growth and development which are congruent with the central themes of this book. Some theorists have questioned the applicability of social systems concepts to the person. We subscribe to the premise that the individual human's existence is essentially a socially defined one. Without the individual, there would be no society and without the society there would be no individual. The one determines the other. Social systems concepts are explanatory of the interactive phenomena.

Our approach to the person as a human system is developmental and cyclical, and we draw from the works of a wide range of theorists, especially Erik H. Erikson and Jean Piaget. Erikson's and Piaget's formulations are particularly congruent with our systems approach.

A. Psychosocial Approach to Human Behavior

The psychosocial view of human behavior is introduced first since this is the major theme of the content about the life cycle. From a systems viewpoint, the individual person is a human system who is both cause and effect of social systems. As the cycle of life unfolds, the person broadens his/her interaction into systems of ever larger magnitude. Here are two of the many possible diagrams of this direction (Figure 12).

In either figure, the person's growth and development is in a pattern of

160

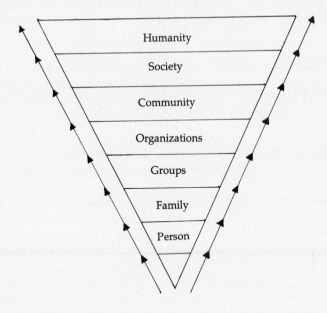

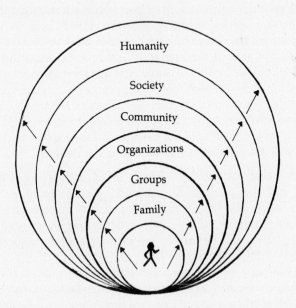

Fig. 12. Diagrams of a person's interactions with systems of increasing scale.

expansion, a movement outward. The life cycle framework of Erik Erikson is a pragmatic way to organize and describe elements of that growth process—at least in Western culture where the emphasis is on the individual.

In examining individual growth and development within a systems context, it is important to make connections between developmental theories and societal provisions. The interaction among research findings, theories, and societal determinants shape the social provisions that will be made available.

1. ERIKSON. Erik H. Erikson was born of Danish parents in Frankfurt, Germany, in 1902. He attended the humanistic gymnasium and began to prepare himself for a career as an artist. As an artist–tutor in Vienna, he became acquainted with persons in the emerging Psychoanalytic Institute. He acquired psychoanalytic training, working most closely with Dorothy Burlingham and Anna Freud. Interestingly, he also earned a certificate from the Maria Montessori School and was one of the few men with membership in the Montessori Academy. In 1933, he emigrated to the United States, where he still lives (Coles, 1970; Maier, 1978:71ff.).

Erikson's major work has been to create and extend a conceptual framework for the total life cycle of humans. His scheme was originally set forth in *Childhood and Society* (1950, 1963). Major revisions, refinements, and expansions were published in *Insight and Responsibility* (1964), *Identity: Youth and Crisis* (1968), and *Life History and the Historical Moment* (1975). He has also pioneered in the field of psychohistorical biography with his two monumental works, *Young Man Luther* (1958) and *Gandhi's Truth* (1969). He was awarded the Pulitzer Prize for his work on Gandhi.

Erikson's eight ages of the human life cycle are used as the organizing theme for this chapter for two reasons. First, his seems to be the only extant theory of human development that encompasses the total lifespan. Second, his psychosocial approach to human development is particularly in accord with the human services with their simultaneous attention to the individual and the environment. A few of the key ideas of the Eriksonian formulation of the life cycle are enumerated to introduce his thinking.

  a. Erikson's view of the life cycle. This is based on the epigenetic principle. *Epigenesis* ("epi" means "upon," "genesis" means "emergence") means that one developmental stage occurs on top of, and in relation to, another in space and time (Evans, 1967:21–22). Since this is a hierarchy of stages, not a simple sequence, the potentials for growth and development are all present in the human organism. The parts arise out of the whole, each component having a special time for ascendency, until all the processes have run their course and have developed into a functioning whole. Thus the human personality is seen as an evolving system comprising potential matrices, which arise according to some sort of ground plan. Correlated

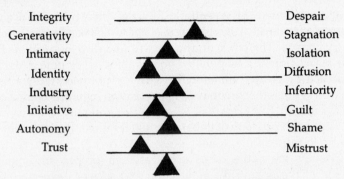

Integrity		Despair
Generativity		Stagnation
Intimacy		Isolation
Identity		Diffusion
Industry		Inferiority
Initiative		Guilt
Autonomy		Shame
Trust		Mistrust

FIG. 13. Stages of life cycle according to Erikson.

with this is the interdependence of the emergent matrices; the development of a subsequent matrix is somewhat dependent on that which has gone before. Each alters the previously achieved balances. The stages are not discrete, nor are they simply the result of an additive process.

The stages may be pictured simplistically as a set of teeterboards balanced upon each other (see Figure 13). Each level (or stage) depends upon the balance achieved in the preceding stage, and an adjustment of any level involves an adjustment of all the others. The point at which each level is balanced is the ratio of polar qualities achieved in each stage.

b. Erikson's life cycle formulation. This is based on human genetic energy but is totally dependent on social experiences. Three principles of organization and process are: (1) *physical:* constitutional or somatic organization; (2) *ego:* the self as organizing force; and (3) *social:* organizing responsive to the rules and expectations of society and culture. In other words, the somatic process, the ego process, and the societal process equal the human life. The similarities and differences between this triad and the Freudian triad are important. Someone commented that Erikson's is an ego psychology and Freud's is an id psychology. Erikson has said, "a human being, thus, is at all times an organism, an ego and a member of society and is involved in all three processes of organization" (Erikson, 1963:36). In our view, of course, these are three systems levels.

Within this scheme, the unfolding of the human system is seen as a combination of maturation, socialization, and education. The eight stages of the life cycle represent a synthesis of developmental (maturation) and social (learning) tasks. *Maturation* is "the process of growth for all members of the species, with predictable characteristics." *Learning* is "individual growth, new behavioral acquisitions based on the organism's experience rather than its structure" (Stone and Church, 1957:38). Growth, then, derives from the constant interaction of maturation and learning. The organism's *readiness* is determined by maturational considerations, while its *learning* is a function of social experiences.

  c. *The idea of crisis.* This is central to Erikson's theory. His use of this term is quite similar to the idea of crisis in *crisis intervention* and refers to a time of necessary change. The crises during growth and development, as Erikson uses the term, connote a heightened potential for development (or change) accompanied by greater vulnerability. Crisis is not necessarily a negative state of affairs but rather an unavoidable occasion requiring coping of some type. This meaning of crisis has existed since antiquity. Hippocrates describes crisis as an occasion of imbalance that required the "constitution" of the person to respond (i.e. cope) (Jones, 1923:1i–1v).

  In Erikson's view, the crises occur at their proper time out of the interaction of the organism's maturation and society's expectations. The outcome (not *resolution* necessarily) is dependent upon the personality resources the individual has accrued up to that point *and* the opportunities and resources available in his/her social situation.

  Erikson has written extensively and thoroughly on two of the eight crises of development — basic trust versus basic mistrust and identity versus diffusion. Attention to these particular periods of child development is not unique to Erikson, since infancy and adolescence have attracted the attention of much of child development research. His theories about the first critical task of life, trust versus mistrust, are compatible with the work of René Spitz (1965) in his studies of the establishment of an initial object relationship. Erikson's formulation is also consistent with the extensive literature on maternal deprivation and even with the work on imprinting. His ideas about adolescence are compatible with a host of theorists including Friedenberg (1962), Keniston (1970), and Paul Goodman (1960). In fact, one gets the impression that infancy and adolescence are indeed the two most critical phases of personality development.

  The critical developmental tasks that Erikson enumerates and describes are expressed as bipolarities. This formulation is consistent with general systems theory that the dynamism of life derives from the fact of negative and positive charges with tension and, therefore, movement existing between them. It is most important to bear in mind that these bipolarities are not achievement scales to serve as measurable criteria of growth and development. One does not achieve *complete* trust and then move on to the next plateau, autonomy. The outcome of each of the developmental crises is a relative mix of the polar qualities, and the developing person must cope with the subsequent task at its proper time as dictated by maturation and social expectations. In one sense these critical tasks of development are present at all times in each person's life and are directly related to one another. They are sequential as to when they emerge as crises.

  Figure 14 illustrates the interrelatedness of the various crises. This figure focuses on the crisis of adolescence and identity versus identity diffusion and illustrates how each of the earlier crises contributes to the readiness to cope with this one and how it, in turn, influences the subsequent crises. Theoretically, it should be possible to take any of the crises represented on the diagonal and fill in the related boxes to show the relationship of that crisis to the preceding and the following steps.

Erikson's worksheet (Figure 15) illustrates his eight stages of man on five dimensions. The second dimension (B, radius of significant relations) indicates the progression of interrelationships from the dyad of the infant and nurturing persons through the ever-expanding hierarchy of social systems. The eighth stage includes all of mankind. Columns C, D, and E concern social order, psychosocial modalities, and psychosexual stages and indicate the relatedness of these dimensions.

Erikson's life cycle scheme can validly be described as a systems viewpoint based in the "natural" epigenetic principle. As the individual's life cycle unfolds, it has the maturational potential and the social necessity to be involved in ever-wider social systems and ever-changing social conditions. To fulfill their functional density, persons must, of necessity, be engaged in transactions with these other social systems.

In summary, then, Erikson's eight ages of the human life cycle represent the necessary occasions for the individual uniting biological, psychological, and social forces. He stresses the adaptive and creative power of the person and respects each individual's unique capacity to forge his/her own way of life. His faith in human social creativity is reflected in his optimistic comment, "there is little that can not be remedied later, there is much that can be prevented from happening at all" (Erikson, 1950:164).

B. Cognitive Theory

1. PIAGET. Phillips begins his book on Piaget by saying

> I hope that you will take from all this a conception of the human brain as a vastly complicated system for the storage and retrieval of information; a system that becomes capable of increasingly complex operations; a system that changes in ways that are at least to some degree similar to the constructions that Piaget has given us (Phillips, 1969:xii).

From this suggestion that Piaget was a systems theorist of sorts, we can advance to Maier's statement that

> Piaget believes in universal order and suggests a single unity of all things biological, social, psychological, and ideational in living as well as non-living systems. . . . Science is interrelated and a theorem established in one branch of science is directly relevant to the laws and principles of other branches. Altogether, Piaget insists upon cosmic unity . . . (Maier, 1978:19).

Maier goes on to describe how Piaget relates parts to wholes within systems.

Piaget was a systems theorist whose area of concentration has been

FIG. 14. The adolescent crisis, "Identity vs. identity diffusion."

	1.	2.	3.	4.	5.	6.	7.	8.
I. Infancy	Trust vs. mistrust				Unipolarity vs. pre- mature self-dif- ferentia- tion			
II. Early child- hood		Autonomy vs. shame, doubt			Bipolarity vs. autism			
III. Play age			Initiative vs. guilt		Play identi- fication vs. (oedipal) fantasy identities			
IV. School age				Industry vs. inferior- ity	Work identi- fication vs. identity foreclo- sure			

	Time perspective vs. time diffusion	Self-certainty vs. identity consciousness	Role experimentation vs. negative identity	Anticipation of achievement vs. work paralysis	Identity vs. identity diffusion	Sexual identity vs. bisexual diffusion	Leadership polarization vs. authority diffusion	Ideological polarization vs. diffusion of ideals
V. Adolescence	Time perspective vs. time diffusion	Self-certainty vs. identity consciousness	Role experimentation vs. negative identity	Anticipation of achievement vs. work paralysis	Identity vs. identity diffusion	Sexual identity vs. bisexual diffusion	Leadership polarization vs. authority diffusion	Ideological polarization vs. diffusion of ideals
VI. Young adult					Solidarity vs. social isolation	Intimacy vs. isolation		
VII. Adulthood							Generativity vs. self-absorption	
VIII. Mature age								Integrity vs. disgust, despair

SOURCE: Reprinted with permission from Erik H. Erikson, "Identity and the Life Cycle: Selected Papers," *Psychological Issues* (Monograph). New York: International Universities Press, 1959, Volume 1, p. 120.

167

FIG. 15. Erikson's worksheet.

	A Psychosocial crises	B Radius of significant relations	C Related elements of social order	D Psychosocial modalities	E Psychosexual stages
I.	Trust vs. mistrust	Maternal person	Cosmic order	To get To give in return	Oral–respiratory, sensory–kines- thetic (incorpora- tive modes)
II.	Autonomy vs. shame, doubt	Parental persons	"Law and order"	To hold (on) To let (go)	anal–urethral, muscular (reten- tive–eliminative)
III.	Initiative vs. guilt	Basic family	Ideal prototypes	To make (=going after) To "make like" (=playing)	Infantile–genital, locomotor (intrusive, inclu- sive)
IV.	Industry vs. inferiority	"Neighborhood," school	Technological elements	To make things (=completing) To make things together	"Latency"

V.	Identity and repudiation vs. identity diffusion	Peer groups and outgroups; models of leadership	Ideological perspectives	To be oneself (or not to be) To share being oneself	Puberty
VI.	Intimacy and solidarity vs. isolation	Partners in friendship, sex, competition, cooperation	Patterns of cooperation and competition	To lose and find oneself in another	Genitality
VII.	Generativity vs. self-absorption	Divided labor and shared household	Currents of education and tradition	To make be To take care of	
VIII.	Integrity vs. despair	"Mankind" "My kind"	Wisdom	To be, through having been To face not being	

SOURCE: Reprinted with permission from Erik H. Erikson, "Identity and the Life Cycle: Selected Papers," *Psychological Issues* (Monograph). New York: International Universities Press, 1959, Volume 1, p. 164.

cognitive development. Cognitive theory concentrates on the process of knowing and learning. In comparison to the work that has been done on the first two views of the personal system, far less has been done in formal research exploration of the cognitive processes.

Much of what has been done in this field can be traced to Jean Piaget and his collaborators. Piaget was born in Switzerland in 1896, and died there in 1980. A precocious student, he published his first scientific paper at the age of 10 and was offered a museum directorship (which he declined). His early interest was in biology, but this broadened to philosophy and psychology during his training at the University of Neuchatel. He sought to combine these three fields in a "psychological and biological epistemology," or theory of knowledge. He kept at this task constantly with thousands of research studies during the past 50 years.

Piaget only slowly gained a reputation in the United States because he did not fit neatly into any of the established disciplines. Psychology reluctantly acknowledged him, and philosophy hardly recognized his work. Oddly enough, and for reasons we mention later, his greatest impact was on educational theory and practice.

Piaget's research methods have been criticized because they are not always orthodox. He used psychoanalytic interviewing style, exploring children's responses, especially their mistakes. Piaget questioned the child while he or she was doing various tasks and while not doing them and also, on occasion, observed in silence. In his career, he invented over 50 new research techniques. Here is one brief example. The child is presented with a group of coins and a bunch of flowers. The child is then asked how many flowers can be purchased if each flower costs one coin.

> Gui (four years, four months) put 5 flowers opposite 6 pennies, then made a one-for-one exchange of 6 flowers (taking the extra flower from the reserve supply). The pennies were in a row and the flowers bunched together: "What have we done? — *We've exchanged them.* — Is there the same number of flowers and pennies? — *No.* — Are there more on one side? — *Yes.* — Where? — *There* (pennies). (The exchange was again made, but this time the pennies were put in a pile and the flowers in a row.) Is there the same number of flowers and pennies? — *No.* — Where are there more? — *Here* (flowers). — And here (pennies)? — *Less* (Phillips, 1969:5).

This exchange illustrates the flexible interview style and searching for concepts in the child's thinking that was typical of Piaget's methods. In this instance, it appeared to the child that if the objects were spread out there were more of them than if they were bunched up, indicating that the concept of transferability of numbers from one set of objects to another was beyond the knowledge of this 4½-year-old child. Piaget also took the "unscholarly" approach of studying his own children and performing small experiments to test their development.

The topics of Piaget's major work are evident in these titles: "the construction of reality," "judgment and reason," "language and thought," "logic and psychology," "moral judgment," "the origin of intelligence," and "the psychology of intelligence." His major work is *Genetic Epistemology* (1970). He refined and added to this work since then.

Although not widely known in the United States, Piaget's reputation has accelerated in recent years. In Europe, he is regarded as "Mr. Child Psychology"; he is, however, something more than the Dr. Spock of the intellect. Phillips says of him and his collaborators:

> The publications of the Geneva school constitute by far the largest repository of knowledge about the cognitive development of children that is available anywhere; students of psychology should be familiar with Piaget's theory even if it turns out to be basically wrong, because it will undoubtedly serve as a base for many future studies of children's thinking (Phillips 1969:11).

Piaget is regarded by some theorists as being equal to Freud in his eventual impact on personality theory. He dealt in concrete detail with the major problems of logic, thought, and philosophy that have hindered our understanding of humans in this century. His major impact, as noted earlier, has been on education.

> Piaget has said some pretty important things about children, and anyone who says important things about children ultimately must be important to educators. Teaching is the manipulation of the student's environment in such a way that his activities will contribute to his development (toward goals whose definitions are not our present concern). It should be obvious . . . that the effect of a given environment on a child is as much a function of the child as of the environment. If a teacher knows that, his behavior will be affected by his conception of what students are like. Indeed, his very definition of teaching will be so determined. Mine was (Phillips, 1969:107–108).

Piaget's emphasis on first-hand involvement, experience, and grappling with problems appropriate to the child's intellectual development was consistent with the view of John Dewey, whose influence on American education has been profound.

The implications of Piaget's work are important for the human services. He stressed invention and creativity and the ability of the person to grow rather than remain handicapped by past deficiencies or conflicts. His view of teaching is that "every time you teach a child something you keep him from reinventing it" (Phillips, 1969:120).

> The principal goal of education . . . is to create men who are capable of doing new things . . . men who are creative, inventive and discoverers. The second goal of education is to form minds which can be critical, can verify, and not accept anything they are offered . . . we need pupils who are active, who learn early to find out by themselves, partly by their own spontaneous activity and partly through materials we set up for them; who learn early to tell what is verifiable and what is simply the first idea to come to them (Elkind, 1968:80).

The basic ideas of Piaget are relatively easy to understand from a systems viewpoint:

a. Equilibrium. Equilibrium, in Piaget's view, is a steady state of the cognitive processes. Specifically, he regards equilibrium as a balance between the person and his environment in which the person's knowledge adequately explains what he experiences. Equilibrium as Piaget viewed it may be defined as a state of active compatibility between the needs of the person and the demands and supplies from the environment. That is, there is feedback that confirms and continues to reinforce the person's developing capacity to understand and master his environment. The similarity to Erikson here is obvious.

b. Intelligence. Piaget defined intelligence as a "special form of biological activity." "For Piaget, the one-time biologist, intelligence can be meaningfully considered only as an extension of certain fundamental biological characteristics" (Flavell, 1963:41). Intelligence arises from the biological makeup and is always a part of the individual as a biological being. Its function is the same as that of other system processes: to preserve the organism. According to Piaget, intelligence is both the activity of coping with the environment *and* the end state of "compatibility." Intelligence, by the latter definition, is the maximum potential of the adaptive capacities; it is never fully realized.

c. Schemas. The structural units that lie at the heart of Piaget's system are *schemata* or *schemas* (both are plural forms, but we prefer the latter). Schemas function as mediating processes, forming a kind of framework onto which data can, indeed must, fit. But the framework continually changes its shape, the better to assimilate those data (Phillips, 1969:9). Intelligence has a structure and this structure is stable and predictable. It is systematic and orderly. At any particular time it maintains an equilibrium which changes — that is maintains a steady state.

Since Piaget believed that thought begins as action, he said that thought structures are patterns of internalized actions, ranging from the most

See definition
of schema
p. 233

elementary reflex pattern to profound philosophical thought. Schemas are organized action sequences and behavior patterns. Schemas arise by association. The reflexes become associated with other experience, and such isolated behaviors as sucking, grasping, looking and hearing become larger and more comprehensive. For example, looking and sucking are coordinated into seeing–grasping–sucking the bottle simultaneously. Progressive refinements of schemas allow the child to see the bottle, hold it, turn it around, tilt it, lay it down, pick it back up, see that it is empty, cry, and so forth.

The later, larger schemas are more highly developed. Eventually the child will be able to think of these operations instead of really perform them — that is, to carry on the action internally, think it through, correct it mentally, and then try it, all without picking up the bottle. Piaget said that thought is precisely such actions and schemas, refined and modified endlessly by intelligence. He carried this a step further by stressing that reality as we know it can only be this structure of associated and coordinated experiences. In other words, reality is structured by the schemas we have built up. Our schemas include time and space and are the frame for our understanding. We are bound by these frameworks except when dreaming and under the influence of drugs or hallucinating, when our usual schemas are loosened and other associations occur. (Here the relation to Freudian "associations" seems very close.)

There are two fundamental characteristics of schemas, *"organization and adaptation.* Every act is organized and the dynamic aspect of organization is adaptation" (Phillips, 1969:7). These are the same in all biological processes and are consistent with systems ideas.

Adaptation takes two forms: *assimilation* and *accommodation.* The person attempts to fit new experience into the old schemas, to accept it as similar to previous experience. This is assimilation. Accommodation refers to the person's modification of his old schema to accommodate the new experience. These are similar, then, to what Buckley calls *morphostasis* and *morphogenesis* (see Chapter 1 and glossary), the maintenance or change of a system's structure in order to achieve a new steady state after the input of new energy. These two tendencies, like other polarities, are never mutually exclusive; there is always some balance of the two.

Piaget's view of the structure of intelligence is quite consistent with the systems view. Just as Freud's concepts of id, ego, and superego came from classical mechanical physics, so Piaget's concept of schema comes from Einstein's theory of relativity and is compatible with Whitehead's and Dewey's philosophies. Piaget specifically refers to physics as being analogous to his own ideas, and many of his experiments deal with children's understandings of such physics concepts as velocity, time, and distance. Piaget has explicitly acknowledged a similarity between his own theories and those of Bertalanffy, the foremost general systems theorist (Koestler and Smythies, 1971:65).

2. PIAGET'S THEORY AND MORAL JUDGMENT. Lawrence Kohlberg, a psychologist, has applied Piaget's theory to the development of moral judgments in children and adults. Piaget's studies of this aspect of human development date from the 1920's; Kohlberg's studies date from the late 1950's and still continue. Kohlberg's methodology has been administration of verbal and written situations that ask children or adults to state what is "right" in each situation. For example, in the "Heinz" case, Heinz's wife is dying and the pharmacist has the rare medicine to cure her but will sell it only at an exorbitant price, which Heinz cannot afford. The respondent must decide what is "right," and why. Should Heinz steal the medicine? If not, why not? If so, why? Because he loves his wife or simply because she is a human being in jeopardy? What are the rights of the pharmacist? Should he be able to set any price he wishes? What of the pharmacist's right to private property that he created? Should Heinz or the pharamacist act according to "the golden rule?" or act according to some other universal rule? The answers given to this and other situations indicate the stage of moral development that the respondent has achieved.

Kohlberg identified six stages (and most recently, a seventh that seems highly speculative), the first four of which emerge from his research. The fifth and sixth stages are logical extensions of the preceding stages, but they are criticized by other investigators for the lack of empirical evidence to substantiate them. The stages are grouped in pairs under three major headings.

a. Preconventional. Kohlberg identified the majority of the population, which fall in stages 3 and 4, as being "conventional" in their moral judgments. Accordingly, stages 1 and 2 are "preconventional," centering upon self, and stages 5 and 6 are "postconventional," centering upon wider systems, either societal or universal (all of humanity), in making moral judgments.

Stage 1. In this earliest stage, judgments are based upon the direct consequences the child is likely to suffer. "Will I be punished for this or rewarded?" The calculation is simple and straightforward. Clearly, this stage corresponds with the earliest stages identified by Piaget.

> Stage 1 represents the moral reasoning of the child who has taken his first step beyond egocentrism. If the egocentric child cannot take the role or perspective of any other person, the next step in development is the ability to take the perspective of one other person at a time (Hersh *et al.*, 1979:65).

Stage 2. In this stage, the child incorporates the desire to please those who provide nurturance. Judgments are based upon the anticipated pleasure or displeasure of these "significant others." The child has now, as in

The Person

Piaget's stages, differentiated self from other and views self in relation to other.

> The child's conception of right at stage 2 is essentially one of stark reciprocity. An exactly equal exchange of goods or favors seems to be the guiding light of this stage. . . . Reciprocity at this stage does not flow from a respect for the rights or dignity of the other, but merely from a pragmatic expectation of receiving similar treatment (Rosen, 1980:75–76).

The child begins to understand that the will or desires of the other person can change—that they can be changed by the child's actions, and that there is some standard of "fairness" or reciprocity used by the other and to which the child can appeal.

b. Conventional. Stages 3 and 4 comprise the levels of development of most of the population. One can, supposedly, assume that the distribution of the general population falls within a classic bell-shaped curve. However, the "bell" would be quite high and quite narrow, since Kohlberg and his fellow researchers estimate that no more than 5% of the population have progressed as far as stage 6.

Stage 3. This stage is characterized by an advance beyond strict reciprocity. The child now takes the role of the other, and can see the situation (and self) from the other's perspective.

> A desire to receive praise and avoid blame will influence the judgment of what constitutes right and wrong action. Kohlberg refers to this sometimes as the "Good-boy/Nice-girl" stage. One is motivated to observe rules in order to maintain relationships. The individual's conception of right at this stage is limited to people within his own circle and does not extend to a broad societal level. . . . This new role-taking ability will enable him to modify his intended behavior on the basis of how he anticipates the other might respond to it (Rosen, 1980:76).

Stage 4. This stage can be called "Social System and Conscience" (Rosen, 1980:77).

> The scope of this stage encompasses the complete network of the entire society. There is a sense of obligation to obey laws and perform duties. Laws are construed as necessary to maintain society. The allegiance to following laws now springs from a conception of a moral order which goes beyond one's own circle of friends and relatives (Rosen, 1980:77).

Judgments in this stage are based upon the rights of society. Vengeance, for example, is the right of society and is interpreted as "paying your debt to society." In a cogent sentence, Kohlberg suggests what underlies the attitude of the general public toward welfare and those who receive it: "Social inequality is allowed where it is reciprocal to effort, moral conformity, and talent, but unequal favoring of the 'idle' and 'immoral,' poor, students, etc., is strongly rejected" (Rosen, 1980:77). This, then, is the stage of conventional morality.

Kohlberg and his collaborators identified a substage (cleverly labeled "stage 4B"), which is a "moratorium" (borrowed from Erik Erikson) or period of limbo. During this substage, the person is in transition from stage 4 to stage 5 and, in confusion, alternates between relativism and absolutism in moral judgments. Apparently, this period falls between high school graduation (i.e., age 18) and the mid-twenties. Kohlberg says that there are periods of "disequilibrium" between stages (similar to Piaget) and that the person in substage 4B is in such a disequilibrium, having lost the stability (we would say steady state, of course) of stage 4 without yet achieving stability in stage 5. Kohlberg believes that stage 5, if it is achieved, occurs during the mid-twenties, and that stage 6 does not occur before age 20 (Rosen, 1980:93). If these stages were substantiated by further research, they would tend to confirm Erikson's stages of adulthood as well as Kohlberg's.

  c. *Postconventional.* Stages 5 and 6 are the most controversial of Kohlberg's stages, since there is less supporting evidence for them. Kohlberg is accused of deriving these from philosophical premises, rather than psychological, empirical research.

  Stage 5. In stage 4, the person accepts and maintains the status quo, for the most part. In stage 5, the person entertains the possibility of changing unjust laws. The person looks beyond the laws to the principles that they embody and can question whether the laws adequately fulfill those principles. Kohlberg's opinion is that the logical outcome of stage 5 is a democratic society. The person becomes aware that there may be two or more valid moral or legal choices and must choose between them. In this sense, the person in stage 5 seeks justice as a principle rather than simply obedience to the law. Equity is preferred over equality; it is clear that Kohlberg has been influenced by philosopher John Rawls. Kohlberg uses capital punishment as an example. If there is no proof that capital punishment deters crime, then the person in stage 5 would conclude that this law does not protect society and would oppose capital punishment. If, on the other hand, there is evidence that it deters crime, the person in stage 5 could conclude that capital punishment serves a valid purpose in protecting society and be in favor of it. The primary criterion in this stage, then, is the social utility of the particular law.

  Stage 6. Rosen identifies the characteristics of the person who has attained stage 6:

post-conventional [handwritten marginal note]

The rare person whose sociocognitive moral development has brought him to this stage of moral reasoning is fully autonomous. He is completely decentered from society's expectations and bases his resolutions to ethical conflicts upon universal principles of justice which are prescriptively consistent without exception. Universality, consistency and logical comprehensiveness are the central attributes. . . . Conscience, in this sense, does not connote guilt, but the purely rational quality of his justice structure. Respect for the dignity of each individual, regardless of station in life, has reached a zenith (Rosen, 1980:80–81).

Kohlberg cites a philosopher's solution to the "Heinz" situation as an example of stage 6 moral judgments:

IF THE HUSBAND DOES NOT FEEL VERY CLOSE TO OR AFFECTIONATE WITH HIS WIFE, SHOULD HE STEAL THE DRUG? *Yes. The value of her life is independent of any personal ties.*

The value of human life is based on the fact that it offers the only possible source of a categorical moral "ought" to a rational being acting in the role of a moral agent.

SUPPOSE IT WERE A FRIEND OR AN ACQUAINTANCE? *Yes, the value of a human life remains the same* (Hersh *et al.*, 1979:80).

The fact that Kohlberg cites a philosopher as an example of the most advanced stage, may seem to betray a bias in his theory. Kohlberg cites Socrates, Lincoln, Jesus, and Martin Luther King as other examples. Rosen comments that, "It only takes a moment's reflection on the fate of the four men identified as examples to raise the intriguing question about the possible inherent danger of being at stage 6 in a predominantly conventional society" (Rosen, 1980:93).

Kohlberg has also recently identified a seventh stage, which Rosen calls "The Cosmic Perspective," which supersedes the humanistic sixth stage. Kohlberg readily acknowledges that there is no research data to support this, as yet. His speculation in the absence of evidence tends to support his critics, who do not find convincing evidence for stages 5 and 6 either. Kohlberg acknowledges being influenced by Erikson and believes that this seventh stage occurs in aged persons who experience despair and doubt about life's meaning. The person finds meaning by "identifying the self with the cosmic perspective of the infinite" (Rosen, 1980:88). Kohlberg does not claim that this is a verifiable stage similar to the earlier ones, but he does believe that spiritual growth occurs among the aging that is qualitatively different from earlier moral judgments.

Kohlberg's theories receive thorough and frequently harsh reviews (Hersh *et al.*, 1979; Rosen, 1980), but he is acknowledged to have created the largest body of research literature on moral judgments and for that reason alone to be significant. Some comments upon his scheme are in order for the reader's understanding. Persons do not inevitably progress through the stages, as contrasted to Erikson's stages. Kohlberg states that most of the population remain in stage 4.

One serious criticism of Kohlberg is that his idealized persons in stages 5 and 6 (and certainly 7) are conceived to be "beyond culture" or "culture-free." This contradicts what we have said earlier regarding the pervasiveness of culture. Socrates, Lincoln, Jesus, King, and, one could add, Ghandi, were certainly not free of their respective cultures. One could maintain that they transformed their cultures through exemplifying certain principles that, in each case, underlay the law, but one cannot accurately maintain that they were culture-free.

The continuing debate over Kohlberg's theory should clarify whether either he or Piaget (or in certain respects, Erikson) are correct in concluding that there are certain genetically "programmed" stages in the development of moral and cognitive capacities.

II. THE CRITICAL PHASES OF THE LIFE CYCLE

A. Establishment of Primary Attachment (Dependency and Trust) in the Parent–Child Dyad

The newborn infant enters the world in a totally dependent state. The major part of the first year is devoted to the effort to survive and to the formation and elaboration of the adaptation devices directed toward survival. The infant during this early period is helpless and incapable of surviving by its own efforts. The nurturing person (or persons) compensates for and supplies what the newborn lacks. The newborn is initially in a state of undifferentiation. Physiological organization is rudimentary, and there is no demonstrated psychic organization. In the world of the newborn, there is no object or object relation. This will develop during the course of the first year (Spitz, 1965).

1. Trust versus Mistrust. Erikson describes the first critical social task as "a sense of basic trust versus a sense of basic mistrust." By this, he means the necessity for the development of a *feeling* of trust in others and in one's self and for healthy mistrust of one's environment (and of oneself, perhaps). Spitz refers to this first task as the initiation of an object relationship. In the Erikson formulation of the dimension of trust, the following elements are of importance.

1. The nurturing person(s) become an inner certainty as well as an outer predictability. This is a state that has included in it the qualities of consistency, continuity, and sameness of experience.

2. The infant develops a sense of being able to trust self and the capacity of his/her own organs to cope with urges.

3. This sense of trust in self and others forms the foundation for the later development of a sense of identity.

4. Since the sense of trust/mistrust is essentially social, it is based in communication (particularly tactile, nutritive, and emotional) between the infant and the caring person(s).

Ever since Spitz's work in the 1930s on the effects of maternal deprivation, controversy in the literature has focused on whether the primary social attachment need be formed between the infant and the mother. It is fairly well accepted that the mother in this sense does not necessarily mean the biological mother. Some authors refer to the caring person, rather than mother, holding to the necessity for continuity, consistency, and predictability but not seeing this necessarily embodied in any one particular person. Consequently, there is fairly general agreement that the climate within which an infant can adapt to the first social task is of the utmost importance, but the question of who the person or persons need be to establish this climate remains controversial. This has been a central question in the recent development of day-care centers.

The infant's primary needs that must be met are the oral, nutritive needs. The mouth is the initial receptor; it is the most sensitive and demanding tissue in the body at this time. Sensitive tissues develop in other erotogenic zones later, and these form the basis of Freud's stages of oral, anal, and genital. Erikson also employs the idea of zones and refers to the zonal sensitivity of the "sense of trust versus sense of mistrust" period as oral–respiratory, and sensory–kinesthetic. He stresses that these are incorporative modes. At any rate, the first social activities of the infant are concerned with incorporation, getting and learning to get. During the later portion of the first critical stage, the infant begins to give in return.

Formation of the primary social attachment is accomplished in a dyadic field wherein the infant and caring person or persons "are one." Contemporary birthing practices that foster "bonding" strive to highlight the immediacy of mutual attachment between infant and parent(s). Initially, at least, we should not refer to the infant as an autonomous entity in itself. It is helpless, dependent, and must be cared for; it is as one with the other party to the dyad. It is now primarily a component, a component of a system — something that cannot be said at any later time. It is possible to think of the "connectiveness" of the human organism to other humans. In the prenatal environment, the developing organism is connected through the umbilical cord; in the first months of life, it is connected by a psychological "cord" that must be severed to permit later movement to wider social connections. To paraphrase Erikson, the child in the first months of life could well say "I am what I am given," next say, "I am what I can get," and finally say "I am what I can give."

Within the dyad, the infant does not long remain a passive recipient. In her definitive theoretical review of object relations, dependency, and attachment, Mary Ainsworth emphasizes the important role of infant behaviors both in eliciting parental responses and in active proximity-seeking (Ainsworth, 1969:981). Quite early in life, the infant must respond and interact through the formation of a primary social attachment. From a systems stance, it can be said that the transactions between the human system and the environment are a necessary condition for the definition of boundary of self. In other words, it is through the recognition of and interaction with "other" that the boundaries of self can be defined. If this process is not sufficiently engaged in, the boundaries of self are not defined, which may result in the condition known as infantile autism. If the latter part of this process is not forthcoming, that is, the differentiation of self within the social attachments, the resulting condition is referred to as symbiosis (see 4b below).

a. Maternal deprivation. A number of aysfunctional dyadic forms have been identified and grouped under the rubric of maternal deprivation (Bowlby, 1962). Maternal deprivation can be described in both quantitative and qualitative aspects. The term generally refers to an insufficiency of interaction between the child and the nurturing persons and the conditions under which this insufficiency seems to develop. The term *maternal deprivation* should not be taken literally but as an expression of the effect on the child. Some of the conditions under which it becomes apparent are:

1. Institutionalization or hospitalization of the infant with no provision for substitute parenting. This is a circumstance where the infant is indeed deprived of a mothering agent. It has been documented by René Spitz in his writings and films (Spitz, 1965).
2. Circumstances where the child is with a mother or mother substitute who provides insufficient opportunity for interaction.
3. Sufficient care is available to the child, but the child is unable to interact because of previous deprivations, maturational deficiencies, or unknown causes. Not infrequently, parents of disturbed preschool children report that almost from birth, an infant was not responsive to cuddling and "gentling." Frequently, a neurological deficit is suspected by the physician.
4. Distorted relationships:
   a. Situations where the child is not differentiated from the parent. The parent does not distinguish the boundary between self and child.
   b. Interlocking dependency, a symbiotic relationship wherein the parent must have a totally dependent infant and the child requires total mothering. This is the normal circumstance of the neonatal infant but prolongation is distorting.
   c. The parent may assimilate the child as being certain aspects of

herself (or himself) or identify the child completely with the qualities of another person. Again a measure of this is normal, as seeing an infant as having Uncle John's eyes or Aunt Clara's hair, but when the total child is viewed as possessing the qualities of another, there is little opportunity to differentiate self and establish self as a separate person.

d. The parent(s) perceives the child as the embodiment of a single quality, such as stupid, bad, or totally demanding.

5. Insufficient relationships:

a. The parenting person(s) is unable to give emotionally because of own isolation or coldness as a person.

b. The parent may be narcissistic and involved with self so that no more than physical care is provided. Her/his human system is closed to an extent that permits little or no transaction of feeling with her/his child.

c. Situational factors exhaust the caring person's energies, and little love is available for nurturance of the child. These demands may come from within the family system or from the surrounding environment (e.g., conditions of poverty or parental illness).

One or more of the above listed distorted or insufficient relationships are usually found in situations of child abuse.

b. Separation. Another form of defective dyad that complicates the child's efforts to establish a basic sense of trust is labeled *separation.* Whereas deprivation refers to insufficiency of relationship, separation refers to interruption of an already established relationship. It has to do with the need for continuity.

John Bowlby was appointed by the World Health Organization of the United Nations to study the effects of separation (Bowlby, 1962:205–214). In his own studies, he found that juvenile delinquency is highly correlated with separation experiences in the preschool years. His review of other research yielded similar results. He suggests that early childhood separation is a causal factor in some delinquents. Although this causal relationship has been questioned by a number of critics, his general findings have been accepted and incorporated into the body of knowledge of child development. He concludes that a separation in the first 3 months of life is not disturbing if an adequate parent substitute is provided. By the age of 3 months, the child has begun to form a social attachment or dyad with the parenting person and separation begins to present problems to the infant's efforts to cope with this first developmental task. Prolonged separation from the ages of 6–12 months is most deleterious and may not be reversible (Bowlby, 1966:117–119). Bowlby describes the characterological development that results from harmful separation as the "affectionless character," meaning a shallow and untrusting person who is unable to enter into intimate emotional transactions with other persons.

2. CONCLUSION. As the first major task of the life cycle, the first foundation in psychological development, the cornerstone of social functioning, the child must engage in striving to establish an essential, primary, social relationship. The interrelatedness of the physical, psychological, and social is most observable in this stage. The infant must survive as an organism and begin to evolve as a self, a person. The social resources available are largely centralized in the parenting person(s), and these resources must be provided to the infant to begin with; later, the child will seek them out. Inputs must be offered and must be accepted—nutritive inputs for physical survival and emotional inputs for psychological survival. The child will emerge from this interaction with a sense of being able or unable to count on others and self, a mixture of trust and mistrust, hope and hopelessness. It should be noted that this outcome is a blending, not necessarily of equal parts, of a basic sense of trust and a basic sense of mistrust.

B. *Differentiation of Self within the Family System*

The family system is the scene of the second and third of Erikson's crises of psychosocial growth. The mother–child dyad of the earlier task becomes a three-or-more-person system for these tasks. We review these crises as Erikson presents them.

1. AUTONOMY VERSUS SHAME AND DOUBT. This psychosocial crisis carries the special requirement for the establishment of a sense of self as an entity distinguished from the environment. This social expectation is congruent with the maturational development wherein the child is beginning to have the physical capacity to manage certain of his or her functions (e.g., ambulation and elimination). Conflicting desires to assert self as an autonomous being and to be uncertain of capacity to do so complete within the child who must risk relinquishing some of the comfortable dependency of the primary dyad.

The first assertion of self as separate is through communicating, "No, I can *will* not to do what you want me to do." The well-known negativism of the 2-year-old child is expression of the assertion of will. In the dominant culture of the United States, this became attached to the cultural dictates about toilet habits, neatness, and respect for property. In other cultures, such negative behavior is responsive to other themes important to those cultures. The corollary of negative assertion is self-control and independence. If the family environment does not provide limits for assertive behavior, the child may be stranded out on a limb beyond the capacity for self-management and direction. If the family environment overly restricts the available opportunities to test the capacity of his or her own behavior, the child will not have the chance to experience self as a separate and sovereign entity. In case of either extreme, the child will develop a sense of shame and doubt about the capacity to be a self-determining human system.

These preschool years are centered in the family system, the primary social unit of the culture. It is within this social climate that the child becomes a person, a social being. The autonomy crisis occurs in a field of experience with certain characteristics.

a. Sense of Self. It is necessary for the developing person to differentiate self within the nurturer – nurturee dyad. There must develop an awareness of existence separate from the sources of nurturance. The question must be dealt with, "Where do they end and where do I begin?"

b. Order. Sensitivity to order is characteristic of this age. Children frequently insist on sameness in their environment and become distraught when important objects are relocated. Predictability, continuity, and consistency of the physical environment assume a special meaning, analogous to these same qualities of the nurturing person in the first stage. The environment must be trustworthy because the child, partly at least, self-constructs from the environment. Learning to name objects provides a degree of control over them (Brown, 1965:267 – 276). Organization of the energies of the self-system is possible only when the suprasystem (immediate environment, in this instance) is organized sufficiently.

c. Assertion of Will. This occurs first in negation and then in positive ways. The child diligently attempts to experience being a self-directing entity. First physiologically, then psychologically, and finally socially, children find they can will to hold on or let go. Physiologically, there develops the capacity to hold on to or let go of sphincter musculature.

If toilet habits are of sensitive importance to the culture, a major battle may develop around this socializing task. Often toilet training is referred to as "breaking" the child, training in the same sense as breaking a wild mustang. To persuade the child to submit its will to that of the culture as represented by the family becomes of crucial importance. The child then is encouraged to feel a willing capacity through self-control according to cultural dictates.

Psychologically, a child can hold on to or let go of feelings. There is the choice of expressing frustration and anger directly through behavior or controlling it to please "others." If others communicate that these feelings are too dangerous to let out, there may be doubt of capacity to deal with them or a feeling of omnipotent powers. If others are unable or unwilling to provide any ground rules, the child may feel internal anarchy and shame.

Socially, one can hold on to or let go of self in relation to other systems. In holding on, the child may not engage in enough transactions with others and have insufficient feedback to enable the establishment of self within a social context. In letting go, self-boundaries may not be established, and the environment continues to be indistinguishable from self.

d. Ambivalences. Dichotomies of feeling (ambivalences) are a characteristic of this crisis. Polarities are a part of a process of differentiation. A child may alternately express a sense of love and hate, a sense of independence and total dependence, or a sense of pleasure and displeasure. This proximity of opposites must be coped with for the first time now, and how this is resolved will serve as the prototype for later life tasks. Erikson states that the cultural solution for this dilemma is embodied in the culture's approach to law and order.

e. Communication. Although language development has begun, much communication continues to be on a nonverbal level. Approval and disapproval are more important reinforcers of behavior and are conveyed by feeling more than word. The prohibitive "no-no" may convey prohibition or permission, approval, or disapproval, challenge or censure. The sensitive 2 or 3 year old may well be more responsive to parental feeling than to word meaning. Piaget finds the child's thought processes to be concrete and fragmentary; the concepts grasped are specific and often literal in their interpretation. At any one time, the child may feel all "good" or all "bad." It is essential at these times that the parents not view the child as either all "bad" or all "good."

The child who does not develop a sufficient sense of autonomy may have little or no sense of self. Manifestations of this include cloying dependency, general anxiety, foolhardy behavior, expecting others to always be in control, or severe withdrawal. Severe and pervasive negativism may also indicate lack of sufficient autonomy. A sense of autonomy is manifest in a measure of self-regulation and a capacity to enter into social transactions as a discrete entity.

In the latter preschool years, the child's primary social system continues to be the family, but he or she is beginning to establish linkages outside the family, such as playmates, neighbors, and extended family or family friends, and increasingly, adults and peers in organizational settings such as Headstart, day care, and preschool.

2. INITIATIVE VERSUS GUILT. This psychosocial crisis, refers to the second social task that must be coped with in and through the family system. The child must now be concerned with who she or he is qualitatively. With the accrued sense of autonomy, shame and doubt as to the capacity to self-will his or her own behavior, the child must next explore who he or she is. The oedipal conflict is central, as is the introjection of right and wrong. As Erikson views this task, the modalities are "to make" (to get) and "to make like" (to play). The bisexuality of the child, which has been apparent up to this time, is directed toward a gender as the culture defines it. The masculine "making" is intrusive, the insertion of self into the social world to accom-

plish purposes. The feminine form of "making" is inclusion of the social world to accomplish purposes. The genital tissue is hypersensitive at this stage, consistent with Freud's phallic stage.

Active insertion of self or inclusion behavior brings anticipated rivalry and threat of punishment. Identification, in the imitative sense, is a frequent method of coping with the child's inner compulsion to define self as a person and the culture's expectations that the boy will be like his father and the girl will be like her mother. Erikson states that the child could say to himself or herself, "I am what I can imagine I will be" (Erikson, 1968:122). The outcome of this crisis will be a mixture of a sense of initiative and a sense of guilt. The person with a goodly measure of sense of initiative will have purpose and direction as a part of her/his character, will be self-motivating, and will be able to initiate social behavior and transactions.

The "initiative" crisis has certain common characteristics.

a. Self. The essential psychosocial task is to create a qualitative sense of self. This exploration begins in the family and then expands outward into other social systems. Because of the arousal of awareness of genital sensations and the cultural expectations of sex differentiation, much of this is played out in the oedipal context. The child of each sex forms identification with the cultural role for that sex as represented by the parent of the same sex. Furthermore, each relates sexually to the parent of the opposite sex. The outcome of the oedipal complex (the complex refers to the sets of relationships) is, ideally, the child's relinquishment of the sexual interest in the parent of the opposite sex and identification with the parent of the same sex. This situation is complicated by the absence of cultural clarity about sex-differentiated behaviors, which affects the parents as well as the child. Sometimes the child identifies with the "stronger" parent regardless of sex, and sometimes the child does not know whom to identify with. Sometimes the child continues to wallow in the complexities of this task into the periods of subsequent crises. Energies are preempted and the later crises are inadequately dealt with. Ideally, however, a solution is reached, and the child expands the field of activity beyond the family and becomes occupied somewhat in other social transactions.

b. Play. Play becomes an important mode during the initiative crisis. Cognitive development has progressed to the extent that imagination can be controlled and used in various ways. Erikson considers play as "auto-therapeutic" in the sense that it is a rudimentary form of the adult capacity to create models and experiment with alternative behaviors without committing oneself to those behaviors. There are three stages in the hierarchical forms of play:

    i. autocosmic: the child's play begins with and centers on his or her own body

    ii. microspheric: the small world of manageable toys

iii. macrospheric: the sharing of play with others, first in parallel fashion and then in concert (Erikson, 1963:220–221).

In this phase, two kinds of play are important. One is the solitary, day-dreaming variety wherein the child can experiment with his or her fantasies and try out imaginings of what he or she would like to do and be. The second is peer play, wherein children together can work on solving their common concerns. Occasionally, play may carry fantasy beyond control or comfort and be very frightening. Pretending is a reassuring way to help establish the boundaries of reality, especially when adults occasionally enter into the "let's pretend" activities.

c. Consolidation and Integration. The initiative crisis is a time of transitional consolidation and integration. The exertion of self into environment with hope and expectation of influencing environment involves a measure of trust in the predictability of environment and one's own predictability, as well as a measure of control or will. To be able to do this enables children to imagine how they might eventually influence the world. Because they are concerned about their intactness and bodily integrity, they may be sensitive to anything that threatens this. They may be frightened by their own fantasies of power and hold themselves responsible for any calamity that befalls others close to them.

Again it is well to mention that the outcome of this particular crisis is a balance between initiative and guilt. This is the critical time for the development of conscience, which can be a tolerant guide or a punitive slavemaster, but a conscience there will be. It is hoped that the initiative will be directed toward "making" things work, people and objects, in the sense of integrated behaviors. But it can be "making" things and people in the exploitative sense. If the child can emerge from these family-centered growth tasks with a degree of trust in others and self, a sense of separateness as a person linked to others, and a sense of purpose, the child is well on the way to a fulfilling life plan congruent with his or her nature as a human being.

C. Definition of Self within Secondary Social Systems

1. INDUSTRY VERSUS INFERIORITY. The next labeled psychosocial crisis occurs in interaction with the organized components of the community: formal organizations (such as the school and church) and informal organizations (such as the neighborhood and the peer group). Physiological and cognitive maturation provide the capacities, and the culture furnishes the expectations. This is the period of development that Freud labeled *latency,* and that Piaget calls the phase of *concrete operations.* Erikson describes this fourth bipolarity as a sense of "industry versus inferiority." There are certain dominant characteristics of this particular crisis.

a. The theme is mastery. Mastery is sought over physical objects, one's physical self, social transactions, and ideas and concepts. It is the time to get about learning the technology and ways of one's culture. Institutionalized means are supplied by the culture whose investment is its own survival. The school is an institution charged with transmission of the cultural technology. The Future Farmers of America and 4H are organizations for communicating the culture of the agricultural community, and the "block gang" exists to transmit the ways of another specialized culture. Games, contests, and athletics are also examples of institutionalized culture carriers. The school-aged child participates in various of these organizations and in the process creates a sense of self as competent and incompetent.

b. Peer group experience is a necessary element in the crucible of testing mastery. It provides a social system parallel to the adult society with its own organization, rules, purposes, and activities. It is with the peer group that the child can test self and grow to mastery in social relationships with equals.

c. The outcome is again a mixture or balance of the two polar feelings. A dominant sense of inferiority may result from a lack of ability, but most frequently it derives from either insufficient accrual from previous crises or unclear or unreasonable adult or peer expectations and criteria of mastery. The idea of *sense* of industry or inferiority is important. It is the *feeling* the child has about his or her own competence that is crucial, not *actual* competence as measured by parental or adult standards. The person who embarks into adolescence with a feeling that he or she can do at least one thing very well is in a favorable position indeed.

a. Mastery. Entry into school is an important step to the child, to the parents, and to the culture. One of the very few clearly demarked way stations on the long trail to adulthood, it is the occasion when society insures that each of its young members becomes a participant in an organized, institutionalized culture. In the Midwest, the phrase "Kindergarten Roundup" well conveys the cultural investment in collecting together the mavericks and commencing the long process of acculturation to technological society. An arbitrary age is set for such entry, 2 years younger than the legal requirement for compulsory school attendance in most states, and there exists the social expectation that the child will be ready. If children are indeed ready, they are eagerly looking forward to entry into this new world. If unready because energies are still devoted to defining self in the family system or maturation is lacking, the child will have "problems." The child and parent(s) may not be ready for separation. The kindergartener may not be able to distinguish teacher from parent, or may not have self sufficiently organized to comply with expectations for settled and cooperative behavior.

If the culture transmitted by the school is alien or oppositional to the culture of the child's family, the young person is in a difficult, indeed untenable, position. The technology and ways of doing things the child has become familiar with and the development of an emerging sense of self and other within has, by this time, been incorporated as a part of self. To accept a differing way may be felt as an act of betrayal of self and family. If so, efforts toward mastery may well be invested outside of the school, seeking mastery of their own culture, not that of others.

Various writers have documented the existence of this dilemma as experienced by racial minorities in America: ghetto blacks (Baratz and Baratz, 1971), American Indians (Cahn, 1969:175–185) and Chicanos (Acuña, 1972). Acuña explains how the educational system serves to socialize the student into accepting and supporting the way things are. He states this is accomplished by "erasing the Chicano's culture, language and values and replacing them with Anglo-American culture, language and values" (Acuña, 1972:146). Such socialization is clearly a means of social control. This places the child in the untenable position of having to choose between cultures: family or school.

The school has evolved as an overinvested carrier of culture as changes in technology and family functions have occurred. As society has been bureaucratized so, too, has the school. On the one hand, the school has taken on the form of a bureaucratic organization, being a highly complex institution. On the other hand, the school has the charge of preparing the young for participation in the existing cultural ways. The child in the school is experiencing himself as a functioning participant in a bureaucratic organization. His success is seen as predictive of later success in adult life, whereas his lack of success is seen as predictive of adult failure. All of the current program-planning of a preventive nature is based on this premise and aimed at earlier identification of difficulty (Goertzel and Goertzel, 1962), even though there is minimal evidence to support this belief. Many persons who are successful in schooling are unsuccessful in other aspects of living, and the obverse is also true.

Society, then, expects the child to demonstrate mastery and competence primarily in the single institution of the school. This includes not only the technology of literacy but also physical mastery (gym class, intramurals, and athletic teams), arts and music, social mastery (social dancing, family life education), and domestic skills. There can be little wonder that the public schools find it very difficult to fulfill all the assignments the culture delegates. The school has even been required to deal with this society's primary problems, racism, sexism, and poverty.

b. Peer Group. The culture expects the child to proceed with the construction of a sense of competence primarily in the school. The next available secondary social system is the peer group. During latency, the child's primary connections continue to be within the family system; it is later in adolescence that the peer group may well take precedence over the family. The peer group of latency is modeled after the culture within which it exists. At its best, it is not very visible to the adult world and has its own parallel culture passed from generation to generation (2 or 3 years to a generation) with continuity, but frequent innovations, as well. The peer group is likely to be strongest in direct relation to the stability of the population it draws from. The peer group of suburbia is likely to be weak and transitory, whereas the peer group in the small town or city neighborhood probably will be stronger. In recent years, there has been a progressive undermining of the latency peer groups through adult take-over of them. In large sectors of the American culture, peer activities are increasingly organized and conducted by adults. The wider scope of school functions is a part of this; Little League baseball exemplifies another part; the day camp and "away camp" are yet others. The attention to individual fulfillment manifested by lessons in swimming, driving, tennis, golf, dancing, music, skiing, and so on has also served to diminish the availability of the child-run peer group. These adult managed and supervised activities undoubtedly serve to enable children to develop competence in a range of skills, but in the process, they minimize the child's opportunities to find out about self through interacting freely in a peer culture. This may be one reason why some disgruntled offspring of upper-middle-class parents head for communes and other experiments in peer living and why such experimentation continues later and later into the adult years.

   c. Outcome. Mastery of the ground rules of life seems important to the latency-age child. Piaget has investigated the development of moral judgment in the child and found that children of this age are quite occupied with justice and accept arbitrary or expiatory punishment as warranted (Piaget, 1932). As they grow older, the idea of retribution connected to the offending act and its natural consequences is favored. Grasp of the schema for moral judgment forms the basis for organized social relations.

   Problems of latency-age children can be grouped under three general headings. The one-word description most often heard is "immaturity." The largest portion of children referred to child guidance clinics and school special services are aged 8–11. The reasons for referral are:

   1. *Poor school performance.* Achievement of mastery of cultural technology does not measure up to the standards of school and/or parents. The child's school behavior disrupts his/her learning or the learning of others.

   2. *Symptoms* not expected at this age but not unusual in a younger child. Some of these are incontinence, fears, short attention span, hyperactivity, daydreaming, and not assuming expected responsibilities.

   3. *Social inferiority.* This may be the isolated child or the child who consistently associates only with younger children. A sense of social inferiority may be manifested by over-compensatory behavior (e.g., bullying or braggadocio). In the event societal expectations are excessive or opportunities for development of competence are too limited, a kind of cultural inferiority may result.

2. CONCLUSION. The middle years of childhood are the years for development of a sense of competence — to master self, social relationships, and the technology of the culture. The human system is relatively open to inputs from and transactions with the institutions of the community beyond the family system while retaining a primary linkage to the family. The growing person emerges from this with a sense of being somewhere on the continuum from industry to inferiority. Erikson opines that the child's expression of a sense of competence could be stated, "I am what I can learn to make work" (Erikson, 1968:127).

D. Transitional Self: Identity beyond Social Systems

This is the pivotal growth crisis in the Eriksonian formulation. It is the time when the biological and social imperatives demand that the evolving person pull herself or himself together and create an identity that goes beyond the accumulation of social roles. In our culture, this more or less coincides with that period of life referred to as adolescence. We prefer to use the term *adolescenthood* to convey the idea of more than a transitory hiatus. The adolescent span of life has become a distinct life phase with its own culture, role expectations, and style.

The concept of identity has entered into the conventional wisdom, and references are replete to individual "identity," group "identity," and even national "identity." Erikson's use of this concept is precise and applies primarily to the individual. He sees the social–psychological task as one of integration, or more precisely reintegration, of the various components of the person into a whole. It is a process of ego synthesis that culminates in ego identity, meaning an internal consistency and continuity of meaning to others. This goes beyond the sum of childhood identifications and is not merely a synthesis of social roles.

Again the concept is that of *sense* of identity. It is not a state of being that can be objectively evaluated by observers. "An optimal sense of identity . . . is experienced merely as a sense of psychosocial well being. Its most obvious concomitants are a feeling of being at home in one's body, 'a sense of knowing where one is going' and an inner assuredness of anticipated recognition from those who count" (Erikson, 1968:165).

Erikson first labeled the opposite pole *identity diffusion*, later *role confusion*, and in later writings (Erikson, 1968) he settled on *identity confusion*. This term conveys the antithesis of integration, the dispersion of selves, the alienation of the self. From a systems viewpoint, one could say that internal and external tensions press the human system to reintegrate its component parts to undertake new purposes and responsibilities. If the components of personality are not brought together, the person is fragmented and has no solid sense of self. Energy is incapable of being put to concerted use — the person is entropic. Schizophrenia, with its disorganization of personality components and particular disparity between thought and feeling, is the extreme form of such fragmentation. Interestingly, the earlier term for schizophrenia was *Dementia Praecox,* meaning "insanity of the young." Some theorists, Erikson among them, hold that true schizophrenia cannot appear until adolescence, since it is foremost a condition of pathology of identity and identification. A sensitive expression of this condition is:

> I am learning peacefulness, lying by myself quietly
> As the light lies on these white walls, this bed, these hands.
> I am nobody; I have nothing to do with explosions.
> I have given my name and my day-clothes up to the nurses
> And my history to the anesthetist and my body to the surgeons (Plath 1966:10).

Erikson has focused much of his study and writing on the adolescent crisis, and the reader is presumed to be familiar with this from any of the available sources, especially *Identity: Youth and Crisis* (1968), *Childhood and Society* (1965), or "The Problem of Ego Identity" (1959). Two of the characteristics of adolescence he identifies, the moratorium and negative identity, are particularly worthy of emphasis.

The idea of *moratorium* refers to a socially sanctioned period of delay wherein the person is allowed to, or forced to, postpone assumption of the full responsibilities of adult commitments. The culture relaxes its expectations and is more permissive. It is then a time when the person can try out a variety of identifications, modes of behavior, and roles without a total commitment to see them through. The moratorium is both necessary and desirable to allow for integration, regrouping of forces, and the setting of life goals. The extension of adolescence in United States culture can be viewed as a socially imposed moratorium that may be of an unnecessarily long duration for some. Moratoria may occur at times other than adolescenthood for some individuals. Often, they are part of the making of decisions or major changes in life goals. If the individually determined moratorium is more prolonged than societal expectations allow, there is reason for concern, for example, Biff in *Death of a Salesman.*

> HAPPY: Well, you really enjoy it on a farm? Are you content out there?
> BIFF: WITH RISING AGITATION: Hap, I've had twenty or thirty different kinds of jobs since I left home before the war, and it always turns out the same. . . . And whenever Spring comes to where I am, I suddenly get the feeling, my God, I'm not gettin' anywhere!. . . . I'm thirty-four years old, I ought to be makin' my future. That's when I come running home. And now, I get here, and I don't know what to do with myself. AFTER A PAUSE: I've always made a point of not wasting my life, and everytime I come back here I know that all I've done is to waste my life.
> HAPPY: You're a poet, you know that, Biff?You're a—you're an idealist!
> BIFF: No, I'm mixed up very bad. Maybe I ought to get married. Maybe I oughta get stuck into something. Maybe that's my trouble. I'm like a boy. I'm not married, I'm not in business, I just—I'm like a boy (A. Miller, 1955:18–19).

Negative identity is another important Eriksonian concept. Negative identity is an identity that occurs in a situation in which available positive identity elements cancel each other out. This can occur because any identity is better than no identity at all. Negative identity is "an identity perversely based on all those identifications and roles which, at critical stages of development, had been presented to them as most undesirable or dangerous and yet also as most real" (Erikson, 1968:174). The confirmation of the person's identity comes from within (this is what I feel like) and from without (this is what you say I am). This confirming feedback cycle operates in like manner for any identity. Although one's sense of identity can and does change subsequent to adolescence, this is the crucial time for identity formulation, the greatest opportunity for such development, and the time of greatest vulnerability.

1. ADOLESCENTHOOD. There are more definitions of adolescence than there are definers. For a time, adolescence was synonymous with the teen years, but that is no longer an adequate definition. The idea of the "between years" is frequently encountered, but that has an implication of "floating." For our purposes at this time, we will employ the following definition, recognizing that it, too, is open to dispute. "Adolescence is probably in all societies that period which comes after the biological and hormonal changes of puberty have set in but before the individual's incorporation into society as an independent adult" (Ktsanes, 1965:17).

Adolescence then begins with biology and ends by social definition. The commencement is organism, the process is organism interacting with culture, and the termination is culturally determined. The seemingly unique element in adolescenthood in the society of the United States is the increasing evidence of adolescence becoming a distinct cultural phase of life in the same sense as childhood and adulthood.

Rather than reviewing all the elements of this crisis, we will approach it from one angle. Freud has been widely quoted as holding the belief that the two elements of a successful life were the capacities to love and work. The task of identity formulation can be viewed as the prerequisite for loving and working. We will discuss briefly some of the characteristics of the adolescent and the culture that are important to development of these capacities.

a. The Peer Group. The associations of the adolescent with peers are extremely necessary experiences. The peer groups take over some of the parental roles of support and value-giving. Peers absorb much of the available social energy of the youth and become a primary reference group. The person can use his/her peers to find him/herself through the mechanism of projecting his/her own ego fragments onto others. The person can experience and express his feelings of tenderness toward others, beyond the family system, on new planes. Various roles are available to be tried and either accepted or discarded. Friedenberg finds an attitude of respect for competence developing in the peer group (Friedenberg, 1962:39) and experience wherein power and influence can be tasted (Friedenberg, 1962:59). In the peer society, the adolescent can begin to be a lover and a worker in close interaction with others. This experience occurred within the family system but only in the role of the child. Adulthood requires more of the person than continuance as a loving, working child within the primary family system. For some youths, the peer group becomes of overriding importance, totally replacing the family. Such substitution of one kind of childlike dependency for another does not suffice for the creation of a unique identity. Some youths remain largely separated from a peer group and still manage to pull together an identity. Peers are, however, an essential part of the adolescent's struggle to find out who he/she is, what he/she values, and what he/she wants to become.

b. Education. The school continues to be the primary social institution as it was during latency. Increasingly, occupational choices are centered in the school experience. As occupational choice has become broader and minimally determined by parents' occupations, it also has become more imbedded in the school. Curricula are constructed to expose the youth to a range of potential occupations, performance is self-evaluated and judged by peers, parents, and guidance counselors, and the youth is guided in certain directions. A number of factors enter in determining the "real" possibilities for any given youth. Some of these are race, sex, socioeconomic status, and "intelligence." In a society where persons are signified by what they do rather than by who they are, one's choice of work role or, more precisely, occupational aspiration takes on great meaning to one's sense of who one is and what one may become (see the discussion of bureaucracy and personality in Chapter 5, "III. Structure: The Bureaucratic Situation." While Paul Goodman, Erich Fromm, Ivan Illich, John Holt, and others have commented upon the absurdity of this institutionalization of identity development, it continues to be, for most youth, the sole situation for acquiring a sense of self as a "worker" and a potential worker.

2. ADOLESCENTHOOD AND CULTURE. The adolescent (a person between puberty and full adult status in matters of love and work) is an important person in our culture. There are certain evident manifestations of this importance.

Economically, the adolescent has the status of a part-time worker and a full-time consumer. The jobs allotted to youth are service rather than production and often are substitutes for parental role performance (e.g., babysitting, food preparation and serving, carrying grocery bags, and home maintenance). This age group is a primary target of advertising and merchandising. Whole industries in fashion and leisure-time facilities cater to an adolescent market. Pop culture, fashion, food, and music styles originate in the youth culture and permeate the broader culture through the impetus of the advertising and distribution industries.

There is a dual ambivalence that exists between the world of adulthood and the world of adolescenthood. This manifests itself in the family system, where parents and youth are both torn between wanting the youth to grow up and wanting him/her to remain children. The ambivalence appears in the community and broader culture as the adult envies the vitality of youth, whereas youth envies the power and control possessed by adults. Adults may covet youthfulness as a denial of death as increasing evidences of age cause this denial to be more difficult to maintain. Similarly, youth may covet power and control because of the prolonged dependence the culture dictates. This dual ambivalence complicates the forming of a sense of identity because the separation into camps may contribute to the foreclosure of adolescent identity rather than adult identity. Such identity foreclosure is problematic in a society wherein choices are many or increasing in scope. It places the person, who early in life made a commitment to a total identity, in the position of, at some point in his/her life cycle, seeking a moratorium to experiment with other identity possibilities. This may be highly problematic when others are expecting the person to continue to be the foreclosed identity.

As Erikson views this, adolescence requires the culture to make adjustments because the generation coming up has absorbed the past, lives in the present, and must confront the future with new forms of living constructed of material not available to their parents. Margaret Mead (1970) points out that youth in fact is the arbiter of our culture. Youth thus finds this construction of both its own lifestyles and those of the culture a bewildering task. Mead helps to explain why youth experiments widely in lifestyles and countercultural activities.

As many writers conclude, each generation has a wide range of characteristics from which the culture can select those best suited to cultural survival. Considering culture as a social system, youth can be considered a component of that system and, as such, a source of energy and tension. As the system seeks steady state, this component must stand in working relationship to other components. In order for this to happen, the system will change (accommodate) or seek to maintain the status quo (assimilate). Within this dynamic interaction, the individual must seek an identity, and the culture its survival.

Ideology is a special concern of the person in the throes of the identity crisis. The adolescent has a special sensitivity toward, as well as a particular vulnerability about, ideology. As Erikson puts it so clearly, "It is through their ideology that social systems enter into the fiber of the next generation and attempt to absorb into their lifeblood the rejuvenative power of youth" (Erikson, 1968:134). Erikson's psychohistorical studies of Martin Luther and Gandhi demonstrate how individual solution of ideological aspects of their personal identity crises provided creative innovations that profoundly affected the total culture. Certainly Malcolm X may be a more recent example of personal identity crises transmuted into the ideology of a subculture.

The special virtue attached to identity is *fidelity*. The proclivity of youth to invest self and substance in a belief, an idea, or a person with total commitment and faith is generally acknowledged. The search for the Holy Grail, the Crusades, the willingness to follow the knight in shining armor be he Arthur Pendragon or Eugene McCarthy are examples. To experience total and complete volitional commitment seems a necessary element of an emerging identity.

The characteristic troubles of the adolescent identity crisis are legion. For convenience they may be grouped under the following headings.

1. *Psychosis* usually appears in the form of schizophrenia. This is a condition of identity confusion in the extreme. The traits may be considered as exaggerations of "normal" traits.
   a. feelings of dislocation and estrangement
   b. total docility or exaggerated rebelliousness
   c. emotional lability, rapid mood swings
   d. feelings of everyone being against one
   e. idealism that seems to be a denial of reality
   f. confused body image and sexual identification
2. *Neurosis* can also be described as identity confusion in that there is a conflict between the ideal self and other selves. Stone and Church define neurosis as "a state of conflict between antagonistic and often unformulated inner tendencies that drains his energies and hampers his functioning" (Stone and Church, 1968:550). The alternating excitability and lethargy of adolescents may well be examples of this tendency.
3. *Delinquency* is a socially defined deviant adaptation to inner demands and outer expectations. It may be the result of particular internal conflicts ("acting out" behavior), or it may be an individual or group rejection of cultural values of a larger system. The negative identity previously referred to may be manifested by delinquent behavior. While delinquency may be pathological, it may, as said earlier, be better than no identity at all. One view of delinquency holds that some antisocial behavior may represent a striving for growth.

In summary, it can be said that the growth crisis of adolescence is the necessity of trying to pull together who one is. "To be or not to be, that is the question" states part of the issue confronting the adolescent. *What* to be or *what not* to be is the second part of the question. The later tasks of adulthood are to a large degree dependent on the outcome of this crisis. A person must be fairly certain and comfortable with self before he or she can enter into a sustained intimate relationship with another.

E. *Perpetuation and Sharing of Identity*

This is the phase of the lifespan generally referred to as the adult years. Adulthood as a period of life development (personality growth) has seldom been dealt with in theories of personality development. Erikson is notable for his attempt to conceptualize the adult "productive" period as an integral part of his lifecycle formulation. Pertinent here are the sixth and seventh growth crises, "Intimacy versus Isolation" and "Generativity versus Self-absorption."

The critical task of "intimacy versus isolation" is to enter in an involved, reciprocal way with others sexually, occupationally, and socially. One's sense of identity is merged with another to form a new primary social system. To put it another way, the person completes the transition from the family of origin to the family of procreation. This social crisis addresses itself to the activities of love and work. If one is unable to merge an intact sense of self with others, the outcome is a sense of isolation and polarization of affect. The concept of alienation (discussed later in this section) is another expression of a sense of isolation. The theme of love, genital and reciprocal, is central to this crisis.

The two adult crises Erikson delineates are closely related, and the second describes the task of "generativity versus self-absorption." This involves the task of active participation in establishing the next generation. In his discussion of this crisis, Erikson explains why he chose to express the quality of feeling as *generativity* rather than creativity or productivity (Erikson, 1959:97). He sees the term *generativity* as being derived from "genitality" and "genes." This particularly emphasizes responsibility for perpetuation of the species and the culture. The theme of this task is caring, caring in the sense of nurturance and caring in the sense of concern for others. In his 1973 Jefferson Lecture, Erikson further elaborated his notion of the adult virtue of caring (Erikson, 1974). The polar sense of stagnation refers to caring primarily and essentially for one's self, with pseudointimacy with others and indulgence of one's self. Stagnation can be viewed as the "closed" human system, defending its equilibrium and minimally engaging in transactions of feelings with others.

The adult period, then, requires the person to perpetuate his/her own ego identity while sharing this sense of identity with others. The culture establishes social institutions, particularly procreative and child-rearing, through which this task can be accomplished. At stake is a sense of well-being for the person, continuity for the culture, and survival for the species.

Other approaches to describing personality development in the mature years generally take one of two forms: either an idealized definition of maturity or a listing of the problems to be overcome. A popular book,

Passages, by Gail Sheehy (1976), uses Erikson's adult stages as a vehicle for commenting on the experiences of the many adults she interviewed. Her findings support Erikson's contention that a person can, and does, "go back again," in the sense of redressing the balances of earlier stages.

It is possible to group the central social expectations for adults under four related headings:

1. SEXUALITY. Adult sexuality is an important aspect of intimacy and the sharing of identity. Genitality, in the sense of the capacity for full and mutual consummation of sexual potential, is only characteristic of adulthood. Sexual mutuality forms the foundation of the procreative family system. Erikson says, "love then, is mutuality of devotion forever subduing the antagonisms inherent in divided function" (Erikson, 1964:129). Sexuality is not confined to sexual activities and includes generativity and child rearing.

2. GENERATIVITY AND CHILD REARING. The assumption of responsibility for transfer of the culture and nurturance of the young fulfills the destiny of the adult of a species. This requirement is particularly stressful for those without a firm sexual identity and the capacity to merge self-interest with the interest of others. This, of course, is not confined to being a biological and rearing parent. It includes a participatory generative role that is gratifying to self and others, such as child care, teaching, or a role that benefits future generations. This is one form of participation in social processes.

3. PARTICIPATION IN SOCIAL PROCESSES. To further the purposes of society and culture requires a measure of subordination of personal needs to the needs of others. This is particularly stressful to those who isolate and retain a primarily self-indulgent orientation. An additional complicating factor here is the omnipresent dilemma of the conflict between the values of individualism and social responsibility. Milton Mayer has formulated a provocative position statement on this dilemma (Mayer, 1969). One of the most important aspects of social participation is work.

4. WORK. A work function is required that is gratifying to self and to society. In our culture, work has become a major organizing theme, and we construct our life styles around it. The usual response of the adult to a "Who am I?" kind of question is more often than not an occupational response. When we meet a person who does not work, it is usually difficult to relate to him/her until it is determined *why* he/she does not work. Something must be "wrong." Recent writings on the rehabilitation of schizophrenics have emphasized the necessity of employment if there is to be hope of continued remission. Work provides an identification, represents social usefulness, and is the means of organizing a life. A recent study of unemployed workers in Great Britain concluded:

According to the findings, a prolonged and fruitless search for work is, in general, accompanied by the following emotions in sequence: first, shock at being out of a job; second, optimism, during search for work; third, when the search fails, pessimism, anxiety and distress follow; and finally, a fatalistic attitude toward life ensues (World of Work Report, 1977:24).

Certain work identifications are still tied to the place of work ("I work in the mines" or "I work in the quarry"), but other designations are also used. Now most people express work identification as either "I do" or "I am." Traditionally the "I am" designation belonged to the classical professions of law, the clergy, and medicine. The "I do" description is usually a shorthand job description ("I sell shoes" or "I wire circuit boards"). The press toward professionalization in a wide variety of occupations is an attempt to establish a work identification of the "I am" type.

The escalation of occupational titles is another indication of the significance of work as a determinant of status and position. The farmer has become the agribusiness person, the undertaker is now the mortician or funeral counselor, the barber has become the hair stylist, and the salesman is an account executive.

Erich Fromm presents a clear and concise exposition of the idea that the marketplace orientation of our society determines and maintains work identity (Fromm, 1962). Fromm suggests that one is valued not for what one is but for what one seems to be; this is then related to supply and demand. "Image" becomes crucial and the person must project the "right" image to be successful. Advertisers are concerned with product image, campaign managers with candidate image, National Association of Social Workers with social work image, and National Education Association with teacher image. One's value as a person is not self-defined but is dependent on value definitions by others within the criteria of the marketplace. Fromm describes how this has led to the cult of adaptability, with the prime value invested in changeability. Work, then, has permeated our social systems to an extent we seldom recognize. The "problem" segments of society are defined and labeled by work status:

a. *The nonworkers.* These include the age groups of youth and the aged. These are not unemployed persons; they are clearly identified as non-workers, not eligible for work identification. The aged are in a worse plight than the young, since school is viewed as a kind of pseudowork and "student" serves as a work status. It is likely that organizations of, and in support of, the elderly will be successful in redefining their status to allow them to continue to be active workers. Changes in practices regarding retirement and pensions permit older workers to continue the socially valued status of worker. This may be acceptable not only because of the difficulty of elders in finding useful roles but also because of the financial strains of providing retirement benefits to the rapidly increasing numbers of retired workers.

b. The unemployed. These are society's greatest concern. Proposed welfare programs, such as workfare, place primary emphasis upon putting the unemployed to work and rewarding persons who make the effort to seek and sustain work. The able-bodied unemployed person violates social prescriptions. That person is without a work identification—in fact, the primary social identity may well be *unemployed.* Since the idea of "right to work" holds sway, such unemployment is attributed either to lack of opportunity or to individual deficiency.

c. The unemployable. These people present a particular problem because of the humanitarian values held by society. Changing the ground rules and expectations of the worker, as Goodwill Industries and sheltered workshops do, makes it possible to remove some people from this classification. This fulfills the promise of the right to work and provides an opportunity structure wherein this right can be realized. Even so, there remains an irreducible residue of unemployables. Although they are "pitied rather than censured," the lack of work identification is judged an important personality deficiency by the person and his significant others.

Unemployment is a significant source of alienation. Alienation is a phenomenon of adulthood, since it is a condition of one's identity. It is, in some respects, the adult counterpart of maternal deprivation. Alienation means the absence or insufficiency of those vital, intimate connections with one's social environment that call forth and sustain one's identity. "Structural unemployment" itself fosters alienation as it breaks the connection between the person and the work environment. In most definitions, alienation also includes the feelings and perceptions that accompany these lacks, including the following:

1. There may be lowered self-esteem, a gulf between societal expectations and perceived self. The person may also experience *self-estrangement* and *self-alienation,* a gulf between ideal and actual self, as though one were someone (or something) other than oneself.

2. *Anomie* is a term coined by Emile Durkheim to convey what, in systems terminology, may be viewed as absent or faulty linkage with larger social systems. This is experienced as "rootlessness," "normlessness," or "meaninglessness." The person does not experience a culture of shared meanings, or a sense of shared norms of behavior.

3. The person may perceive (correctly or not) that her/his deeply held values are not shared or supported by his/her social environment, and the converse, that one does not share society's (or family's) values. It is from such polarized tensions that creativity emerges in persons and the social system with which they are in conflict and for which they care deeply.

One of the most frequently examined forms of alienation is *work-alienation*. The federal study, *Work in America* (1973), found a high proportion of workers who found their work to be stifling and unrewarding. Reactions to the publication of these findings were mixed; some questioned their validity (Gomberg, 1976:401–411), but others, such as Studs Terkel, found the findings congruent with their own observations and studies. Terkel had earlier described an alienated work situation as a "Monday through Friday kind of dying" (Terkel, 1975:xiii). *Work in America* noted three particular alienating conditions: lack of autonomy, in the sense of freedom to perform assignments without close, arbitrary supervision; lack of advancement or opportunity for personal growth; and lack of opportunity to make decisions.

The largest group of alienated workers is probably female. In addition to the reasons already mentioned, women face other alienating circumstances. They frequently are not taken as seriously as career-oriented workers. They usually are not paid as well as men for performing the same jobs. They are underutilized, less frequently advanced, and less frequently chosen for specialized training.

In conclusion, the crises of adulthood are focused in the socially defined expectations for the person to intimately involve himself or herself with others in the creation and maintenance of the social systems that enable the culture and species to survive. An adult who does not do this will be isolated, self-seeking, and stagnant. To paraphrase Erikson, the adult may say, "I am what I can love and care for and about."

F. Conservation of Identity (Elderhood)

This is the concluding task of the life cycle and, as such, can be characterized as the crisis of aging. *Conservation* refers to consolidation, protection, and holding on to the ego integrity one has accrued over a lifetime in the midst of loss and divestment of usual roles and functions. The positive sense of conservatism is that identity passes from one social context to another and yet remains the same. The self maintains its continuity and consistency from one social system to another.

Erikson's polarity during the waning years of life is "Ego integrity versus disgust and despair." This is the culmination of the previous seven crises. Integrity refers to "the ego's accrued assurance of its proclivity for order and meaning—an emotional integration faithful to the image-bearers of the past and ready to take, and eventually to renounce, leadership in the present" (Erikson, 1968:139). It is the capacity of persons to accept their life histories, to see the effect they have had on their world through their relationships, and to accept their mortality. The other pole, the sense of disgust, is characterized by bitterness and refusal to accept death as the finite boundary of the personal life cycle.

A definition of "aging" or "age" is difficult to formulate to everyone's satisfaction. In one sense, the aging process begins at birth. Socially, age is defined by function. For example, most professional athletes are "old" by the time they are 35 (coincidentally, the same as the minimal age qualification for President), while a Supreme Court Justice is thought to be still functional at 80. Some industries consider the 40-year-old worker as too old to be hired. Social Security currently sets the age of retirement as 65 for men and 62 for women, although this will increase in the next century, as is now planned. A utilitarian definition is suggested by Birren.

> A person is "old" or, better perhaps, "aging" when he is so regarded and treated by his contemporaries and by the younger generation and when he himself has read the culturally recognized individual and social signs symbolic of membership in the generation of elders. The only matter of individual choice open to the old person has to do with whether he wishes to accept or postpone belief in his new identity and act accordingly (Birren, 1959:280).

Erikson comments that "it is perfectly obvious that if we live long enough, we all face a renewal of infantile tendencies—a certain childlike quality, if we're lucky, and senile childishness, if we're not. The main point is again a developmental one: only in old age can true wisdom develop in those who are thus 'gifted'" (Evans, 1967:53–54).

The tasks of aging in our culture are nicely summarized by Birren in quoting Simmons' cross-cultural studies. These are:

> 1. To live as long as possible, at least until life-satisfaction no longer compensates for its privation, or until the advantages of death seem to outweigh the burden of life.
> 2. To get more rest, relief from the necessity of wearisome exertion at humdrum tasks, and protection from too great exposure to physical hazards— opportunities, in other words, to safeguard and preserve the waning energies of a physical existence.
> 3. To remain active participants in personal and group affairs in either operational or supervisory roles—any participation, in fact, being preferable to complete idleness and indifference.
> 4. To safeguard or even strengthen any prerogatives acquired in long life, i.e., skills, possessions, rights, authorities, prestige, etc.
> 5. Finally, to withdraw from life, when necessity requires it, as honorably as possible, without too much suffering, and with maximum prospects for an attractive hereafter (Birren, 1959:864–865).

As earlier stated, aging is characterized by the theme of conservation. It involves relinquishment of certain patterned investments of self. The nature of transactions with other human systems is necessarily modified. The involved elements of identity can be discussed under a few general headings.

1. WORK ROLE AND OCCUPATIONAL IDENTIFICATION. This has a more profound effect on those with the "I do" work identification than it does on those with an "I am" identification. The retired doctor continues to be seen as a doctor, but the retired shoe salesman is no longer a salesman. Willy Loman in *Death of a Salesman* is an example of a man faced with such a loss of work identity. The relinquishment of the work role is particularly difficult for such a man because so much feedback about his worth is tied to this role. Loss of work role usually is accompanied by a marked reduction in income and the necessity of readjustment in standard of living. Such persons are deprived of membership in their former work system. The situation may be somewhat different for women, who may face losses of roles (children leave home or husband dies) earlier. On the other hand, many of both sexes who retire from their work roles easily make the transition to a more leisurely pace of living. The time is available to pursue other interests; the economic means may or may not be. In view of the large percentage of people who opt for early retirement, it is conceivable that the work identification of "retired" substitutes for the identification as active worker.

2. INTIMATE TIES. As the person's friends, acquaintances, and spouse die, that person is again faced with separation experiences faced as a child or young adult. Those who were part of one's personality system are gone. One must undergo the painful process of withdrawing (decathecting) attachments to them at a time when it is most difficult to establish new linkages to replace the former ones. One may not be able to modify one's own structure sufficiently to accommodate new attachments. One's environment narrows, and perhaps the intensity of the remaining attachments is increased. Such attachments may become "overinvested"; for example, a pet or a formerly casual acquaintance may suddenly become all-important. If no replacements or reinvestments are accomplished, the person may turn inward, seeking energy internally, or may "bank the fires," attempting less and seeking equilibrium on a lower level of interaction with the environment.

3. SEXUAL INTERESTS. Research on the sexual activity of the aged, limited as it is, indicates a gradual decline in frequency over the entire adult period. There is no sharp decline at any particular age. As overt sexual engagement declines, the aged may find it difficult to express or receive tenderness or affection in other ways; grandchildren frequently serve this function for grandparents. Because socially our stereotype of the aged indicates that such needs somehow disappear, we are often unrealistic about the behavior of the aged.

Unfortunately, society's understanding of this is blocked by our tendency to deny sexuality in the elderly persons. For example, some residences for the elderly prohibit physical manifestations of affection, do not allow the closing of doors when one has a visitor of the opposite sex, and in a few reported instances, prohibition of holding hands. The available evidence indicates that sexual companionship (with or without sexual activity) is as important to most elderly persons as it is to those of earlier adult years.

4. PHYSICAL ABILITIES, PARTICULARLY SENSORY AND MOTOR. Physiologically, the number of taste buds declines with age, eyesight and hearing may suffer impairment, and walking may become difficult. These limitations necessarily handicap the aging person in maintaining contact with the accustomed social environment. The person's world may be narrowed to the walls of his or her own home, and to the television set.

The older person's self-concept may be threatened by these losses. An example is the 60-year-old man who refuses to be beaten at tennis. The person's reaction may be to deny the losses and to demand of himself what she/he was capable of at a younger age, or the reaction may be depression and unrealistic refusal to do what one is still capable of. It is common among the aged to make reasonable adjustments to less acute faculties — to read larger type, to be more accurate rather than fast — in other words, to make the best of one's abilities. Such realistic adjustments are part of the person's integrity and maintenance of self.

5. INTELLECTUAL ABILITIES. Borrowing from Piaget, it could be concluded that as one's schemas multiply and more adequately account for one's experience, they become progressively less modifiable. Accommodation declines, while assimilation increases. The aged may exclude stimuli from awareness, to limit the energy interchange with those in their environment. He/she may become less concerned with interpreting and storing new information and more concerned with preserving previous information, sometimes literally in the form of scrapbooks, possessions of a deceased spouse, or a house that was the family dwelling. Either of these intellectual patterns, becoming more closed or remaining open, may be performed to allow integrity. Erikson's "wisdom" implies, in one's past, the accrued identity of a lifetime. "Despair and disgust" implies closure but may well include feedback that indicates the person's alienation from his environment. Thus it implies openness as well.

6. LIFE REVIEW. Life review may include the feeling that time is running out. There are no alternatives possible "at this late date." In *Death of a Salesman*, Willy depends upon his son, Biff, to reassure him of his own integrity, but Biff has neglected to write to his father:

> BIFF: I was on the move. But you know I thought of you all the time. You know that, don't you pal?
> LINDA: I know, dear, I know. But he likes to have a letter. Just to know that there's still a possibility for better things (A. Miller, 1955:55).

With the United States' cultural emphases on youth, external appearance, and robust health, to the neglect of wisdom, experience, and the ability to cope with travail, the frail elderly may find themselves in a disadvantaged state and their integrity unnoticed. This poem sensitively describes such a state:

GREY, WRINKLED AND KNARLED

You look at me
And quickly turn away.
You see a living corpse,
Both hair and skin are grey.

    You see
Wrinkled, knarled hands,
    Grasp feebly,
At the wheel of my chair,
    Which propel me at an incredibly
    slow
      erratic
      pace,
To the dismal table
    where
    with
Sixty others, I take my meals.

You note the acrid stench
    of stale
Crusted
    Urine
      Ignored
    By an apathetic staff,
      Overiding
The other nonspecific odors,
    Best described as
      age.

Every one here either
    Stinks,
    Feels spongy
    Or is ugly.

Our sounds are mingled cacaphonies
    of incoherent mumblings.

Faces of visitors reflect sorrow and pity.
    Even our children
Only notice
    Drooling mouths,
      Yellow teeth
    And
      Vacant stares.

    They think
Our brains
    are also barren and lifeless
Our pain is intensified
    by their patronage.

If only they would realize,
    Our minds are full
    Of sweet memories
Of youthful better times.

Frustration churns within us,
For in this state,
        Of physical deterioration,
        We can not
        Communicate
        or
Express our thoughts
So others may understand.

We only ask you to be sensitive
To the non-verbal signs
        of the
        Love within us.

The tear
    At the corner of
    My eye
    IS
    REAL
                    —Glenn Shaffron

Aged persons as human systems must find their steady state, their identity, among the social systems to which they are related. Erikson says that "man as a psychosocial creature will face, toward the end of his life, a new edition of an identity crisis which we may state in the words, 'I am what survives of me' " (Erikson, 1968:141). What survives are the human systems one has been related to and part of: persons, families, groups, organizations, communities, societies, cultures. These human systems in turn affect other persons who are being born and who are developing. This is why Erikson calls it a *life*cycle — not the life cycle of an individual, alone, but the cycle of life itself: the human system.

> Webster's Dictionary is kind enough to help us complete this outline in circular fashion. Trust (the first of our ego values) is here defined as "the assured reliance on another's integrity," the last of our values. . . . It seems possible to further paraphrase the relation of adult integrity to infantile trust by saying that healthy children will not fear life if their elders have integrity enough not to fear death (Erikson, 1963:269).

In this book, we examine and speculate upon social systems — human systems. We state in the chapter on families, that "a family, then, is to be construed as patterns of relatedness as they converge in a person." We can now say the same about all social systems; systems are patterns of relatedness as they converge in individual persons. Systems do not exist without persons; persons can exist only because of social systems of which they are, or have been at some time in their life, a part. Understanding of the implications of this, and applying that understanding to one's life and practice, are the highest wisdom to which a systems approach can contribute.

SUGGESTED READINGS

Ainsworth, Mary D. Salter.
   1969 "Object Relations, Dependency and Attachment: A Theoretical Review of the Infant-Mother Relationship," *Child Development*, Vol. 40, No. 4, pp. 969–1025.
       The definitive review of early attachment; grouped under headings of Psychoanalytic, Social Learning and Ethological.
Bringuier, Jean-Claude.
   1980 *Conversations with Jean Piaget*, Chicago: The University of Chicago Press. Covering the years 1969–1976, these conversations were first published in France in 1977. Not for the novice student of Piaget since the book presumes some knowledge of Piaget's theory.
Butler, Robert N.
   1975 *Why Survive? Being Old in America.* New York: Harper and Row.
       A landmark work on the plight of the aged in United States society. Dr. Butler, a psychiatrist, was the first director of the National Institute on Aging. This book was awarded a Pulitzer Prize in 1976.
Cottle, Thomas J.
   1972 *The Abandoners: Portraits of Loss, Separation and Neglect.* Boston: Little, Brown.
       A series of detailed cameos sampling the necessary pain and joy of "growing up." Cottle includes his own life experience. He is unusually sensitive to the realities of being.
Erikson, Erik.
   1968 *Identity: Youth and Crisis.* New York: Norton.
       In this book Erikson expands on the critical task of identity formation within the context of contemporary issues. It is also one of many of his writings to discuss the total life cycle. (This book has been used as the small-map text for this chapter.) For a thorough explanation of his life cycle formulation see *Childhood and Society*, 2nd ed. (New York: Norton, 1963).
Freud, Sigmund.
   1949 *An Outline of Psychoanalysis.* New York: Norton.
       The last book that Freud wrote, it is a concise explanation of the principles derived from his life's work. It is *strongly* recommended that the reader be familiar with Freud's own expression of his ideas rather than relying on the interpretations of latter-day critics.
Maier, Henry W.
   1978 *Three Theories of Child Development.* New York: Harper and Row. (Third Edition)
       The author, a social worker, examines, compares, and contrasts the theories of Erikson, Piaget, and Sears. He further looks at them as bases for social work practice.

Newman, Barbara M., and Philip R. Newman.
   1979   *Development Through Life: A Psychosocial Approach.* Homewood, Ill: Dorsey Press.
      This is an excellent text for any student who has not had the opportunity to study human development from a life cycle perspective. It is comprehensive and thorough.
Phillips, John L., Jr.
   1969   *The Origins of Intellect: Piaget's Theory.* San Francisco: W. H. Freeman.
      This is an excellent source for anyone wishing to read further about the contributions of Piaget. Especially good are the Preface, Chapter 1, and Chapter 5.
Rosen, Hugh.
   1980   *The Development of Sociomoral Knowledge.* New York: Columbia University Press.
      While this is largely a presentation, review and critique of Kohlberg's work, it briefly summarizes the work of Piaget and others who preceded Kohlberg. Thorough and impartial.
Sheehan, Susan.
   1977   *A Welfare Mother.* New York: New American Library, Mentor.
      This is the story of Carmen Santana, a welfare mother of indomitable spirit. To the welfare industry she is both consumer and product. The author has written in a documentary form with a minimum of editorializing.

LITERARY SOURCES

Bergman, Ingmar.
   1960   "Wild Strawberries." In *Four Screenplays.* New York: Simon and Schuster.
      An elderly man reminisces about the past as a means of dealing with the present. The film version is sensitively done.
Malcolm X (with the assistance of Alex Haley).
   1966   *The Autobiography of Malcolm X.* New York: Grove Press.
      This moving autobiography exemplifies all levels of human systems and a person's interactions with them. It highlights how systems affect the person and how a person can influence systems.
McCullers, Carson.
   1940   *The Heart Is a Lonely Hunter.* Boston: Houghton Mifflin.
      The story of a man with a severe hearing loss who cares for and about others. The movie version is beautifully done.
Miller, Arthur.
   1949   *Death of a Salesman.* New York: Bantam Books.
      Miller's classic play of everyman caught up in a world of change and attempting to live in the past.
Thompson, Ernest.
   1979   *On Golden Pond.* New York: Dodd, Mead.
      Two elders struggling to maintain their integrity. The interaction between them and the youngster well illustrates Erikson's comment at the conclusion of this chapter, i.e., healthy children will not fear life if their elders have integrity enough not to fear death.

EPILOGUE

He laughed because he thought they could not hit him
He did not imagine that they were practicing how to miss him.

Brecht

This chapter addresses some of the implications of a social systems view of the world. Does it make a difference what we perceive and believe? Unequivocally and emphatically, yes! Within each of the realms in which helping professions operate (either literally or figuratively), there exists divergence of opinions regarding the most efficacious means of effecting change. In the health fields, for example, there is contention as to which will be more effective: basic research into the physiology of disease processes or greater concentration devoted to environmental conditions affecting public health? Which will improve patient care more, intensified training of the nurse practitioner or restructuring the organizations that deliver health care services? In the field of social services, should there be expansion of clinical training of social workers or should efforts be directed toward restructuring social agencies to permit more participation and self-determination by clients?

The listing of such choices could be an inexhaustible exercise. The relevant point here is that the practitioner, or student, often chooses his or her means of intervention on the basis of beliefs and values that have not been articulated, examined, analyzed and evaluated.

The "helping professions" and professional disciplines that are oriented toward practical application of theory are often accused of shallowness and lack of philosophical clarity. Those who practice these professions are condemned by both external and internal critics for failure to be explicit about their assumptions and suppositions, their definition of their competencies, the nature of their helping processes and the goals of their activities.

There is, beyond a doubt, some truth to these charges. We, in the helping professions, share idealism, impatience, and dissatisfaction with the world as it is, and we seek pragmatic approaches to action. Frequently, our desire for change outdistances our willingness to thoughtfully examine the philosophical and intellectual structures that are the foundations of our practice. In this chapter, we comment briefly on these intellectual and ethical foundations.

I. THE ESSENCE OF A SOCIAL SYSTEMS APPROACH

You have noted a number of concepts, introduced in the first chapter and developed in subsequent chapters, dealing with the dimensions of partness and wholeness; of oppositeness, duality and polarities. Whether we are examining the idea of holon (Chapter 1, "I. The Systems Model") or seeking the locus of change in the individual or society, we remain in the realm of part – whole relatedness, examining how the one is interdependent with the other. Systems thinking provides a means to appraise, understand, and accept the inevitable unity and separateness of part and whole. As Ronald Jones succinctly states the "problem:"

From approximately 3,000 B.C. in the East when Emperor Fu Hsi is believed to have discovered the idea of Yin and Yan as they are embodied in T'ai Chi, and since about 400 B.C. in the West when Heraclitus and Plato struggled with the problem of opposites, scholars have tried to resolve the mystery of how many parts come to be a unified whole. This adds up to 5,000 year old problem. Throughout the history of ideas the problem of the One and the Many, of part-whole relations, of order and structure has appeared over and over again. Names we are all familiar with identify this as the *pons asinorum.* Nicholas of Cusa (15th Century), Giambattista Vico (17th Century), and more recently Cassirer, Whitehead, von Bertalanffy, Koestler, Sorokin, and Polanyi have made this problem *the* problem. The problem of the integration of differentiated parts, of harmony in diversity, is not merely a problem for idle, remote, and academic speculation.

To make certain that this connection is clearly before us, let me elaborate a bit. It seems to me that the *sine qua non* of man's knowledge, happiness, and existence is to be found in the idea of the reconciliation of differences. It matters little whether we talk about mental health and personality structure or whether we talk in the context of society. It matters little what the size of the society is. It makes little difference whether the society is a marriage, a small group, a large industrial organization, a community, a nation, or many nations, the basic issue is that of the reconciliation of the individual with the group, the organization, the integration of parts into a unified whole. These issues are all matters of totality, wholeness, completeness, unity, order, structure (Whyte, Wilson and Wilson, 1969:284).

But this is not a "problem" in the sense of solving, curing, or otherwise having done with it. It is rather a perplexing mystery of human existence. Systemic thinking is a means toward perceiving the issue of the one and the many as a foundation for systems well-being. In fact, the one cannot exist without the many and the many cannot exist without the one.

The question of differences and opposites has always puzzled humankind. Aristotle dealt with it by holding that an entity, quality, or phenomenon must be one thing or another. A contemporary statement of that belief is, "If you aren't part of the solution, then you are part of the problem."

Earlier Greek philosophers, Anaximander and Heraclitus, postulated that differences must be merged or balanced into a state of wholeness. Hippocrates drew from the thought of Anaximander in developing the doctrine of "coction." According to the Hippocratic formulation, in the course of each disease, there occurs a "crisis" when either coction occurs or the patient dies. Strictly speaking, coction is the action that combines the opposing humours so that there results a perfect fusion of them all. According to Hippocrates, "a disease was supposed to result when the equilibrium of the humours, from 'some exciting cause' or other was disturbed, and then nature, that is the constitution of the individual, made every effort through coction to restore the necessary balance," (Jones, 1923, p. 1ii). "Balance" is equivalent to steady state.

In Warmington's and Rouse's translation of *Phaedo*, Plato reports a passage wherein Socrates insists that the Hippocratic method is right and then discourses on the nature of opposites.

> "Then don't consider it as regards men only," he said; "if you wish to understand more easily, think of all animals and vegetables, and, in a word, everything that was birth, let us see if everything comes into being like that, always opposite from opposite and from nowhere else; whenever there happens to be a pair of opposites, such as beautiful and ugly, just and unjust, and thousands of others like these. So let us enquire whether everything that has an opposite must come from its opposite and from nowhere else. For example, when anything becomes bigger, it must, I suppose, become bigger from being smaller before."
> "Yes."
> "And if it becomes smaller, it was bigger before and became smaller after that?"
> "True," he said.
> "And again, weaker from stronger, and slower from quicker?"
> "Certainly."
> "Very well, if a thing becomes worse, is it from being better, and more just from more unjust?"
> "Of course."

"Have we established that sufficiently, then, that everything comes into being in this way, opposite from opposite?"

"Certainly."

"Again, is there not the same sort of thing in them all, between the two opposites two becomings, from the first to the second, and back from the second to the first; between greater and lesser increase and diminution, and we call one increasing and the other diminishing?"

"Yes," he said.

"And being separated and being mingled, growing cold and growing hot, and so with all; even if we have sometimes no names for them, yet in fact at least it must be the same everywhere, that they come into being from each other, and that there is a becoming from one to the other?"

"Certainly," said he (*Plato Dialogues:* 475–476).

The one and the many is just such a set of unified opposites and partakes in the nature of opposites. Each system, as the observer recognizes it and separates it from its environment, is simultaneously part/whole or one/many (i.e., holon) and contains a duality within itself; it also can be viewed as one pole of a larger duality. Again, it should be stressed that these are ways of thinking, not descriptions or discoveries of "reality."

It follows, then, that controversies over whether it is better to work toward changing individuals (the one) or to work toward changing society (the many) are of little practical consequence unless the inseparability is fully taken into account. When that is so, it becomes apparent that both (one and many) are inextricably responsible for change. Systems thinking provides a means to observe, understand, and intervene into these interactive processes.

II. IMPLIED VALUE AND ETHICAL POSITIONS

Most of the recurring questions about our social-systems approach have had to do with values and ethics. Are there implicit values that should be explicated? Can a perspectivistic model be value free? Does a social-systems approach remain at a descriptive level and thus mitigate against change? Does it foster maintenance of status quo?

In our judgment, there are certain value stances implicit in a social systems perspective. Holding no brief for the specific labels, we will discuss five aspects under the following rubrics:

1. interdependence
2. interaction
3. conservation and conflict
4. change
5. egalitarianism

A. Interdependence

The systems view presented in this book begins with the postulate that each human or social entity exists and thrives as both whole and part. It cannot continue existence in isolation and, therefore, must participate in interdependent relatedness with other entities.

A dramatic example can be drawn from medieval times. The walled castle-keep, surrounded by a moat with a bridge that could be drawn closed and sealed, was designed to protect a community from attack. It proved, often, to be virtually unassailable with the weaponry available. However, the adversary could simply make sure the boundary was not crossed and that the castle remained isolated to draw the occupants out, for in time the only other alternative was death. The modern day naval blockade follows the same strategy. A system then cannot be completely autonomous indefinitely. Neither can it exist without some measure of autonomy. Without some distinguishable quality of separateness it could not be defined or identified within its environment. To deny the quality of autonomy and separateness is to deny human and social existence. "They all look alike to me" is an expression of such denial of humanity. Interdependent relatedness is a melding of dependence and autonomy (independence) and is both desirable and necessary to the well-being of social systems.

B. Interaction

Similiarly, interaction is essential and, therefore, desirable to systems' well-being. Energy exchange and feedback (as a regulatory mechanism) require and depend upon interaction. Furthermore, the quality of mutuality is, and will be, assumed to be a necessary aspect of interaction. Systems interactions are reciprocal and cyclical. That which is valued is mutuality of interaction: systems affecting and being affected by other systems of the same magnitude (horizontal) and differing magnitudes (vertical). Certainly interdependence and interaction are closely related, but they are not precisely the same.

The Old Order Amish continue to employ the social sanction of "shunning" with members who have seriously violated expectation of behavior. The practice of shunning allows the person to remain in the community system but prohibits others from mutual interaction with the person being shunned. Within this custom, the quality of interdependence remains largely unchanged whereas the quality of mutual interaction is greatly diminished.

C. Conservation and Conflict

Conservation of system integrity is necessary and desirable to system vitality and well being. Conservation is defined as "the act of preserving, guarding or protecting; preservation from loss, decay, injury or violation" (Webster, 1980:389). It is important to discriminate between conservation as so defined and conservatism, "the practice of preserving what is established; disposition to oppose change in established institutions and methods" (Webster, 1980:389).

Paradoxically, conservation and conflict stem from the same systemic source: a system seeks to protect its integrity in ways that well might interfere with or prevent the protection of another system's integrity. The achievement of synergy, or constructive interchange, occurs only with effort and expenditure of energy. Entropy occurs without effort; conflict requires effort. In those situations where conflict can be avoided, it can be averted only with effort. Conflict, then, is not merely accidental and unfortunate; it is an inherent, legitimate, and frequently unavoidable event that is a direct result of system(s) striving for integrity (i.e., wholeness). As Stafford Beer (1981) puts it, "Resistance is only people continuing to be who they are."

D. Change

Change, too, is necessary and desirable to systems vitality. Without change, systems tend to "feed" on themselves or their environment, depleting the internal or external resources, shrink, and eventually cease to exist (i.e., become entropic). Our view of systems presupposes an interactive balance between change and conservation, the mixture varying according to circumstances. In some instances, conservation requires change, especially for purposes of preservation from decay, injury, or violation. Change is the means to the genesis of "new life" for systems purposes, while conservation maintains or augments the "life stream" of the system.

E. Egalitarianism

Our systems view is permeated by values of equality and equity. Interdependence and mutuality of interaction dictate that systems of varying magnitudes be perceived as being equally necessary to systemic functioning. Within a systems approach, the centrality of the concept of hierarchy strikes some as inimical to an egalitarian value. In point of fact, "hierarchy" is a structural aspect of systems organization that implies no value or power differential.

Egalitarianism does not imply maintenance of a status quo or an absence of conflict. As stated earlier, conflict is inherent within and between systems; and the fact that each system strives to maintain its integrity inevitably leads to conflict. Thus, egalitarianism does not denote absolute equality but rather a recognition that each system posseses its own "will to live," its place in the sun; and thus has, existentially, as much right as any other system, subsystem, or suprasystem to survive. It is the carrying-out of this survival that engages the system in the other values/ethical positions of interdependence, interaction, conservation, conflict, and change. It could be interpreted as tragedy, in the Greek sense, for in order to preserve itself, any system must risk "losing itself."

This conundrum applies to all systems. In order to survive, each must change to some degree. This is the ultimate egalitarian imperative of a social systems approach.

BIBLIOGRAPHY

Ackerman, Nathan W. (1958). *The Psychodynamics of Family Living: Diagnosis and Treatment of Family Relationships.* New York: Basic Books.

Acuña, Rodolpho. (1972). *Occupied America: The Chicano Struggle Toward Liberation.* San Francisco: Canfield.

Adams, Margaret. (1971). "The Compassion Trap—Women Only." *Psychology Today.* November: 71ff.

Agger, Robert E. (1978). *A Little White Lie.* New York: Elsevier.

Ainsworth, Mary D. Salter. (1969). "Object Relations, Dependency, and Attachment: A Theoretical Review of the Infant–Mother Relationship." *Child Development* 40(4): 969–1025.

Albee, Edward. (1963). *Who's Afraid of Virginia Woolf?* New York: Pocketbook Cardinal.

Alissi, Albert S. (1980). *Perspectives on Social Group Work Practice.* New York: The Free Press.

Anderson, Ralph E. (1981). Book Review of Jeremy Rifkin, *Entropy,* In *Social Development Issues,* Vol. 5, No. 1, 1981.

Ardrey, Robert. (1966). *The Territorial Imperative.* New York: Atheneum. (1970). *The Social Contract.* New York: Atheneum.

Arendt, Hannah. (1962). *The Origins of Totalitarianism.* Cleveland: World Publishing Co.

Argyris, Chris. (1968). "Personal vs. Organizational Goals." In Robert Dubin (ed.), *Human Relations in Administration.* Third Edition. Englewood Cliffs, NJ: Prentice-Hall.

Asimov, Isaac. (1970). "In the Game of Energy and Thermodynamics You Can't Break Even." *Smithsonian,* August.

Auger, Jeanine Roose. (1976). *Behavioral Systems and Nursing.* Englewood Cliffs, NJ: Prentice-Hall.

Bailey, Joe. (1980). *Ideas and Intervention: Social Theory for Practice.* London: Routledge & Kegan Paul.

Bales, Robert F. (1950). *Interaction Process Analysis.* Cambridge: Addison-Wesley.

Banfield, Edward. (1961). *Political Influence.* New York: The Free Press.

Baratz, Stephen, and Joan Baratz. (1971). "Early Childhood Intervention: The Social Science Base of Institutional Racism." In Norman R. Yetman and C. Hoy Steele (eds.), *Majority and Minority.* Boston: Allyn and Bacon.

Barnard, Chester. (1968). "Dilemmas of Leadership in the Democratic Process." In

Robert Dubin (ed.), *Human Relations in Administration.* Third Edition. Englewood Cliffs, NJ: Prentice-Hall.

Barnes, John. (1954). "Class and Committees in a Norwegian Island Parish." *Human Relations* 7, February, 1954.

Barnet, Richard, and Ronald E. Müller. (1974). *Global Reach.* New York: Simon and Schuster.

Beer, Stafford. (1981). "Death is Equifinal." Eighth Annual Ludwig Von Bertalanffy Memorial Lecture. *Behavioral Science* 26: 185–196.

Bell, Colin, and Howard Newby. (1972). *Community Studies:* An Introduction to the Sociology of the Local Community. New York: Praeger.

Bennis, Warren G. (1969). "Post-Bureaucratic Leadership." *Transaction* 6: 44ff.

Bennis, Warren G., and Herbert A. Shepard. (1956). "A Theory of Group Development." *Human Relations* 9(4): 415–437.

Bensman, Arthur J., and Joseph Vidich. (1958). *Small Town in Mass Society.* Revised Edition, 1968. Princeton: Princeton University Press.

Berne, Eric. (1966). *The Structure and Dynamics of Organizations and Groups.* New York: Grove.

Berrien, F. K. (1971). "A General Systems Approach to Human Groups." In Milton D. Rubin (ed.), *Man in Systems.* New York: Gordon and Breach.

Bertalanffy, Ludwig Von. (1967). *Robots, Men and Minds.* New York: George Braziller, Inc.

Bierstedt, Robert. (1961). "Power and Social Organization." In Robert Dubin (ed.), *Human Relations in Administration.* Englewood Cliffs, NJ: Prentice-Hall. Second Edition.

Billingsley, Andrew. (1968). *Black Families in White America.* Englewood Cliffs, NJ: Spectrum.

Bird, Caroline. (1966). *The Invisible Scar.* New York: David McKay.

Birdwhistell, Ray L. (1970). *Kinesics and Context: Essays on Body Motion Communication.* Philadelphia: University of Pennsylvania Press.

Birren, James E. (1959). *Handbook on Aging and the Individual.* Chicago: University of Chicago Press.

Blau, Peter M. (1956). *Bureaucracy in Modern Society.* New York: Random House.

Blumer, Herbert. (1967). "Society as Symbolic Interaction." In Jerome G. Manis and Bernard N. Meltzer (eds.), *Symbolic Interaction.* Boston: Allyn and Bacon.

Boehm, Werner. (1965). "Relationship of Social Work to Other Professions." In *Encyclopedia of Social Work.* New York: National Association of Social Workers.

Boguslaw, Robert. (1965). *The New Utopians.* Englewood Cliffs, NJ: Prentice-Hall.

Bohen, Halcyone H., and Anamaria Viveros-Long. (1981). *Balancing Jobs and Family Life.* Philadelphia: Temple University Press.

Bormann, Ernest G., and Nancy C. Bormann. (1980). *Effective Small Group Communication.* Minneapolis: Burgess Publishing Company.

Boulding, Elise. (1972). "The Family as an Agent of Change." *The Futurist* 6(5): 186–191.

Bowen, Murray. (1978). *Family Therapy in Clinical Practice.* New York: Jason Aronson.

Bowlby, John. (1962). *Deprivation of Maternal Care.* Geneva: World Health Organization. (1966). "Child Care and the Growth of Love." In Morris L. Haimowitz and Natalie Reader Haimowitz (eds.), *Human Development.* Second Edition. New York: Crowell.

Brill, Charles. (1974). *Indian and Free.* Minneapolis: University of Minnesota Press.

Bringuier, Jean-Claude. (1980). *Conversations with Jean Piaget.* Chicago: The University of Chicago Press.

Brodey, Warren M. (1977). *Family Dance: Building Positive Relationships through Family Therapy.* Garden City, New York: Anchor.

Brown, Roger. (1965). "How Shall a Thing Be Called?" In Paul Mussen *et al.* (eds.), *Readings in Child Development and Personality.* New York: Harper and Row.

Bruner, Jerome. (1968). *Toward a Theory of Instruction.* New York: Norton.

Buckley, Walter. (1967). *Sociology and Modern Systems Theory.* Englewood Cliffs, NJ: Prentice-Hall. (1968). *Modern Systems Research for the Behavioral Scientist* (ed.). Chicago: Aldine.

Butler, Robert N. (1975). *Why Survive? Being Old in America.* New York: Harper and Row.

Cahn, Edgar S. (1969). *Our Brother's Keeper: The Indian in White America.* Cleveland: World Publishing.

Califano, Joseph A., Jr. (1981). *Governing America.* New York: Simon and Schuster.

Campbell, D. T. (1958). "Common Fate, Similarity and Other Indices of the Status of Aggregates of Persons as Social Entities." *Behavioral Science* 3: 14–25.

Capelle, Ronald G. (1979). *Changing Human Systems.* Toronto: International Human Systems Institute.

Capra, Fritjof. (1977). *The Tao of Physics.* New York: Bantam Books, Inc.

Cartwright, Darwin, and Alvin Zander. (1960). *Group Dynamics.* Evanston, Illinois: Row, Peterson.

Caudill, Harry M. (1963). *Night Comes to the Cumberlands.* Boston: Little, Brown.

Chatterjee, Pranab, and Raymond A. Koleski. (1970). "The Concepts of Community and Community Organization: A Review." *Social Work* 15(3): 82–92.

Christaller, Walter. (1966). *Central Places in Southern Germany.* Englewood Cliffs, NJ: Prentice-Hall.

Christenson, James A., and Jerry W. Robinson, Jr. (1980). *Community Development in America.* Ames, Iowa: Iowa State University Press.

Churchman, C. West. (1968). *The Systems Approach.* New York: Dell.

Coles, Robert H. (1970). *Erik H. Erikson: The Growth of His Work.* Boston: Little, Brown.

Cooley, Charles Horton. (1967). "Looking Glass Self." In *Symbolic Interaction.* Jerome G. Manis and Bernard Maltzer, eds. Boston: Allyn & Bacon.

Corey, Gerald, Marianne Schneider Corey, Patrick J. Callanan, and J. Michael Russell. (1982). *Group Techniques.* Monterey, CA.

Coser, Lewis. (1964). *The Functions of Social Conflict.* New York: The Free Press.

Cottle, Thomas J. (1972). *The Abandoners: Portraits of Loss, Separation and Neglect.* Boston: Little, Brown. (1974). *A Family Album: Portraits of Intimacy and Kinship.* New York: Harper/Colophon.

Coyle, Grace. (1948). *Group Work with American Youth.* New York: Harper and Row.

Dahl, Robert A. (1957). "The Concept of Power." *Behavioral Science* 2: 201–215.

Davenport, Judith, and Joseph Davenport III. (1982). "Utilizing the Social Network in Rural Communities." *Social Casework* 63(2): 106–113.

Dessler, Gary. (1980). *Organization Theory: Integrating Structure and Behavior.* Englewood Cliffs, NJ: Prentice-Hall.

Dewey, John. (1966). *Democracy and Education.* New York: The Free Press.

Domhoff, G. William. (1967). *Who Rules America?* Englewood Cliffs, NJ: Prentice-Hall. (1971). *The Higher Circles.* New York: Vintage Books. (1974). *The Bohemian Grove and Other Retreats.* New York: Harper and Row.

Drucker, Peter. (1982). *The Changing World of the Executive.* New York: Truman Talley Books.

Dubin, Robert. (ed.). (1961). *Human Relations in Administration.* Second Edition.

Englewood Cliffs, NJ: Prentice-Hall. (1968). *Human Relations in Administration.* Third Edition. Englewood Cliffs, NJ: Prentice-Hall.

Dunn, Edgar S. (1980). *The Development of the U.S. Urban System.* Volume I. Baltimore: The Johns Hopkins University Press.

Durkheim, Emile. (1968). "Division of Labor and Interdependence." In Robert Dubin (ed.), *Human Relations in Administration.* Third Edition. Englewod Cliffs, NJ: Prentice-Hall.

Durkin, James E. (1981). *Living Groups: Group Psychotherapy and General System Theory.* New York: Brunner/Mazel.

Elkind, David. (1968). "Giant in the Nursery—Jean Piaget." *New York Times Magazine,* May 26.

Engel, George. (1977). "The Need for a New Medical Model: A Challenge for Biomedicine." *Science* 196: 129–136.

Engels, Friedrich. (1902). *The Origin of the Family, Private Property and the State.* Chicago: C. H. Kerr.

Epstein, Norman. (1982). "A Residence for Autistic and Schizophrenic Adolescents." *Social Casework* 63(4): 109–214.

Erikson, Erik H. (1950). In M. J. E. Senn (ed.), *Symposium on the Healthy Personality.* New York: Josiah Macy, Jr. Foundation, Passim. (1958). *Young Man Luther.* New York: Norton. (1959). "The Problem of Ego Identity." In George S. Klein (ed.), *Psychological Issues.* New York: International Universities Press. (1963). *Childhood and Society.* Second Edition. New York: Norton. (1964). *Insight and Responsibility.* New York: Norton. (1968). *Identity: Youth and Crisis.* New York: Norton. (1969). *Gandhi's Truth.* New York: Norton. (1974). *Dimensions of a New Identity.* New York: Norton. (1975). *Life History and the Historical Moment.* New York: Norton.

Etzioni, Amitai. (1964). *Modern Organizations.* Englewood Cliffs, NJ: Prentice-Hall.

Evans, Richard. (1967). *Dialogue with Erik Erikson.* New York: Harper and Row.

Farb, Peter. (1968). *Man's Rise to His Civilization as Shown by the Indians of North America from Primeval Times to the Coming of the Industrial State.* New York: Dutton.

Feldman, Frances Lomas, and Frances H. Scherz. (1967). *Family Social Welfare.* New York: Atherton.

Flavell, John H. (1963). *The Developmental Psychology of Jean Piaget.* Princeton: Van Nostrand.

Flink, James J. (1976). *The Car Culture.* Cambridge: MIT Press.

French, Robert Mills. (1969). *The Community.* Itasca, Illinois: Peacock.

Freud, Sigmund. (1949). *An Outline of Psychoanalysis.* Translated by James Strachey. New York: Norton.

Friedenberg, Edgar Z. (1962). *The Vanishing Adolescent.* New York: Dell.

Friedman, Edwin H. (1971). "Family Systems Thinking and a New View of Man." *Central Conference of American Rabbis Journal* 28(1).

Fromm, Erich. (1942). *The Fear of Freedom.* London: Routledge & Kegan Paul. (1955). *The Sane Society.* New York: Rinehart. (1962). "Personality and the Market Place." In Sigmund Nosow and William H. Form (eds.), *Man, Work, and Society.* New York: Basic Books.

Galbraith, John Kenneth. (1968). *The New Industrial State.* New York: Signet Books.

Galper, Jeffry. (1970). "Nonverbal Communication in Groups." *Social Work* 15(2): 71–78.

Gardner, Hugh. (1978). *The Children of Prosperity: Thirteen Modern American Communes.* New York: St. Martin's Press.

Garland, James A. (1965). "A Model for States of Development in Social Work Groups." In Saul Berstein (ed.), *Explorations in Group Work*. Boston: Boston University School of Social Work.

Giner, Salvador. (1976). *Mass Society*. London: Martin Robertson.

Gintis, Herbert. n.d. *Neo-Classical Welfare Economics and Individual Development*. Cambridge, MA: Union for Radical Political Economics, Occasional Paper No. 3.

Glazer, Nathan, and Daniel P. Moynihan. (1970). *Beyond the Melting Pot: The Negroes, Puerto Ricans, Jews, Italians, and Irish of New York City*. Cambridge: MIT Press.

Goertzel, Victor, and M. B. Goertzel. (1962). *Cradles of Eminence*. Boston: Little, Brown.

Goffman, Erving. (1961). *The Presentation of Self in Everyday Life*. Indianapolis: Bobbs-Merrill. (1973). *Asylums: Essays on the Social Situations of Mental Patients and Other Inmates*. New York: Doubleday. (Originally published in 1961 by Aldine.)

Goldberg, Lorna, and William Goldberg. (1982). "Group Work with Former Cultists." *Social Work* 27(2): 165–171.

Golembiewski, Robert T., and Arthur Blumberg. (1970). *Sensitivity Training and the Laboratory Approach*. Itasca, Illinois: Peacock.

Gomberg, William. (1976). "Job Satisfaction: Sorting Out the Nonsense." In Robert A. Sutermeister (ed.), *People and Productivity*. New York: McGraw-Hill.

Goode, William J. (1964). *The Family*. Englewood Cliffs, NJ: Prentice-Hall.

Goodman, Paul. (1960). *Growing Up Absurd*. New York: Random House.

Gordon, Robert A., and James E. Howell. (1968). "Current Opinions about Qualifications for Success in Business." In Robert Dubin (ed.), *Human Relations in Administration*. Third Edition. Englewood Cliffs, NJ: Prentice-Hall.

Gouldner, Alvin W. (1961). "Organizational Analysis." In Warren G. Bennis *et al.*, (eds.), *The Planning of Change*. New York: Holt, Rinehart, and Winston.

Granovetter, Mark S. (1977). "The Strength of Weak Ties." Pp. 347–367 in Samuel Leinhardt (ed.), *Social Networks*. New York: Academic Press.

Gusfield, Joseph R. (1975). *Community: A Critical Response*. New York: Harper and Row.

Hacker, Andrew. (1982). "Farewell to the Family." *New York Review of Books* XXIX: 37–45.

Hall, Edward T. (1961). *The Silent Language*. Greenwich, Conn.: Fawcett. (1969). *The Hidden Dimension*. Garden City, New York: Doubleday. (1977). *Beyond Culture*. Garden City, New York: Doubleday Anchor Press.

Hare, A. Paul. (1976). *Handbook of Small Group Research*. New York: The Free Press.

Hearn, Gordon (ed.). (1969). *The General Systems Approach: Contributions Toward An Holistic Conception of Social Work*. New York: Council on Social Work Education.

Heraud, Brian J. (1970). *Sociology and Social Work*. Oxford: Pergamon.

Hersh, Richard H., Diana Pritchard Paolitto, and Joseph Reimer. (1979). *Promoting Moral Growth: From Piaget to Kohlberg*. New York: Longman.

Herzberg, Frederick, Bernard Mausner, and Barbara Bloch Synderman. (1959). *The Motivation to Work*. New York: Wiley.

Hewitt, John P. (1979). *Self and Society*: Second Edition. Boston: Allyn and Bacon.

Hillery, George A., Jr. (1968). *Communal Organizations: A Study of Local Societies*. Chicago: University of Chicago Press.

Hollingshead, August. (1969). *Elmtown's Youth*. New York: Wiley.

Holt, John. (1972). *Freedom and Beyond*. New York: Dutton.

Homans, George. (1950). *The Human Group.* New York: Harcourt, Brace and World.

House, R. J. (1975). "Etzioni's Theory of Organizational Compliance." Pp. 74–80 in Henry L. Tosi (ed.), *Theories of Organization.* Chicago: St. Clair Press.

Hunter, Floyd. (1953). *Community Power Structure.* Chapel Hill: University of North Carolina Press.

Huxley, Julian. (1964). *Man in the Modern World.* New York: Mentor Book.

Ichheiser, Gustav. (1949). "Misunderstandings in Human Relations: A Study in False Social Perception." *American Journal of Sociology* 55(2).

Illich, Ivan. (1973). *Tools for Conviviality.* New York: Harper and Row.

Jackson, Don. (1970). "The Study of the Family." In Nathan W. Ackerman (ed.), *Family Process.* New York: Basic Books.

Jaffee, Adrian H., and Virgil Scott (eds.). (1960). *Studies in the Short Story.* New York: Holt, Rinehart and Winston.

Johnson, David W., and Frank P. Johnson. (1982). *Joining Together: Group Theory and Group Skills.* Englewood Cliffs, NJ: Prentice-Hall.

Jones, W. H. S. (translator). (1923). *Hippocrates: With an English Translation.* London: William Heinemann.

Kahn, Alfred J. (1969). *Theory and Practice of Social Planning.* New York: Russell Sage Foundation.

Kahn, Si. (1982). *Organizing.* New York: McGraw-Hill.

Kanter, Rosabeth Moss. (1970). "Communes." *Psychology Today* (2): 53ff.

Katz, Alfred H., and Eugene I. Bender. (1976). *The Strength in US.* New York: New Viewpoints.

Keniston, Kenneth. (1970). "Youth: A 'New' Stage of Life." *The American Scholar* 39(4): 631–654.

Kephart, William M. (1976). *Extraordinary Groups: The Sociology of Unconventional Lifestyles.* New York: St. Martin's Press.

Kimberly, John R., Robert H. Miles, and Associates. (1981). *The Organization Life Cycle.* San Francisco: Jossey-Bass.

Kinkade, Kathleen. (1973). *A Walden Two Experiment: The First Five Years of Twin Oaks Community.* New York: Morrow.

Kinton, Jack (ed.). (1978). *American Communities Tomorrow.* Aurora, Illinois: Social Science Services and Resources.

Kleiman, Carol. (1980). *Women's Networks.* New York: Ballantine Books.

Knowles, Louis L., and Kenneth Prewitt (eds.). (1969). *Institutional Racism in America.* Englewood Cliffs, NJ: Prentice-Hall.

Koestler, Arthur. (1967a). *The Act of Creation.* New York: Dell. (1967b). *The Ghost in the Machine.* London: Hutchinson. (1979). *Janus: A Summing Up.* New York: Random House.

Koestler, Arthur, and J. R. Smythies (eds.). (1971). *Beyond Reductionism: New Perspectives in the Life Sciences.* Boston: Beacon.

Kovel, Joel. (1976). *A Complete Guide to Therapy: From Psychoanalysis to Behavior Modification.* New York: Pantheon Books.

Kroeber, Alfred Louis, and Clyde Kluckhohn. (1952). *Culture: A Critical Review of Concepts and Definitions.* Cambridge, MA: The Museum.

Ktsanes, Thomas. (1965). "Adolescent Educational Values and Their Implications for the Assumption of the Adult Role." In *Adolescence: Pivotal Period in the Life Cycle.* Tulane Studies in Social Welfare, 8.

Kvaraceus, William C. (1959). *Delinquent Behavior, Culture and the Individual.* Volume 1. Washington, D.C.: National Education.

La Barre, Weston. (1954). *The Human Animal.* Chicago: University of Chicago Press.

Landsberger, Henry A. (1961). "Parsons' Theory of Organizations." In Max Black (ed.), *The Social Theories of Talcott Parsons.* Englewood Cliffs, NJ: Prentice-Hall.

Lasch, Christopher. (1979a). *The Culture of Narcissism.* New York: Warner Books. (Originally published in 1979 by W. W. Norton & Company.) (1979b). *Haven in a Heartless World: The Family Besieged.* New York: Basic Books.

Laszlo, Ervin. (1972). *The Systems View of the World.* New York: Braziller. (1974). *A Strategy for the Future: The Systems Approach to World Order.* New York: Brazille.

Lauffer, Armand *et al.* (1977). *Understanding Your Social Agency.* Beverly Hills, CA: Sage Publications, Inc.

Lenski, Gerhard. (1970). *Human Societies.* New York: McGraw-Hill.

Leslie, Gerald. (1967). *The Family in Social Context.* New York: Oxford University Press.

Levine, Baruch. (1979). *Group Psychotherapy.* Englewood Cliffs, NJ: Prentice-Hall.

Lewis, Oscar. (1959). *Five Families.* New York: Basic Books.

Lidz, Theodore. (1963). *The Family and Human Adaptation.* New York: International Universities Press.

Linton, Ralph. (1945). *The Cultural Background of Personality.* New York: Appleton-Century-Crofts.

Lipset, David. (1980). *Gregory Bateson: The Legacy of a Scientist.* Englewood Cliffs, NJ: Prentice-Hall.

Loeb, Martin. (1961). "Social Class and the American Social System." *Social Work* 6(2): 12–18.

Loomis, Charles P., and Zona K. Loomis. (1961). *Modern Social Theories.* Princeton NJ: Van Nostrand.

Lorenz, Konrad. (1963). *On Aggression.* New York: Harcourt, Brace and World.

Lyman, Stanford M., and Marvin B. Scott. (1967). "Territoriality: A Neglected Sociological Dimension." *Social Problems* 15: 236–245.

Lynd, Robert S., and Helen Merrell Lynd. (1929). *Middletown.* New York: Harcourt, Brace and World. (1937). *Middletown in Transition.* New York: Harcourt, Brace and World.

Mabry, Edward A., and Richard E. Barnes. (1980). *The Dynamics of Small Group Communication.* Englewood Cliffs, NJ: Prentice-Hall.

McCullers, Carson. (1972). "A Tree. A Rock. A Cloud." In *The Shorter Novels and Stories of Carson McCullers.* London: Barrie and Jenkins.

McGregor, Douglas. (1960). *The Human Side of Enterprise.* New York: McGraw-Hill.

McLuhan, Marshall. (1965). *Understanding Media: The Extensions of Man.* New York: McGraw-Hill.

McRobie, George. (1981). *Small Is Possible.* New York: Harper & Row.

Maier, Henry W. (1978). *Three Theories of Child Development.* Third Edition. New York: Harper and Row.

Malcolm X. (1966). *The Autobiography of Malcolm X.* New York: Grove.

Manis, Jerome G., and Bernard M. Meltzer (eds.). (1967). *Symbolic Interaction.* Boston: Allyn and Bacon.

March, James G., and Herbert A. Simon. (1968). "Significance of Organizations." In Robert Dubin (ed.), *Human Relations in Administration.* Third Edition. Englewood Cliffs, NJ: Prentice-Hall.

Marrow, Alfred J. (1969). *The Practical Theorist: The Life and Work of Kurt Lewin.* New York: Basic Books.

Marshall, T. H. (1964). *Class, Citizenship, and Social Development.* New York: Doubleday.

Maruyama, Magorah. (1966). "Monopolarization, Family and Individuality." *Psychiatric Quarterly* 40(1): 133–149.

Maslow, Abraham. (1964). "Synergy in the Society and in the Individual." *Journal of Individual Psychology* 20: 153–164. (1968). *Toward A Psychology of Being.* Princeton: Van Nostrand.

Maturana, Humberto R., and Francisco J. Varela. (1980). *Autopoiesis and Cognition.* Dordrecht, Holland: D. Reidel Publishing Company.

May, Rollo. (1969). *Love and Will.* New York: Norton.

Mayer, Milton. (1969). *On Liberty: Man vs. The State.* Santa Barbara, CA: The Center for the Study of Democratic Institutions.

Mayo, Elton. (1945). *The Social Problems of an Industrial Civilization.* Boston: Harvard University Press.

Mead, Margaret. (1970). *Culture and Commitment.* Garden City, NY: Natural History Press. (1972). *Blackberry Winter.* New York: Simon and Schuster.

Meadows, Donella *et al.* (1972). *Limits to Growth.* New York: Universe Books.

Meenaghan, Thomas M. (1972). "What Means 'Community'?" *Social Work* 17(6): 94–98.

Menninger, Karl. (1963). *The Vital Balance.* New York: Viking.

Merton, Robert K. (1957). *Social Theory and Social Structure.* Revised Edition. New York: The Free Press.

Miller, Arthur. (1955). *Death of a Salesman.* New York: Bantam. (Originally published in 1949.)

Miller, James G. (1955). "Toward a General Theory for the Behavioral Sciences." *American Psychologist* 10: 513–531. (1965). "Living Systems: Basic Concepts." *Behavioral Science* 10: 193–237. (1972). "Living Systems: the Organization." *Behavioral Science* 17(1): 1–182. (1978). *Living Systems.* New York: McGraw-Hill.

Mills, C. Wright. (1948). *The New Men of Power.* Harcourt, Brace and World. (1951). *The Power Elite.* New York: Oxford University Press.

Mills, Theodore. (1967). *The Sociology of Small Groups.* Englewood Cliffs, NJ: Prentice-Hall.

Minuchin, Salvador. (1974). *Families and Family Therapy.* Cambridge: Harvard University Press.

Monane, Joseph H. (1967). *A Sociology of Human Systems.* New York: Appleton-Century-Crofts.

Monge, Peter R. (1977). "The Systems Perspective As a Theoretical Basis for the Study of Human Communication." *Communication Quarterly* 25 (1): 19–29.

Moore, Barrington. (1958). *Political Power and Social Theory.* Cambridge: Harvard University Press.

Mumford, Lewis. (1961). *The City in History.* New York: Harcourt, Brace and World. (1970). *The Myth of the Machine: II. The Pentagon of Power.* New York: Harcourt Brace Jovanovich.

Newman, Barbara M., and Philip R. Newman. (1979). *Development Through Life: A Psychosocial Approach.* Homewood, IL: Dorsey Press.

Nimkoff, Meyer. (1965). *Comparative Family Systems.* Boston: Houghton Mifflin.

Nisbet, Robert A. (1966). *The Sociological Tradition.* New York: Basic Books.

Northen, Helen. (1969). *Social Work with Groups.* New York: Columbia University Press.

Nye, F. Ivan, and Felix M. Berardo. (1968). *Emerging Conceptual Frameworks in Family Analysis.* New York: Macmillan.

Olmsted, Michael. (1959). *The Small Group.* New York: Random House.

Olsen, Marvin. (1968). *The Process of Social Organization.* New York: Holt, Rinehart, and Winston.

Ouchi, William G. (1981a). "A Framework for Understanding Organizational Failure." In John R. Kimberly, Robert H. Miles, and Associates, *The Organizational Life Cycle.* San Francisco: Jossey-Bass. (1981b). *Theory Z: How American Business Can Meet the Japanese Challenge.* Reading, MA: Addison-Wesley.

Papademetriou, Marguerite. (1971). "Use of a Group Technique with Unwed Mothers and Their Families." *Social Work* 16(4): 85–90.

Park, Robert E. *Human Communities.* Glencoe, Illinois: The Free Press, 1952.

Parsons, Talcott. (1960). *Structure and Process in Modern Societies.* New York: The Free Press. (1964a). "The Normal Family." *Family Mental Health Papers.* Los Angeles: County Bureau of Public Assistance. (1964b). *The Social System.* New York: The Free Press.

Parsons, Talcott, R. F. Bales, and E. A. Shils. (1953). *Working Papers in the Theory of Action.* New York: The Free Press.

Pei, Mario. (1966). *The Story of Language.* New York: Mentor Book.

Perlman, Helen Harris. (1968). *Persona.* Chicago: University of Chicago Press.

Phillips, John L. Jr. (1969). *The Origins of Intellect: Piaget's Theory.* San Francisco: Freeman.

Piaget, Jean. (1932). *The Moral Judgment of the Child.* Translated by Marjorie Gabain. London: Kegan Paul. (1970). *Genetic Epistemology.* Translated by Eleanor Duckworth. New York: Columbia University Press.

Pirsig, Robert M. (1975). *Zen and the Art of Motorcycle Maintenance.* New York: Bantam Books.

Plath, Sylvia. (1966). "Tulips." In *Ariel.* New York: Harper and Row.

Pollak, Otto. (1968). "Contributions of Sociological and Psychological Theory to Casework Practice." *Journal of Education for Social Work* 4: 49–54.

Presthus, Robert. (1962). *The Organizational Society: An Analysis and a Theory.* New York: Vintage Books. (1964). *Men at the Top.* New York: Oxford University Press.

Ramsoy, Ødd. (1962). *Social Groups As System and Subsystem.* Oslo: Norwegian Universities Press.

Reik, Theodor. (1948). *Listening with the Third Ear.* New York: Farrar, Strauss.

Rifkin, Jeremy. (1981). *Entropy: A New World View.* New York: Bantam Books.

Roberts, Robert W., and Helen Northen (eds.). (1976). *Theories of Social Work With Groups.* New York: Columbia University Press.

Rodman, Hyman (ed.). (1966). *Marriage, Family and Society.* New York: Random House.

Roethlisberger, F. J., and W. L. Dickson. (1947). *Management and the Worker.* Cambridge: Harvard University Press.

Rogers, Carl. (1970). *Carl Rogers on Encounter Groups.* New York: Harper and Row.

Rogers, Martha E. (1970). *An Introduction to the Theoretical Basis of Nursing.* Philadelphia: F. A. Davis Co.

Rose, Arnold M. (1967). *The Power Structure.* New York: Oxford University Press.

Rose, Reginald. (1955). *Twelve Angry Men.* Chicago: Dramatics Publications Co.

Rosen, Hugh. (1980). *The Development of Sociomoral Knowledge.* New York: Columbia University Press.

Ross, Murray G. (1955). *Community Organization.* New York: Harper and Row.

Rowan, John. (1978). *The Structured Crowd.* London: Davis Poynter.

Sager, Clifford, and Helen Singer Kaplan (eds.). (1972). *Progress in Group and Family Therapy.* New York: Brunner/Mazel.

Sandburg, Carl. (1955). "Chicago." In Oscar Williams (ed.), *The New Pocket Anthology of American Verse.* New York: The Pocket Library.

Sanders, Irwin T. (1958). *The Community.* New York: Roland Press.

Sarri, Rosemary C., and Meade J. Galinsky. (1967). "A Conceptual Framework for Group Development." In Robert D. Vinter (ed.), *Readings in Group Work Practice.* Ann Arbor: Campus Publishers.

Saxton, Dolores F. *et al.* (eds.). (1977). *Mosby's Comprehensive Review of Nursing.* Ninth Edition. St. Louis: The C. V. Mosby Co.

Scheflen, Albert E. (1972). *Body Language and the Social Order.* Englewood Cliffs, NJ: Prentice-Hall.

Schumacher, E. F. (1973). *Small Is Beautiful: Economics As If People Mattered.* New York: Harper and Row.

Scott, William G., and David K. Hart. (1980). *Organizational America.* Boston: Houghton Mifflin.

Senn, M. J. E. (ed.), (1950). *Symposium on The Healthy Personality.* New York: Josiah Macy, Jr. Foundation.

Sennett, Richard. (1974). *Families Against the City.* New York: Vintage Books.

Shaffron, Glenn. n.d. "Grey, Wrinkled and Knarled." Unpublished manuscript.

Shaw, Marvin E. (1981). *Group Dynamics: The Psychology of Small Group Behavior.* New York: McGraw-Hill.

Sheehan, Susan. (1977). *A Welfare Mother.* New York: New American Library, Mentor.

Sheehy, Gail. (1976). *Passages.* New York: Dutton.

Shepherd, Clovis R. (1964). *Small Groups.* San Francisco: Chandler.

Silk, Leonard, and Mark Silk. (1981). *The American Establishment.* New York: Avon Books.

Simon, H. A. (1945). *Administrative Behavior.* New York: Macmillan.

Simon, Paul. (1966). *I Am a Rock.* New York: Charing Cross Music, Inc.

Skinner, B. F. (1948). *Walden Two.* New York: Macmillan.

Slater, Philip. (1974). *Earthwalk.* New York: Anchor.

Southey, Robert. (1959). *The Doctor.* In *Oxford Dictionary of Quotations.* Second Edition. London: Oxford University Press.

Spitz, René. (1965). *The First Year of Life.* New York: International Universities Press.

Stack, Carol B. (1974). *All Our Kin: Strategies for Survival in Two Black Families.* New York: Harper and Row.

Stein, Maurice R. (1960). *The Eclipse of Community.* Princeton: Princeton University Press.

Steiner, Gilbert. (1981). *The Futility of Family Policy.* Washington, D.C.: The Brookings Institution.

Stone, L. Joseph, and Joseph Church. (1957). *Childhood and Adolescence.* New York: Random House. (1968). *Childhood and Adolescence.* Second Edition. New York: Random House.

Tarrytown Newsletter. (1982). "Virginia Hine: Complete at Last." No. 14, April.

Tausky, Curt. (1970). *Work Organizations: Major Theoretical Perspectives.* Itasca, Il: Peacock.

Teicher, Morton I. (1958). "The Concept of Culture." *Social Casework* 39: 450–455.

Terkel, Studs. (1975). *Working.* New York: Avon.

Toffler, Alvin. (1970). *Future Shock.* New York: Random House.

Tönnies, Ferdinand. (1957). *Community and Society.* Translated by Charles P. Loomis. East Lansing: Michigan State University Press.

Townsend, Robert. (1970). *Up the Organization.* New York: Knopf.

Trecker, Harleigh. (1955). *Social Group Work Principles and Practices.* New York: Whiteside.

Tropp, Emanuel. (1976). "A Developmental Theory." In Robert W. Roberts and Helen Northen (eds.), *Theories of Social Work With Groups.* New York: Columbia University Press.

Vattano, Anthony J. (1972). "Power to the People: Self-Help Groups." *Social Work* 17(4): 7–15.

Veninga, Robert, and James P. Spradley. (1981). *The Work-Stress Connection.* Boston: Little, Brown.

Vidich, Arthur J., and Joseph Bensman, *Small Town in Mass Society.* Princeton University Press, 1958.

Vogel, Ezra, and Norman Bell. (1960). *A Modern Introduction to the Family.* New York: The Free Press.

Voiland, Alice L., and Associates. (1962). *Family Casework Diagnosis.* New York: Columbia University Press.

Warmington, Eric H., and Philip Rouse. (1956). *Great Dialogues of Plato.* Translated by W. H. D. Rouse. New York: The New American Library of World Literature, Inc.

Warren, Roland L. (1963). *The Community in America.* Chicago: Rand McNally. (1971). *Truth, Love and Social Change.* Chicago: Rand McNally. (1977). *New Perspectives on the American Community: A Book of Readings.* Third Edition. Chicago: Rand McNally.

Washburne, Norman F. (1964). *Interpreting Social Change in America.* New York: Random House.

Watts, Alan. (1966). *The Book: On the Taboo Against Knowing Who You Are.* New York: Pantheon Books.

Watzlawick, Paul. (1976). *How Real is Real?* New York: Random House.

Watzlawick, Paul, Janet Helmick Beavin, and Don Jackson. (1967). *Pragmatics of Human Communication: A Study of Interactional Patterns, Pathologies, and Paradoxes.* New York: W. W. Norton and Company, Inc.

Webster's New Twentieth Century Dictionary of the English Language. Unabridged Second Edition. (1980) New York: William Collins Publishers, Inc.

Weisman, Celia B. (1963). "Social Structure as a Determinant of the Group Worker's Role." *Social Work* 8(3): 87–94.

Welch, Mary-Scott. (1981). *Networking.* New York: Warner Books.

Whorf, Benjamin Lee. (1956). *Language, Thought and Reality.* New York: Wiley/Technology Press.

Whyte, William Foote. (1955). *Street Corner Society.* Second Edition. Chicago: University of Chicago Press.

Whyte, Lancelot Law, Albert G. Wilson, and Donna Wilson. (1969). *Hierarchical Structures.* New York: American Elsevier Publishing Company, Inc.

Woodward, Bob, and Scott Armstrong. (1981). *The Brethren.* New York: Avon.

Work in America. (1973). *Report of a Special Task Force to the Secretary of Health, Education, and Welfare.* Cambridge: MIT Press.

World of Work Report. (1977). "Britain's Longtime Unemployed: Most Prefer Work over State Aid," Vol. 2, No. 2, 24.

Wright, J. Patrick. (1979). *On a Clear Day You Can See General Motors.* New York: Avon.

Zaleznik, Abraham, and Anne Jardim. (1967). "Management." In Paul F. Lazarsfield *et al.* (eds.), *The Uses of Sociology.* New York: Basic Books.

Zimmerman, Carle. (1947). *Outline of the Future of the Family.* Cambridge: The Phillips Book Store.

Zukav, Gary. (1979). *The Dancing Wu Li Masters.* New York: William Morrow and Company, Inc. (Also available in Bantam edition, 1980.)

LITERARY SOURCES

Anderson, Robert Woodruff. (1968). *I Never Sang for My Father*. New York: Random House.

Bergman, Ingmar. (1960). "Wild Strawberries." In *Four Screenplays*. New York: Simon and Schuster.

Forster, E. M. (1954). *Howard's End*. New York: Random House. (Originally published in 1921 by Vintage Books.)

Golding, William. (1959). *Lord of the Flies*. New York: Capricorn Books/Putnam.

Guest, Judith. (1976). *Ordinary People*. New York: Viking.

Kesey, Ken. (1962). *One Flew Over the Cuckoo's Nest*. New York: New American Library.

McCullers, Carson. (1940). *The Heart Is a Lonely Hunter*. Boston: Houghton Mifflin.

Mailer, Norman. (1979). *The Executioner's Song*. New York: Warner Books Inc.

Olsen, Tillie. (1976). *Tell Me a Riddle*. New York: Dell/Laurel Edition.

Romains, Jules. (1961). *Death of a Nobody*. New York: New American Library.

Salinger, J. D. (1961). *Franny and Zooey*. Boston: Little, Brown.

Steinbeck, John. (1961). *The Winter of Our Discontent*. New York: Viking.

Thompson, Ernest. (1979). *On Golden Pond*. New York: Dodd/Mead.

Zindel, Paul. (1970). *The Effect of Gamma Rays on Man-in-the-Moon Marigolds*. New York: Harper and Row.

GLOSSARY

Accommodation. Modification of the system to adapt to environmental conditions. See ADAPTATION, ASSIMILATION.

Adaptation. Action by the system to secure or conserve energy from the environment. Parsons' use of this term includes this as well as the achievement of goals in the environment. See ACCOMMODATION, ASSIMILATION, FUNCTIONAL IMPERATIVES.

Alienation. This term has a wide variety of definitions. We consider that, fundamentally, it describes a state in which a person experiences no synergistic linkage with any system (or component) that he judges significant to him.

Assimilation. A form of adaptation in which incoming information is interpreted as being similar to previous information (i.e., fitted into old schemas). See ACCOMMODATION, ADAPTATION.

Autonomy. Independence from other components within a system. The components are related to a common suprasystem but are largely or entirely separate from each other.

Autopoiesis. Literally (from Greek), "self-powered;" self-development and self-creation.

Behavior. Short-term exchanges between components or systems that accomplish specific goals for the system. This includes socialization, communication, and social control. See EVOLUTION, STRUCTURE.

Body Language. Communication of a nonvocal nature expressed through touch, posture, facial expression, and movement.

Bond. The common interest, identification, or feeling of "we-ness" among members of a group that permits the group to exist as a system. See BOUNDARY.

Boundary. The limits of the interaction of the components of a system with each other or with the environment. It is usually defined by intensity or frequency of interaction between systems and components.

Bureaucracy. A distinct form of organization in which there is a relatively high degree of administrative centralization, hierarchical control, specificity of rules, and clearly identified role expectations. This form of organization is usually found in cultures that are highly elaborated, and it usually serves social control functions in the society.

Class. A scheme of classification of a particular society. Usually ordered by indices such as income, occupation, and education. See ROLE, STATUS.

Communication. In a narrow sense, the transportation of information between or within systems; in a broader sense, the transportation of energy, also. In this

229

broader sense, information is considered a special form of energy (see Monane, 1967, Chapter 2 for his use of these terms).

Component. Synonymous with PART (a part of a system). It may or may not be a system in itself, in contrast to a subsystem, which IS a system. See SUBSYSTEM.

Differentiation. Selectivity of function or activity among components of a system. "Division of labor" is one example. A function or activity is "assigned" to one, or some, components and not others. This differs from specialization in that the component may perform other functions or activities in addition to the assigned, differentiated one. See SPECIALIZATION.

Disintegration. "Disintegration means systemic death. With it, components *De*systematize. It is a movement away from organization into entropy and randomness" (Monane, 1967:159). See ENTROPY, ORGANIZATION.

Ecological Approach. This is an approach that is virtually synonymous with a systems approach. Specifically, it refers to "nested" systems, that is, from component to subsystem to system to suprasystem. It probably originated in the "human ecology" approach at the University of Chicago several decades ago. See ECOLOGICAL SYSTEMS.

Ecological Systems. A term used by some systems writers in the broad sense of systems that are hierarchically related. In biology and ecology, the term refers to living organisms in the earth's biosphere that are hierarchically related. See ECOLOGICAL APPROACH.

Elaboration. Used in reference to evolution of groups, this denotes increasing complexity and multiplication of parts of the system.

Energy. Capacity for action; action; or power to effect change. We use this term much as Parsons used action. As increased interaction occurs, there is greater available energy. See ENTROPY, SYNERGY, SYNTROPY, POWER.

Entropy. "The quantity of energy *not* capable of conversion into work" (Asimov, 1970:8). Entropy is the tendency of systems to "run down," to distribute energy randomly so that it becomes less accessible; the system, therefore, becomes less capable of organized work. Some argue that open systems are not subject to the law of entropy. Rudolph Clausius is credited with the origin of the concept in 1865. See ENERGY, ORGANIZATION, NEGENTROPY, SYNTROPY.

Environment. Anything not included within the interaction of the components of a system but that affects the system. It may also be considered as anything that affects the system but over which it has no control (Churchman, 1968:50).

Equifinality. The term derives from systems theory; it means that two different systems, if they receive similar inputs, will arrive at similar end states even though they had different initial conditions. One illustration is that although two children may grow differently, one "undershooting" and the other "overshooting" initially, both will arrive at adulthood in good health and normal size *If* they are fed similarly and adequately.

Equilibrium. Fixed balance in a relatively closed system characterized by little interchange with the environment and avoidance of disturbance. See HOMEOSTASIS, STEADY STATE.

Ethology. The study of animal behavior, especially of innate patterns. In the past two decades, writings of ethologists, including Konrad Lorenz, Desmond Morris, Lionel Tiger and Robin Fox, have gained popularity. See TERRITORIALITY.

Evolution. Change in a system's structure and behavior from one time to another. This term describes which relationships have altered (and which have remained the same) and in what manner a system's functions are being performed differently at the end of some particular period of time. See BEHAVIOR, STRUCTURE.

Feedback. The process in which a system receives internal or environmental responses to its behavior and, in turn, responds to these received responses by accommodating and assimilating the information or energy received. See ADAPTATION, COMMUNICATION.

Focal system. This refers to the system that is the object of attention at a particular moment. It must be specified in order to be consistent with the demand that the perspective of the viewer should be stated. Systems analysts frequently label this the TARGET SYSTEM if the focal system is the system in which change is to be achieved. See HOLON, PERSPECTIVISM.

Functional Imperatives. Parsons specified four functions that are necessary in a system. These are ADAPTATION, GOAL-DIRECTED ACTIVITY, INTEGRATION and PATTERN MAINTENANCE. We identify other energy functions that we consider more descriptive.

Goal. A desired steady state to be achieved by fulfilling a specific function of the system within some relatively short period of time. See PURPOSE.

Goal-Directed Activity (GE and GI functions). One of two kinds of energy functions, the other being SECURING AND CONSERVING ENERGY. The process is the expenditure of energy to achieve system goals, either internally or externally.

Hierarchy. A form of organization that characterizes all viable systems. Hierarchy is a superordinate–subordinate relationship between systems in which any unit is dependent upon its suprasystem for performance of energy functions and must provide direction to its subsystems. See HOLON.

Holon. Arthur Koestler's term, denoting that a system is both a part of a larger suprasystem and is itself a suprasystem to other systems. See FOCAL SYSTEM, SUBSYSTEM, SUPRASYSTEM..

Homeostasis. Fixed balance in a partially open system, characterized by very limited interchange with the environment and by maintenance of the system's present structure. See EQUILIBRIUM, STEADY STATE.

Identity. Erikson defines this in several variations. The central idea is integration of the components of the personality, along with validation through interaction with the social environment. The result of these is ego identity, which is inner assurance of congruence between one's own feelings about self and others' feelings about oneself. The concept has been loosely applied to other systems such as "national identity" and "racial identity." Identity is a steady state of the personality system but is richer in its meaning than steady state. See STEADY STATE, SYNTALITY, SYNERGY.

Information. The content of feedback and communication. In a narrow sense, information includes signs and symbols which are communicated. In a broader sense, information could include energy interchange itself. See COMMUNICATION, FEEDBACK.

Institutionalization. One form of differentiation in which some component or system is assigned responsibility to perform specific major functions for the system (usually a culture, society or community but, in a broader sense, in microsystems as well). The differentiated component or system may specialize in this function. A new component or system may be created to carry out the function, or the assignment may be given to an existing component or system. See DIFFERENTIATION, SPECIALIZATION.

Integration. One of Parsons' four functional inperatives. A system must ensure the harmonious interaction of its components in order to prevent entropy and in order to secure and conserve internal energy sources.

Isomorphic. Similarity of form or function between systems or components of systems. "Isomorph" is used in this book to point to similarities between the behaviors and structures of different levels of systems. For example, "feedback cycle" is applicable to all levels of systems from person to culture and thus can be termed "isomorphic."

Linkage. Energy exchange among and between components and systems.

Loop. This term is from engineering and cybernetics. It is a specific form of feedback in which a system's output becomes input that modifies the system's functioning. That is, the system's own behavior supplies stimuli for system modification. See FEEDBACK.

Mission. See PURPOSE.

Morphogenesis. A system tending toward structural change. In actuality, all systems must simultaneously maintain and change a shifting balance between morphogenesis and morphostasis. See MORPHOSTASIS.

Morphostasis. A system tending toward maintenance of the status quo structurally. See MORPHOGENESIS.

Negentropy. The word is a contraction of "negative entropy," meaning the reduction of randomized, unavailable energy via importing energy from outside the system. See ENERGY, ENTROPY, SYNERGY, SYNTROPY.

Open or Closed System. "Open" denotes energy exchange across a system's boundaries. "Closed" denotes lack of energy exchange across boundaries.

Organization. The process of structuring the exchange of energy in a system. Persistent regularities of relationship between components make up the structure, or organization, of the system. See DIFFERENTIATION, SPECIALIZATION.

Pattern Maintenance. One of Parsons' four functional imperatives. This refers to the necessity of the system to regulate and enforce legitimized behaviors in order to conserve energy and achieve goals. We consider this to include our SI and GI functions.

Perspectivism. In the systems approach, this means that any description or definition of a system must include an explicit statement of one's own position or intention with regard to that system and an explicit identification of the system that one is identifying as the focal system. Philosophically, the term denotes that any viewpoint is relative to one's own perceptions and relations to the system being described or defined and to its environment.

Polarities. Opposite or contrasting qualities. Many of the systems ideas are conceived as polarities at opposite ends of a continuum. Any system at any time is a mixture or ratio of two polar qualities, such as task versus sentiment, adaptation versus integration, basic trust versus basic mistrust. Polarities are opposites that define each other and together form a single quality.

Power. The capacity to achieve goals by the application or deprivation of energy to another system so as to affect its functioning.

Psychosexual. Generally, refers to the Freudian stages of personality development (i.e., oral, anal, phallic, and genital). See PSYCHOSOCIAL.

Psychosocial. Generally, refers to the Eriksonian life cycle formulation of personality development. This is a modification and extension of the psychosexual, with emphasis on the social and cultural influences. See PSYCHOSEXUAL.

Purpose. A desired steady state achieved by assignment of goal(s) to a subsystem and completion of the goal(s). GOAL denotes that the system itself will be the object of change; PURPOSE that the suprasystem will be the object of change. Systems analysis frequently use MISSION to mean the same as purpose. See GOAL.

Role. A set of expectations regarding behavior that can be fulfilled by a person. It carries with it expectations of behavior that are defined and sanctioned by significant environmental systems. The role occupant generally has some leeway in interpretation of assigned behaviors. This is analogous to the theater, in which the playwright prescribes the role but the artist interprets through the performance. See STATUS.

Schema. Precisely used, this is Piaget's term for a single complex, or nexus, or associated responses a person is capable of making. The plural is SCHEMATA, or SCHEMAS. We use the term in a broader sense to emphasize its transferability to systems other than a person (e.g., the repertoire of responses that an organization or community is capable of making). We also use the term to mean the integrated knowledge, experience, and interpretations that underlie a system's responses.

Securing and Conserving Energy. We designate this as one of two kinds of energy functions in a system (the other is GOAL-DIRECTED ACTIVITY). The process is one of expending energy to secure further energy or to reduce the expenditure of energy, as in minimizing intrasystem conflict.

Social Control. The use of energy by a system to assure that its components fulfill assigned functions (see PURPOSES and GOALS). Such activity includes socialization and enforcement of norms of behavior. Enforcement may entail persuasion, authority, or force. The purpose of social control is to permit continued functioning of the system through reducing or preventing deviance among the components. See SOCIALIZATION.

Socialization. One form of social control intended to assure the availability of components' energies to the system. The means to achieve this are primarily through assimilating the culture. Hence education, indoctrination, and enculturation are forms of socialization. See SOCIAL CONTROL.

Specialization. Performance of a function or activity to the exclusion of other functions or activities by a component or part of a system. A system may differentiate its components by allocating functions or activities among them; some perform certain functions, whereas others do not perform the same functions. If the part performs *only* the differentiated function, then it has specialized; if it performs other functions as well, it is differentiated but not specialized. The two are separate. See DIFFERENTIATION.

Status. A vertical dimension of ranking. May be ascribed (assigned by society) or achieved (attained by dint of individual or group activity). See CLASS, ROLE.

Steady State. A total condition of the system in which it is in balance both internally and with its environment but which is at the same time undergoing some degree of change (i.e., it is not static). The word STEADY fails to connote the dynamic nature of systems, while the word STATE fails to connote a succession of conditions of the system. Used fairly loosely and somewhat interchangeably with equilibrium and homeostasis but distinct from them. See EQUILIBRIUM, HOMEOSTASIS.

Structure. The most stable relationships between systems and components (i.e., with the slowest rate of change). This states which components or systems are related to each other during a given time period but does not necessarily give details of the amount of energy exchanged, or in what direction, or the functions being performed for each party to the relationship. It is thus a "snapshot," frozen in time, not a movie. See BEHAVIOR, EVOLUTION.

Subsystem. A component of a system that is itself a system. It is one kind of component. See COMPONENT, SUPRASYSTEM, SYSTEM.

Suprasystem. A larger system that includes the focal system; a "whole" of which the focal system is a "part."

Symbolic Interaction. A theoretical perspective within social psychology that seeks to understand human behavior through study of the "social act." Such study attends to overt behavior and what the act symbolizes within the social context.

Synergy. Increasing the amount of available energy in a system through increased interaction of the components. Loosely, it may be described as the creation of new energy through compounding the actions of the parts, but this is a moot point in the systems approach. See ENERGY, ENTROPY, SYNTROPY, NEGENTROPY.

Syntality. This is the unique character of a group; analogous to the "personality" of a person.

Syntropy. An innate drive in living matter to protect itself, to seek synthesis and wholeness. See ENERGY, ENTROPY, NEGENTROPY, SYNERGY.

System. An organized whole made up of components that interact in a way distinct from their interaction with other entities and which endures over some period of time. See COMPONENT, SUBSYSTEM, SUPRASYSTEM.

Territoriality. Refers to the proclivity of organisms, including man, to seek, obtain, and defend an area of space or action. This serves to order and stabilize behavioral space. See ETHOLOGY.

NAME INDEX

235

SUBJECT INDEX

241